Mental Health - Innovations in Therapy and Treatment

Edited by María-José Martín Vázquez and Cicek Hocaoglu

Published in London, United Kingdom

Mental Health - Innovations in Therapy and Treatment
http://dx.doi.org/10.5772/intechopen.1005998
Edited by María-José Martín Vázquez and Cicek Hocaoglu

Contributors
Ayla Gencan, Ayşegül Yildiz, Cansu Önal, Chaomeng Liu, Cicek Hocaoglu, Didem Bostan Bendas, Emma R. Torncello, Gregory M. Nikogosyan, Hayriye Soytürk, Henry Drasiku, Justin Thomas, Magdalen Akia, Milton Anguyo, Molly Naisanga, Nada Al Juraib, Pınar Harmancı, Samuel I. MacDonald, Shahroo Izadi, Wei Zheng, Xian-Jun Lan, Xin-Hu Yang, Özge Kaya, Ümit Kiliç

First published in London, United Kingdom, 2025 by IntechOpen
IntechOpen is the global imprint of INTECHOPEN LIMITED, registered in England and Wales, registration number: 11086078, 167-169 Great Portland Street, London, W1W 5PF, United Kingdom

For EU product safety concerns: IN TECH d.o.o., Prolaz Marije Krucifikse Kozulić 3, 51000 Rijeka, Croatia, info@intechopen.com or visit our website at intechopen.com.

British Library Cataloguing-in-Publication Data
A catalogue record for this book is available from the British Library

Mental Health - Innovations in Therapy and Treatment
Edited by María-José Martín Vázquez and Cicek Hocaoglu
p. cm.
Print ISBN 978-1-83634-461-2
Online ISBN 978-1-83634-460-5
eBook (PDF) ISBN 978-1-83634-462-9

Meet the editors

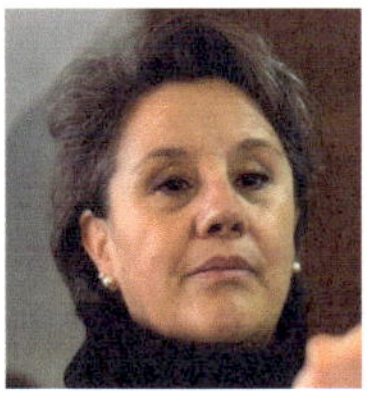

María-José Martín-Vázquez is a psychiatrist and psychologist, with a doctorate in Medicine from Alcalá de Henares University, and a professor of psychiatry at Universidad Europea de Madrid. She has been working as the responsible person for the severe personality disorder program in the area of San Sebastián de los Reyes / Alcobendas, in Madrid (Spain). She has published more than 80 articles and book chapters, and she is the editor of a book, "Manual of use of psychotropic medication in medical illness". She has been an active reviewer for several international publications. Finally, she has a background in psychodynamics, research in Psychology, Bioethics, and Law, as well as experience in EMDR, Transference-Focused Psychotherapy, and Good Psychiatric Management. Her doctoral thesis is a work about bipolar disorder and voice changes. Currently, she is a member of the Assistential Ethics Committee at Hospital Infanta Sofía in Madrid.

Cicek Hocaoglu obtained her medical degree from the Bursa Uludag University Faculty of Medicine in Turkey. She received postgraduate training in psychiatry at the Medical School of Karadeniz Technical University, Trabzon, Turkey. She is currently a professor and head of the Department of Psychiatry, Recep Tayyip Erdogan University Medical School, Rize, Turkey. She has published numerous national and international scientific articles, book chapters, and conference papers. Her interests include consultation-liaison psychiatry, suicide, schizophrenia, anxiety disorders, bipolar disorder, and psychopharmacology.

Contents

Preface

Mental Health is a significant concern worldwide. In the last decades, institutions of all types, clinicians, patients and people in general have understood that a person with mental health problems is neither healthy nor happy. The stigma around mental disorders is still present, but it is reducing in intensity overall in some societies.

The costs related to mental disorders worldwide could represent 4% of global GDP (Gross Domestic Product), in both direct costs (treatment and investigation) and indirect costs (loss of productivity, absenteeism, presentism, and personnel changes), and these costs are increasing year by year [1]. Moreover, mental disorders not only affect the one who suffers from the problem, but also families and communities. This reality implies that society has an increasing interest in reducing the impact of suffering and the costs of mental disorders.

This interest can be demonstrated by the increase in investigation lines related to mental health and the improvement of scientific communication. In this direction, this book features selected works from around the world, examining the latest developments in prevalent and disabling disorders.

Firstly, there is a section dedicated to Obsessive-Compulsive Disorder (OCD), in which the authors will break down the old and new tests and scales that have been developed to measure OCD symptomatology, their pros and cons, and it will provide clinicians with comprehensive information to facilitate their decision on choosing one instrument over the other.

The first chapter in the section is a review of novel approaches for the diagnosis and treatment of OCD, emphasizing new treatments, including transcranial magnetic stimulation. Additionally, we will review pharmacological treatments and new strategies, such as deep brain stimulation, which have shown promising results for the future.

In the second chapter of this section, the authors will review mindfulness-based approaches to problematic technology use, examining mindfulness as a strategy widely used in other disorders for treating problematic technology use, a newly diagnosed condition. This diagnosis can be new, but its prevalence is increasing exponentially in all sectors of society. Therefore, a well-accepted strategy, such as mindfulness, could be a very interesting instrument.

Finally, the section will conclude with a chapter discussing the diverse advanced approaches of transcranial magnetic stimulation in Obsessive-Compulsive Disorder. This new technology has expanded its indications for treating a wider range of disorders. This technology has many advantages, including that it is well-tolerated and effective. The authors will explain different points of application and observed responses in the clinical trials.

The second section of the book is dedicated to bipolar disorder. Bipolar disorder is observed in all populations all around the world. It is a severe mental disorder that can result in a decline in personal functioning and worsen response to treatment.

To open the section, the chapter will explore suicidal behaviour in mania and hypomania. This clinical problem has already been dealt with, because suicidal behaviour is usually related to depressive episodes. Many times, clinicians do not have this serious complication in their minds when they are treating bipolar patients, so this topic has singular importance in mental health prevention.

Another topic of great interest in the treatment of bipolar disorder is recognizing symptom evolution in ageing individuals. Bipolar disorder implies a decline in personal function, and the presentation of the symptoms changes with the age of the patient. In addition, in many cases, the episodes persist and the response to treatment decreases. As bipolar disorder is a chronic disease, clinicians must take into account the ageing of their patients and the changes in the evolution and prognosis.

Moreover, to close the section, the last chapter treats about secondary mania of medical and neurological disorders, a significant clinical problem, not because its prevalence, but due to its severity if a patient has a neurological or medical problem with a psychiatric presentation, which need another approach, not only psychiatric to save the life of the patient. In the clinical setting, it is essential to consider this when improving patients' prognosis.

The final section and chapter of the book discuss the role and importance of neuroinflammation in neuropsychiatry. Inflammatory theory has demonstrated its relevance in many physical problems, but in the last decades, there is more and more evidence of the role that the defence system plays in the development of psychiatric symptoms. This theory will probably change the way we treat mental health disorders.

This book could not be finished without the collaboration of Dr. Hocaoğlu as a co-editor. In addition, the roles of Sandra Maljavac, Karmen Daleta, and Lucija Tomicic-Dromgool have been essential to the good progress of this book. My gratitude to them all.

María-José Martín-Vázquez, PhD, MD. Psychiatrist
Department of Psychiatry and Mental Health,
Hospital Universitario Infanta Sofía,
Madrid, Spain

Faculty of Medicine, Health and Sports,
Department of Medicine,
Universidad Europea de Madrid,
FIIB HUIS-HUHEN,
Madrid, Spain

References

[1] Arias Daniel et al. Quantifying the global burden of mental disorders and their economic value. eClinicalMedicine, Volume 54, 101675

Section 1

What's New in OCD?

Chapter 1

Advancements in Obsessive Compulsive Disorder: Novel Approaches for Diagnosis and Treatment

Milton Anguyo, Henry Drasiku, Magdalen Akia and Molly Naisanga

Abstract

This chapter explores the cutting-edge advancements in the diagnosis and treatment of Obsessive-Compulsive Disorder (OCD). It delves into the complex diagnostic criteria and varying symptom presentations, providing a comprehensive understanding of the disorder. Genetic and neurobiological markers are examined, showcasing personalized medicine's potential through targeted interventions. Cognitive-behavioral therapies, augmented by exposure and response prevention techniques and innovative technologies, offer new avenues for therapeutic success. Neuro stimulation methods, such as Tran's cranial magnetic stimulation and deep brain stimulation, provide hope for treatment-resistant cases. Integrative therapies, including mindfulness-based stress reduction and art therapy, focus on holistic healing. Ethical considerations in novel treatments, disparities in accessibility, and the importance of stigma reduction are explored. The collaborative efforts of researchers, clinicians, and patient advocacy groups are emphasized. The abstract underscores the significance of ongoing research, societal support, and compassion for individuals with OCD. These advancements signal a transformative era in mental healthcare, promising tailored treatments and improved quality of life for those affected by OCD.

Keywords: Obsessive-Compulsive Disorder, OCD, diagnosis, treatment, genetic markers, cognitive-behavioral therapy, neuro stimulation, integrative therapies, personalized medicine, stigma reduction, ethical considerations

1. Introduction

Obsessive-Compulsive Disorder (OCD) is a debilitating mental health condition characterized by persistent, intrusive thoughts (obsessions) and repetitive behaviors or mental acts (compulsions). Individuals with OCD often find their daily lives profoundly impacted by these distressing thoughts and rituals, leading to impaired social functioning and diminished quality of life. As of the latest update, it affects approximately 1–2% of the global population, making it one of the most prevalent mental disorders worldwide [1].

Over the years, the field of OCD research and treatment has witnessed remarkable advancements, leading to a deeper understanding of the disorder's neurobiological underpinnings and the development of innovative therapeutic interventions. This chapter delves into these advancements, exploring novel approaches for both diagnosing and treating OCD. Understanding the intricacies of these developments is pivotal, as it not only enhances our comprehension of the disorder but also opens new avenues for effective interventions, offering hope to millions who suffer from OCD.

1.1 Significance of studying OCD advancements

The significance of studying advancements in OCD diagnosis and treatment lies in the transformative potential these discoveries hold. With the advent of cutting-edge technologies and interdisciplinary collaborations, researchers and clinicians have made substantial progress in unraveling the complex nature of OCD. These advancements not only aid in accurate diagnosis but also pave the way for personalized treatment strategies tailored to individual patients' needs. Such tailored approaches have shown promising results in improving treatment outcomes and reducing the burden of OCD symptoms [2].

1.2 Brief historical context of OCD diagnosis and treatment

Historically, OCD has been a subject of fascination and perplexity for clinicians and researchers alike. The understanding of OCD has evolved significantly from early beliefs that deemed it as a purely psychological phenomenon to the current comprehensive neurobiological model. Early treatments often involved psychoanalytic approaches, but the contemporary landscape of OCD treatment is characterized by evidence-based interventions, including cognitive-behavioral therapies and pharmacological agents [3].

In this chapter, we will embark on a journey through the advancements that have reshaped our comprehension of OCD, exploring the genetic and neurobiological markers that shed light on its origins, the innovative diagnostic tools that aid in precise identification, and the diverse array of therapeutic interventions that have emerged, offering hope and relief to individuals living with OCD.

2. Understanding OCD: a brief review

2.1 Diagnostic criteria and classification

Obsessive-Compulsive Disorder (OCD) is characterized by the presence of obsessions, compulsions, or both, causing significant distress and impairment in social, occupational, or other important areas of functioning. Obsessions are intrusive and unwanted thoughts, images, or urges, while compulsions are repetitive behaviors or mental acts that an individual feels driven to perform in response to an obsession or according to rigid rules. To meet the diagnostic criteria, these symptoms must be time-consuming (taking more than one hour per day) or cause clinically significant distress or impairment in daily functioning [4].

OCD can present in various forms, leading to a classification based on predominant symptoms. These classifications include:

- Contamination obsessions and cleaning compulsions: characterized by fears of contamination and cleaning rituals.
- Harm obsessions and checking compulsions: involving fears of causing harm and checking behaviors to prevent harm.
- Symmetry or exactness obsessions and ordering compulsions: centered on a need for symmetry, order, or precise arrangements.
- Unacceptable taboo thoughts and mental rituals: involving obsessions related to forbidden or taboo thoughts and mental rituals to neutralize these thoughts [4].

Diagnostic criteria for OCD in ICD-10 and DSM-V (Appendix C).

2.2 Common symptoms and variations in presentation

While the diagnostic criteria provide a broad framework, OCD symptoms manifest uniquely in each individual. Common obsessions include fears of contamination, fears of harming oneself or others, fears of making a mistake, and fears of unwanted sexual or aggressive thoughts. Corresponding compulsions often involve washing, checking, counting, repeating actions, or mental rituals. It is crucial to note that the presentation of OCD can vary widely, with some individuals primarily experiencing obsessions, while others primarily exhibit compulsions. Additionally, symptom severity fluctuates over time, often worsening during periods of stress [4].

2.3 Comorbidities associated with OCD

OCD rarely occurs in isolation and is frequently accompanied by other mental health conditions. Common comorbidities include depression, anxiety disorders, tic disorders, and attention-deficit/hyperactivity disorder (ADHD). Understanding these comorbidities is essential as they can influence the course of OCD and impact treatment outcomes. For instance, the presence of depression might necessitate a different therapeutic approach than when OCD occurs without comorbid depression [4].

3. Advancements in OCD diagnosis

3.1 Genetic and neurobiological markers

3.1.1 Genetic predispositions and biomarkers

Recent studies have uncovered potential genetic markers associated with OCD susceptibility. Identifying specific genetic variations can aid in early detection and personalized treatment. Research indicates the involvement of genes related to neurotransmitter regulation, specifically serotonin and glutamate systems, highlighting potential targets for intervention [5]. Furthermore, ongoing research in epigenetics and gene expression patterns is shedding light on the interplay between genetic factors and environmental influences in OCD etiology.

3.1.2 Neuroimaging studies and brain circuitry

Advanced neuroimaging techniques, such as functional magnetic resonance imaging (fMRI) and positron emission tomography (PET) scans, have provided insights into the neural circuits implicated in OCD. Aberrant activity in the orbitofrontal cortex, anterior cingulate cortex, and basal ganglia has been observed in individuals with OCD, offering valuable information for targeted interventions [6]. Additionally, diffusion tensor imaging (DTI) studies have elucidated abnormalities in white matter tracts, enhancing our understanding of the neural connectivity disruptions associated with OCD.

3.2 Behavioral and cognitive assessments

3.2.1 Role of cognitive assessments in diagnosis

Cognitive assessments, including neuropsychological tests and structured interviews, play a vital role in diagnosing OCD and assessing symptom severity. Innovations in cognitive assessments have enabled a more nuanced understanding of cognitive impairments associated with OCD subtypes. These assessments are valuable for treatment planning and tracking cognitive changes over the course of interventions [7].

3.2.2 Behavioral observation and assessment tools

Behavioral observation tools, such as ecological momentary assessment (EMA) and wearables, offer real-time data on individuals' behaviors and emotional states. By integrating technology, clinicians can gain a comprehensive view of patients' daily experiences, helping to identify triggers and patterns. Wearables equipped with biosensors can detect physiological markers associated with anxiety, providing valuable data for both diagnosis and treatment monitoring [8].

Advancements in OCD diagnosis are not only refining our understanding of the disorder but also paving the way for more precise and personalized interventions. By leveraging genetic insights, neuroimaging technologies, and innovative assessment tools, clinicians can tailor treatments to address specific neurobiological markers and behavioral patterns, ultimately improving outcomes for individuals living with OCD.

4. Innovative approaches to OCD treatment

Obsessive-Compulsive Disorder (OCD) poses a significant challenge for clinical psychiatrists, affecting about 1.3% of the population annually and up to 2.7% over a lifetime. The disorder is characterized by distressing obsessions (repetitive, intrusive thoughts) and compulsions (ritualized actions to alleviate distress). While first-line treatments involve cognitive-behavioral therapy and selective serotonin reuptake inhibitors (SSRIs), the need for more effective interventions is pressing.

4.1 Pharmacological interventions: SSRIs as mainstay

SSRIs are the primary pharmacological treatment for OCD. Early evidence showed the efficacy of clomipramine, a tricyclic antidepressant, but its side effects limit its use. Fluvoxamine, introduced in 1989, marked the beginning of SSRI success. Over 20 studies affirmed the efficacy of SSRI monotherapy in OCD. Despite fluvoxamine's historical preference, there's no evidence of differential benefit among SSRIs. The choice depends on factors like side effects, drug interactions, and patient preference.

Higher doses of SSRIs (e.g., 80 mg fluoxetine, 40 mg escitalopram) are often required for efficacy, differing from their use in major depressive disorder (MDD). OCD responses also take longer, requiring 8–12 weeks for an adequate trial. While higher doses show clear benefits, the impact on individual patients is modest. Citalopram, although not FDA-approved for OCD, has been historically used. Still, a 2011 FDA warning against doses over 40 mg/day complicates its use due to ECG abnormalities and arrhythmia risks. Escitalopram, without a similar warning, becomes a reasonable alternative.

4.2 Challenges and considerations

1. Time to response: while the common belief is that SSRIs take 8–12 weeks to work, a nuanced view suggests subjective improvement may occur more rapidly. Meta-analyses examining symptom improvement trajectories reveal benefits starting in the early weeks.

2. Citalopram caution: the FDA warning on citalopram doses above 40 mg/day complicates its use, despite evidence supporting higher doses in OCD. Clinicians often switch to alternatives like escitalopram due to safety concerns.

5. Conclusion

Despite optimal treatment, remission of moderate or severe OCD is rare, necessitating long-term management. The quest for innovative interventions remains crucial to address the persistent symptoms faced by many patients. Continued research and exploration of alternative treatments are essential to enhance the efficacy and outcomes in the management of OCD.

5.1 Children and adolescents

The use of SSRIs in children and adolescents differs in some ways from their use in adults. Although randomized, placebo-controlled trials clearly demonstrate benefits of SSRI in children with OCD, concerns regarding side effects are more substantial. The added benefit from higher doses of SSRIs, which is clear in adults, has not been demonstrated in the pediatric population. Three of the SSRIs are approved by the FDA for use in children: fluoxetine (age 7 and above), sertraline (age 6 and above), and fluvoxamine (age 8 and above). Clomipramine is also FDA-approved for children 10 and above.

5.2 Clomipramine in OCD treatment: balancing efficacy and side effects

Clomipramine, a tricyclic antidepressant, was the first FDA-approved agent for OCD treatment in 1989. As a potent serotonin reuptake inhibitor (SRI), it exhibits efficacy comparable to SSRIs, according to some meta-analyses. However, methodological challenges complicate direct comparisons with SSRIs. While higher SSRIs doses prove more effective, clomipramine's unique benefit may be underestimated due to the risk of cardiac toxicity limiting dose escalation.

Despite its potential efficacy, clomipramine comes with a challenging side effect profile, including significant anticholinergic, anti-histaminergic, and alpha-adrenergic effects. Notably, it poses a risk of arrhythmia and seizures, particularly at doses exceeding 250 mg, requiring ECG monitoring. These side effects make it a non-first-line choice, reserved for cases where SSRI monotherapy fails.

Combination strategies, such as adding clomipramine to an SSRI or vice versa, are occasionally employed to capture clomipramine's benefits without intensifying side effects. However, limited controlled data exist on the efficacy of these strategies, making their use less straightforward. Caution is warranted, especially when combining clomipramine with fluvoxamine, as the latter inhibits clomipramine metabolism, elevating the risk of adverse effects like seizures or arrhythmia.

In summary, while clomipramine offers a modestly greater efficacy in some cases, its side effect profile and safety concerns make it a secondary option when standard SSRIs prove insufficient. Combination strategies require careful consideration, emphasizing the need for individualized treatment approaches in managing OCD.

5.2.1 Exploration of novel drug therapies

Recent research has focused on novel pharmacological agents to target specific neurotransmitter pathways implicated in OCD. Glutamatergic modulators, such as N-acetylcysteine and memantine, have shown promise in reducing obsessive-compulsive symptoms by modulating glutamate levels, a neurotransmitter associated with excitatory signaling [9]. Additionally, ongoing studies on the effects of psychedelics, such as psilocybin and MDMA, offer intriguing avenues for understanding their potential therapeutic role in treating OCD by altering brain connectivity and perception.

5.2.2 Personalized medicine and drug targeting

The emergence of pharmacogenomic research allows for personalized medicine approaches in OCD treatment. Genetic profiling enables clinicians to identify specific gene-drug interactions, ensuring tailored medication choices based on individual genetic makeup. This precision medicine approach minimizes adverse effects and enhances treatment efficacy by matching patients with medications that align with their genetic predispositions [9].

5.3 Cognitive behavioral therapy (CBT) enhancements

5.3.1 Exposure and response prevention

Exposure and response prevention (ERP) a component of CBT involves gradually exposing you to a feared object or obsession, such as dirt, and having you ways to resist the urge to do your compulsive rituals.

Innovations in ERP include virtual reality exposure therapy, immersing patients in computer-generated environments to simulate real-life situations. Virtual reality therapy enhances the effectiveness of ERP by providing a controlled and customizable environment for exposure, fostering a safe space for confronting fears [10].

5.3.2 Integration of technology in CBT

Mobile applications and online platforms have revolutionized the delivery of CBT interventions. Therapy apps offer guided self-help exercises, mood tracking, and interactive modules designed to challenge obsessive thoughts and compulsive behaviors. These digital tools provide continuous support, allowing individuals to engage in therapeutic activities outside of traditional therapy sessions, promoting consistent progress and symptom management [11].

5.4 Neurostimulation and brain modulation techniques

5.4.1 Transcranial magnetic stimulation (TMS)

TMS, a non-invasive brain stimulation technique, involves the use of magnetic fields to stimulate specific brain regions. In OCD treatment, repetitive TMS (rTMS) targeted at the prefrontal cortex has shown promising results in reducing obsessive-compulsive symptoms. Studies indicate that rTMS modulates neuronal activity, restoring aberrant neural circuits associated with OCD [12].

5.4.2 Deep brain stimulation (DBS)

DBS involves implanting electrodes into specific brain regions and delivering electrical impulses to modulate neural activity. In severe and treatment-resistant OCD cases, DBS targeting the anterior limb of the internal capsule has demonstrated significant symptom reduction. By fine-tuning dysfunctional circuits, DBS offers hope to individuals resistant to conventional treatments, providing a life-changing intervention [13].

Innovations in pharmacological interventions, cognitive behavioral therapy techniques, and Neurostimulation methods are transforming OCD treatment paradigms. By embracing these advancements, clinicians can offer more targeted and effective interventions, significantly improving the lives of individuals struggling with OCD.

6. Psychotherapeutic interventions

6.1 Mindfulness-based therapies

6.1.1 Mindfulness-based stress reduction (MBSR)

MBSR, rooted in mindfulness meditation and yoga, has gained recognition in treating OCD. By cultivating non-judgmental awareness of thoughts and sensations, individuals with OCD learn to observe their obsessions without reacting compulsively. MBSR interventions have shown promising results in reducing anxiety and obsessive-compulsive symptoms. Through regular practice, patients develop greater emotional regulation and resilience, easing the grip of obsessive thoughts [14].

6.1.2 Acceptance and commitment therapy (ACT)

ACT combines mindfulness strategies with behavioral techniques, encouraging patients to accept their thoughts and feelings rather than suppressing or avoiding them. By fostering psychological flexibility, individuals with OCD can engage in meaningful life activities despite the presence of obsessions. ACT interventions target values-based actions, helping patients live in alignment with their aspirations rather than being dictated by their fears [15].

6.2 Integrative therapies

6.2.1 Art and music therapy

Creative therapies, such as art and music therapy, provide alternative channels for expression and processing of emotions. Individuals with OCD often struggle to articulate their feelings, making these therapies invaluable. Engaging in creative activities offers a non-verbal outlet, enabling patients to explore and confront their emotions indirectly. Art therapy, in particular, allows individuals to externalize their obsessions and gain perspective, fostering a sense of control [16].

6.2.2 Yoga and mind-body practices

Yoga, along with other mind-body practices like tai chi and qigong, emphasizes the connection between the mind and body. Through controlled movements, breathing exercises, and meditation, individuals with OCD can reduce anxiety and improve overall well-being. Mindfulness incorporated in these practices enhances self-awareness and self-compassion, empowering individuals to navigate obsessive thoughts with greater calmness and resilience [17].

Integrating mindfulness-based therapies and creative interventions into OCD treatment broadens the spectrum of available approaches. By addressing the emotional and psychological aspects of the disorder, these therapies empower individuals to develop coping strategies, fostering a sense of mastery over their obsessions and compulsions.

7. Challenges and ethical considerations

7.1 Ethical concerns in novel treatment approaches

7.1.1 Informed consent and treatment risks

Ethical dilemmas arise in novel treatments like deep brain stimulation (DBS) and psychedelic therapies. Ensuring informed consent is challenging due to the complexity and experimental nature of these interventions. Balancing the potential benefits with risks, including unforeseen psychological consequences or physical side effects, necessitates careful consideration. Ethical guidelines must evolve to address the unique challenges posed by these innovative treatments, safeguarding patient autonomy and well-being [18].

7.1.2 Long-term effects and sustainability

Monitoring the long-term effects of emerging therapies is essential. While short-term studies might demonstrate efficacy, understanding the sustainability of treatment outcomes and potential adverse effects over several years is crucial. Ethical responsibility extends to ensuring ongoing support and follow-up care for patients receiving novel treatments, especially those involving Neurostimulation or psychoactive substances [19].

7.2 Accessibility and affordability of advanced treatments

7.2.1 Financial accessibility and healthcare disparities

Novel treatments often come with high costs, creating disparities in access based on financial means. Addressing these disparities requires advocating for equitable healthcare policies and exploring funding mechanisms to subsidize advanced treatments for underserved populations. Ensuring that cutting-edge therapies are accessible to all, regardless of socioeconomic status, is essential for promoting social justice and equality in mental healthcare [20].

7.2.2 Training and expertise

Implementing innovative treatments requires specialized training for healthcare providers. Ensuring that professionals receive comprehensive education in administering these therapies ethically and effectively is vital. Establishing standardized training protocols and certification processes ensures that patients receive high-quality care, minimizing the risk of malpractice or inadequate treatment delivery [21].

7.3 Stigma reduction and public awareness initiatives

7.3.1 Combatting stigma associated with novel treatments

The unfamiliarity of novel treatments can lead to stigmatization, both within the medical community and society at large. Public awareness campaigns and educational initiatives are crucial for dispelling myths and fostering understanding. By normalizing discussions around advanced therapies, society can reduce stigma, encourage open dialog, and promote acceptance of innovative approaches to mental health treatment [22].

7.3.2 Collaboration between researchers, clinicians, and advocacy groups

Collaborative efforts among researchers, clinicians, and patient advocacy groups are instrumental in challenging societal attitudes. By sharing knowledge, experiences, and success stories, these groups can work together to create a supportive environment. Engaging the public through media, workshops, and community events fosters empathy, dispels misconceptions, and encourages acceptance of diverse treatment modalities [24].

Addressing the ethical challenges, ensuring accessibility, and reducing stigma associated with advanced OCD treatments are essential steps toward fostering an inclusive and supportive environment for individuals seeking innovative therapeutic interventions.

8. Future directions and research opportunities

8.1 Potential breakthroughs in OCD research

8.1.1 Genomic studies and precision medicine

Advancements in genomic research hold the promise of identifying specific genetic markers associated with OCD subtypes. Understanding the genetic basis of the disorder can pave the way for targeted therapies, enabling personalized treatment plans tailored to an individual's genetic profile. Precision medicine approaches, based on genetic and biomarker data, have the potential to revolutionize OCD treatment, optimizing efficacy and minimizing adverse effects [23].

8.1.2 Neuroplasticity and cognitive remediation

Exploring the brain's ability to reorganize and adapt, known as neuroplasticity, offers exciting possibilities for cognitive remediation in OCD. Interventions focusing on enhancing neuroplasticity, such as cognitive training exercises and neuro feedback, could help reshape dysfunctional neural circuits. By encouraging adaptive neural changes, these interventions may promote symptom reduction and improve overall functioning in individuals with OCD [24].

8.2 Importance of collaborative efforts in advancing OCD treatment

8.2.1 Interdisciplinary research collaborations

Collaborative efforts between neuroscientists, clinicians, psychologists, and data scientists are essential for comprehensively understanding OCD. Interdisciplinary research can bridge gaps between genetic studies, neuroimaging findings, and behavioral interventions. By combining expertise from diverse fields, researchers can develop holistic models of OCD, leading to more effective treatment strategies [25].

8.2.2 Patient-driven research initiatives

Involving patients and their families in the research process is invaluable. Patient-driven research initiatives ensure that studies address the most pressing concerns and priorities of individuals living with OCD. Engaging patients as active partners fosters a patient-centered approach; leading to research that is not only scientifically rigorous but also directly relevant and impactful for those affected by the disorder [26].

8.3 Promising areas of study and technological integration

8.3.1 Advanced brain imaging techniques

Continued development of advanced neuroimaging methods, such as functional connectivity MRI (fcMRI) and diffusion spectrum imaging (DSI), allows for more precise mapping of brain circuits associated with OCD. Integrating these techniques with machine learning algorithms can enhance our understanding of the disorder's neural basis, potentially leading to breakthroughs in diagnosis and targeted interventions [27].

8.3.2 Digital therapeutics and Telehealth platforms

The rise of digital therapeutics, including smartphone apps and virtual reality programs, offers accessible and scalable interventions for individuals with OCD. These platforms provide tailored cognitive behavioral interventions, allowing patients to practice exposure and response prevention exercises in virtual environments. Telehealth services, coupled with digital therapeutics, ensure that evidence-based treatments reach individuals in remote or underserved areas, addressing the gap in mental healthcare accessibility [28].

By exploring these future directions and embracing collaborative, patient-centered, and technologically integrated approaches, the field of OCD research and treatment can continue to evolve, offering hope for more effective and accessible interventions for individuals living with OCD.

9. Conclusions

9.1 Recapitulation of key advancements discussed

In this chapter, we have explored the multifaceted advancements in the diagnosis and treatment of Obsessive-Compulsive Disorder (OCD). From understanding the intricate diagnostic criteria and common symptom variations to delving into innovative therapeutic approaches, the landscape of OCD research and treatment has significantly evolved. Genetic and neurobiological markers have illuminated the disorder's underlying mechanisms, paving the way for personalized treatments. Cognitive-behavioral therapies have been enhanced through exposure and response prevention techniques, alongside the integration of technology for more accessible interventions. Neuro stimulation methods, such as trans cranial magnetic stimulation and deep brain stimulation, offer promising avenues for treatment-resistant cases. Additionally, mindfulness-based therapies and integrative approaches, including art and music therapy, provide holistic avenues for emotional expression and regulation.

9.2 Hope for the future: improving lives of OCD patients

As we stand on the brink of an era marked by unprecedented scientific and technological progress, there is immense hope for individuals grappling with OCD. The advancements discussed in this chapter signify more than just scientific milestones; they represent newfound hope and improved quality of life for patients. Personalized treatments, precise diagnostics, and novel therapeutic modalities offer the promise of tailoring interventions to meet individual needs, thereby enhancing treatment efficacy and minimizing adverse effects. Moreover, the ongoing collaborations between researchers, clinicians, and patient advocacy groups underscore a collective commitment to improving mental health outcomes and reducing the burden of OCD.

9.3 Call to action: importance of continued research and support

While the strides made in OCD research and treatment are commendable, there remains a critical need for sustained efforts. Continued research is essential to unravel the complexities of OCD fully. Longitudinal studies exploring the long-term effects of novel treatments, further investigations into genetic and neurobiological markers, and in-depth qualitative research to understand patients' lived experiences are all imperative.

Furthermore, society must foster an environment of acceptance and understanding for individuals with OCD. This includes reducing stigma through education and awareness campaigns and ensuring that mental health services, including innovative treatments, are accessible to all, regardless of socioeconomic status. Support networks, both familial and societal, play a pivotal role in the recovery journey, emphasizing the significance of empathy and compassion in the face of mental health challenges.

In conclusion, the advancements in OCD diagnosis and treatment signify a transformative era in mental healthcare. By embracing these innovations, advocating for continued research, and fostering a compassionate society, we can collectively work toward a future where individuals affected by OCD can lead fulfilling lives, unencumbered by the limitations of their condition.

Acknowledgements

We extend our heartfelt gratitude to all those who contributed to this chapter. Special appreciation to our colleagues and institutions (Gulu University, Kampala International University, and All Saints Institute of Health Sciences Yumbe) for their support. Thanks to the editors and reviewers for their valuable feedback. Lastly, we appreciate our families and friends for their unwavering support.

Conflict of interest

The authors declared no conflict of interest.

Notes/thanks/other declarations

We confirm that this chapter received no external funding. We express gratitude to everyone acknowledged for their invaluable contributions. The views expressed here are solely those of the authors and do not reflect any official stance.

Nomenclature

OCD	Obsessive-Compulsive Disorder
ERP	exposure and response prevention
CBT	cognitive behavioral therapy
rTMS	repetitive transcranial magnetic stimulation
DBS	deep brain stimulation
MBSR	mindfulness-based stress reduction
ACT	acceptance and commitment therapy
EMA	ecological momentary assessment
fcMRI	functional connectivity magnetic resonance imaging
DSI	diffusion spectrum imaging

DOI: http://dx.doi.org/10.5772/intechopen.114260

Appendix A. Glossary of terms

1. Obsessive-Compulsive Disorder (OCD): a chronic mental health condition characterized by persistent, unwanted thoughts (obsessions) and repetitive behaviors or mental acts (compulsions).

2. Genetic markers: specific genes or DNA sequences associated with the risk of developing OCD, providing insights into the disorder's hereditary factors.

3. Neuroplasticity: the brain's ability to reorganize its structure, functions, and connections in response to learning, experience, and injury.

4. Deep Brain Stimulation (DBS): a surgical procedure involving the implantation of electrodes in specific brain regions to modulate neural activity and alleviate OCD symptoms.B.Case studies

Appendix B1. Case Study 1: Sarah's struggle with OCD

Sarah, a 28-year-old professional, experienced severe contamination obsessions, leading to excessive hand washing. Cognitive behavioral therapy (CBT) combined with Exposure and Response Prevention (ERP) gradually reduced her compulsive behaviors, enhancing her daily functioning and overall quality of life.

Appendix B2. Case Study 2: Mark's treatment-resistant OCD

Mark, 35, had treatment-resistant OCD, showing no improvement with standard therapies. Deep Brain Stimulation (DBS) targeted at the anterior limb of the internal capsule significantly alleviated his symptoms, highlighting the potential of neuro stimulation in severe cases.

Appendix C1. Diagnostic criteria and classifications

See **Table AC1**.

ICD-10 Criteria for OCD	
1. Obsessions	Recurrent, intrusive, and unwanted thoughts. Efforts to ignore or neutralize with actions or thoughts. |
2. Compulsions	Repetitive behaviors driven by obsessions. Actions not realistically connected to the feared event.
3. Duration	Takes more than 1 hour per day or causes significant distress.
4. Exclusion	Not due to substance effects or a medical condition. |
DSM-5 Criteria for OCD	
1. Obsessions and compulsions	Presence of intrusive thoughts or repetitive behaviors.
2. Time consuming	Takes up significant time, causing distress or impairment.
3. Specifiers	Differentiates insight levels

Table AC1.
Showing the ICD-10 and DSM-5 Criteria for OCD.

Appendix C2. Classifications based on symptomatology

- Contamination obsessions and cleaning compulsions: fears of contamination leading to extensive cleaning rituals.
- Harm obsessions and checking compulsions: persistent fears of causing harm, leading to repeated checking behaviors.
- Symmetry or exactness obsessions and ordering compulsions: need for symmetry, order, or precise arrangements.

Author details

Milton Anguyo[1*], Henry Drasiku[2], Magdalen Akia[3] and Molly Naisanga[1]

1 Gulu University, Uganda

2 Kampala International University, Uganda

3 Yumbe Regional Referral Hospital, Uganda

*Address all correspondence to: miltonanguyoosk@gmail.com

References

[1] Ruscio AM, Stein DJ, Chiu WT, Kessler RC. The epidemiology of obsessive-compulsive disorder in the National Comorbidity Survey Replication. Molecular Psychiatry. 2010;**15**(1):53-63

[2] McGuire JF, Piacentini J, Storch EA, et al. A multicenter examination and strategic revisions of the Yale global tic severity scale. Neurology. 2015;**85**(11):896-903

[3] Hollander E, Wong CM. Obsessive-compulsive spectrum disorders. Journal of Clinical Psychiatry. 1995;**56** (Suppl. 4):3-6

[4] American Psychiatric Association. Diagnostic and Statistical Manual of Mental Disorders. 5th ed. Arlington, VA: Author; 2013

[5] Pauls DL, Abramovitch A, Rauch SL, Geller DA. Obsessive-compulsive disorder: An integrative genetic and neurobiological perspective. Nature Reviews Neuroscience. 2014;**15**(6):410-424

[6] Milad MR, Rauch SL. Obsessive-compulsive disorder: Beyond segregated cortico-striatal pathways. Trends in Cognitive Sciences. 2012;**16**(1):43-51

[7] Abramovitch A, Abramowitz JS, Mittelman A. The neuropsychology of adult obsessive-compulsive disorder: A meta-analysis. Clinical Psychology Review. 2013;**33**(8):1163-1171

[8] Torous J, Staples P, Shanahan M, Lin C, Peck P, Keshavan M, et al. Utilizing a personal smartphone custom app to assess the patient health Questionnaire-9 (PHQ-9) depressive symptoms in patients with major depressive disorder. JMIR Mental Health. 2015;**2**(1):e8

[9] American Psychiatric Association and American Psychiatric Association. Diagnostic and Statistical Manual of Mental Disorders : DSM-5 Task Force. 5th ed. Washington, DC: American Psychiatric Association; 2013 p. xliv, p. 947

[10] Soomro GM et al. Selective serotonin re-uptake inhibitors (SSRIs) versus placebo for obsessive compulsive disorder (OCD). Cochrane Database of Systematic Reviews. 2008;**1**:CD001765

[11] Hoppen LM, et al. Low intensity technology-delivered cognitive behavioral therapy for obsessive-compulsive disorder: A meta-analysis. BMC Psychiatry. 2021;**21**(1):1-17.5556

[12] Insel TR et al. Obsessive-compulsive disorder. A double-blind trial of clomipramine and clorgyline. Archives of General Psychiatry. 1983;**40**(6):605-612

[13] Rodriguez CI, Kegeles LS, Levinson A, Feng T, Marcus SM, Vermes D, et al. Randomized controlled crossover trial of ketamine in obsessive-compulsive disorder: Proof-of-concept. Neuropsychopharmacology. 2013;**38**(12):2475-2483

[14] Winner JG, Carhart JM, Altar CA, Allen JD, Dechairo BM. A prospective, randomized, double-blind study assessing the clinical impact of integrated pharmacogenomic testing for major depressive disorder. Discovery Medicine. 2013;**16**(89):219-227

[15] Klinger E, Bouchard S, Légeron P, Roy S, Lauer F, Chemin I, et al. Virtual reality therapy versus cognitive behavior

therapy for social phobia: A preliminary controlled study. Cyberpsychology & Behavior. 2005;**8**(1):76-88

[16] Sucala M, Schnur JB, Constantino MJ, Miller SJ, Brackman EH, Montgomery GH, et al. The therapeutic relationship in e-therapy for mental health: A systematic review. Journal of Medical Internet Research. 2012;**14**(4):e110

[17] Mantovani A, Rossi S, Bassi BD, Simpson HB, Fallon BA. Targeted repetitive transcranial magnetic stimulation: A new method for localizing and treating focal cortical dysfunctions. NeuroImage. 2019;**190**:96-104

[18] Greenberg BD, Gabriels LA, Malone DA, Rezai AR, Friehs GM, Okun MS, et al. Deep brain stimulation of the ventral internal capsule/ventral striatum for obsessive-compulsive disorder: Worldwide experience. Molecular Psychiatry. 2010;**15**(1):64-79

[19] Kabat-Zinn J. An outpatient program in behavioral medicine for chronic pain patients based on the practice of mindfulness meditation: Theoretical considerations and preliminary results. General Hospital Psychiatry. 1982;**4**(1):33-47

[20] Hayes SC, Strosahl KD, Wilson KG. Acceptance and Commitment Therapy: An Experiential Approach to Behavior Change. New York: Guilford Press; 1999

[21] Malchiodi CA. Expressive Therapies. New York: Guilford Press; 2005

[22] Khalsa SB, Cope S. Effects of a yoga lifestyle intervention on performance-related characteristics of musicians: A preliminary study. Medical Science Monitor. 2006;**12**(8):CR325-CR331

[23] Racine É, Bar-Ilan O, Illes J. Brain imaging: A decade of coverage in the print media. Science Communication. 2005;**27**(1):5-43

[24] Coveney C, Nerlich B. The demonization of epidemics, or the failure of health promotion. Human Relations. 2004;**57**(8):981-1000

[25] Giddens A. Modernity and Self-Identity: Self and Society in the Late Modern Age. California, United States: Stanford University Press; 1991

[26] Tesh SN. Hidden Arguments: Political Ideology and Disease Prevention Policy. New Jersey, United States: Rutgers University Press; 1990

[27] Barroso C, Corbett AM. Stigma in psychiatric nursing. Perspectives in Psychiatric Care. 2009;**45**(3):196-206

[28] Phelan JC, Link BG. Is racism a fundamental cause of inequalities in health? Annual Review of Sociology. 2014;**41**:311-330

Chapter 2

Mindfulness-Based Approaches to Problematic Technology Use

Justin Thomas, Nada Al Juraib and Shahroo Izadi

Abstract

Mounting societal and clinical concerns about the mental health impacts of personal digital devices/services (social media, smartphones, gaming platforms, etc.) have underscored a need for evidence-based approaches to problematic technology use. Interventions and prevention strategies rooted in mindfulness-based techniques have proven helpful, supporting the development and maintenance of healthier and more adaptive relationships with technology. This chapter explores the literature on mindfulness-based interventions for problematic technology use, providing summative conclusions and identifying areas for further research. The chapter also describes, in detail, mindfulness-based digital balance (MBDB), our novel approach to problematic technology use. We examine the potential therapeutic mechanisms through which MBDB and other mindfulness-based approaches might operate. Finally, we explore the further development of the MBDB approach by considering how adaptive behaviors and healthier technology use might be sustained post-intervention.

Keywords: mindfulness, addiction, technology, gaming disorder, social media

1. Introduction

> *We shape our tools, and thereafter, our tools shape us*
> *[Frequently attributed to Marshall McLuhan]*

Whether people can develop problematic relationships with digital technologies is no longer debated—they can and do. How best to conceptualize (e.g., addiction, compulsion, and maladaptive-coping), treat and prevent such problems, however, remains an open and lively debate. This notion that individuals could develop technology-related disorders started attracting significant clinical concern in the 1990s, coinciding with the dawn (Web 1.0) and rapid proliferation of the publicly accessible World Wide Web [1]. Drawing on insights from pathological gambling, Griffiths [2] describes technology-related disorders as non-chemical (behavioral) addictions involving human-machine interaction. Echoing Griffiths, Young [3] proposed the inclusion of Internet Addiction Disorder (IAD) within the revisions to the 4th edition of the American Psychiatric Association's Diagnostic and Statistical Manual (DSM-IV-TR) [4]. Young's conceptualization of IAD was relatively broad, encompassing numerous subtypes that reflected different facets of problematic internet use, such as cyberrelationship (social media) addiction, cybersexual addiction, gaming addiction and more. Ultimately, IAD was not included in the DSM-IV-TR. However, gaming addiction, renamed internet gaming disorder (IGD), did make it into the revised text. IGD was incorporated as a condition worthy of further research, a status it currently retains in DSM-5-TR [5]. The proposed DSM-5 research criteria for IGD include preoccupation/obsession, withdrawal, tolerance, loss of control, anhedonia, continued overuse, deception, mood repair, and social/occupational impairment. It is stipulated that at least five of these nine symptoms should have been present for at least 12 months to meet the requirements for the proposed IGD diagnosis. Other research teams have adapted the same criteria for "social media disorder" [6].

Going further than the American Psychiatric Association (APA), the World Health Organization (WHO) has included gaming disorder as an official diagnostic entity within its diagnostic system [7]. In 2018, the WHO added gaming disorder to the behavioral addictions section of the International Classification of Disease, 11th Revision (ICD-11). Other internet-related problems (e.g., problematic social media use) can also be diagnosed within the section's residual categories: "disorders due to addictive behaviors, unspecified" and "other specified disorders due to addictive behaviors" [8, 9]. The inclusion of a health problem within the ICD necessitates the development of treatment approaches and preventive measures.

To date, mindfulness-based interventions (MBIs) have proven effective [10–12]. The application of mindfulness-based approaches to problematic technology use and technology-related disorders is a common-sense extension of their effectiveness in the treatment of ostensibly similar, addiction-like problems, such as hypersexuality [13], gambling disorder [14] and substance use disorders [15]. Beyond official diagnostic entities such as "gaming disorder," we also observe subclinical presentations, states not yet significant enough to impair day-to-day functioning but sufficiently distressing to motivate a desire for change. Here, also, mindfulness-based approaches have proven effective.

The remainder of this chapter explores how mindfulness-based approaches might be helpful for individuals struggling with problematic technology use and for those who wish to modify their relationship with technology in pursuit of enhanced digital well-being. Our reliance on digital technologies for work and leisure seems set to increase in the coming decades. Our ability to develop and maintain healthy relationships with digital technologies has become a cornerstone of twenty-first-century psychological well-being.

2. Mindfulness-based approaches to digital illbeing

Derived from Eastern meditative traditions, mindfulness-based interventions (MBIs) were initially developed to help manage chronic pain, with the same techniques later extended to target stress management [16–18]. The essence of mindfulness training is learning to pay attention, on purpose, to present moment experience in a non-judgmental and compassionate way. Ultimately, one of the benefits of such training is that individuals become more curious and accepting of moment-to-moment experiences, reducing habitual reactivity and opening the door to creative responses. Beyond chronic pain and stress management, mindfulness was integrated with cognitive therapy, becoming mindfulness-based cognitive therapy (MBCT), which is particularly effective for preventing relapse in recurrent major depressive disorder [19, 20]. The effectiveness of MBIs is attested by their inclusion in rigorously evidence-based treatment guidelines, such as the UK's NICE guidelines for

Depression in Adults: Treatment and Management. Conditions other than depression have also benefited from MBIs, from eating disorders to substance use disorders and, more recently, technology-related disorders (problematic technology use).

We recently (2024) reviewed all published research studies that used mindfulness-based approaches to address various aspects of problematic technology use. Between 2017 and 2023, using a systematic search strategy described elsewhere [21], we identified 10 published articles reporting on the application of MBIs in the context of problematic technology use. The interventions varied, but all of them contained mindfulness as an active element. Similarly, the stated targets for the interventions also varied, from gaming disorder to internet addiction and problematic social media or smartphone use.

Despite this heterogeneity, all of these studies reported positive outcomes, typically in the form of post-intervention symptom reduction; however, only one employed an active control condition, where participants were randomly allocated to either the intervention or control group [15]. There is an obvious need for further robust randomized controlled trials of MBIs targeting problematic technology use. Another limitation is that almost half of the studies reviewed were undertaken in China, necessitating further research among other cultural groups, especially where meditative/mindfulness-based practices might be perceived as alien.

3. The mindfulness-based digital balance (MBDB) retreat

We will now describe our mindfulness-based intervention targeting problematic technology use. This intervention was developed by the first author of this chapter, a graduate of the mindfulness-based stress reduction teacher training pathway (TTP1) offered by the UK's Centre for Mindfulness-based Research and Practice (CMRP). The intervention was refined with additional input from the chapter's co-authors and a senior faculty member at the CMRP.

The intervention was initially designed and offered as part of a 4- or 5-day intensive retreat experience. There is, however, no reason why it cannot be adapted to be delivered weekly over 4 or 5 weeks. The intervention aims to promote digital well-being (healthy adaptive technology use) in general rather than targeting any particular diagnostic entity or behavioral addiction. At the heart of the intervention is the idea that problematic technology use occurs along a continuum and is essentially a form of maladaptive mood modification strategy, also referred to as experiential avoidance.

Experiential avoidance is essentially a tendency to avoid or escape from unpleasant inner experiences, such as painful emotions, thoughts, and memories [22]. It can become habitual and automatic to the extent that the tendency evades awareness. Such problematic experiential avoidance is often considered a transdiagnostic symptom, that is, a problem associated with various mental health conditions, from anxiety and depression to eating and substance use disorders. MBIs are broadly viewed as effective because they target such transdiagnostic symptoms [23]. Experiential avoidance is characteristic of all behavioral addictions, where it is variously referred to as a mood modification strategy, emotion avoidance or palliative coping [24–27]. Questionnaire-based assessments of gaming disorder and problematic social media use ask questions such as: "Do you play in order to temporarily escape or relieve a negative mood?" and "I often used social media to escape from negative feelings?." Experiential avoidance is central to problematic technology use, and identifying and reducing this tendency is one of the key targets of the MBDB retreat. The following description of each MBDB session is based on the typical content and sequence; this, however, should be viewed as a rule of thumb rather than a rigid plan, while the overall goals of the program and its thematic sequence would remain the same, the specific form of the exercises and activities might change, as might some elements of within-session sequencing.

The orientation for the program socializes participants to the idea of experiential learning, growing by doing and interpersonal sharing, with little room for note-taking, PowerPoint slides, or bookwork. It also disabuses them of the notion that the program is some kind of digital detox with a didactic addendum. With caveats, technology use is encouraged, and most information is elicited *via* Socratic discussion. There is an emphasis on safety (knowing and respecting limits) and privacy (Chatham House rules). The concept of mindfulness/attention training is briefly discussed and illustrated with a brief meditative practice—a pause. Participants are asked to reflect on their intentions for signing up for the program and given information about its expectations of commitment to practice, activities and participation within and between sessions. Ideally, there are two instructors per group, with the optimum group size being between 10 and 20 participants. Both instructors should be explicit about their qualifications, being certified to teach mindfulness-based approaches (e.g., mindfulness-based stress reduction or mindfulness-based cognitive therapy) and experienced in delivering the same with access to regular supervision.

Session/day 1 has the concept of awareness as the central theme. With contextual (problem tech use) modifications, MBDB's session one mirrors session one of the standard mindfulness-based stress reduction curriculum (MBSR). Ideally, all participants are seated in a circle, which helps with group formation and facilitates interpersonal attention exchange (this applies to all sessions). Using a think-pair-share framework, participants are invited to engage in an exercise where they think about some of the challenges that personal digital technologies present in their lives. After individual reflection, participants are encouraged to pair or form small groups to discuss the same. Finally, the whole group reconvenes to share the outcomes of the side discussions more broadly. If appropriate, the instructor maps the outcomes of the broader group discussion to models of behavioral addiction and problematic technology use.

This activity is followed by an introduction to mindfulness and examples of mindlessness (autopilot), with reflections on how technology use is often mindless, intention-less, habitual and automatic. This is followed by the raisin exercise (mindful eating) to foster an appreciation of the links between paying attention and awareness and demystifying meditation. Participants are next introduced to the body scan mediation, with all meditative practices typically followed by an inquiry (how was that, what was that like, what did we notice?). This is where the instructor models curiosity about the minutiae of the experience, being equally attentive and interested in pleasant and unpleasant experiences, ideally modeling "experiential approach," the antonym of experiential avoidance. Each session ends with the assignment of "homework" (intersession tasks and practices). At the end of session one, participants are invited to practice mindful eating, body scan meditation, and bringing mindful awareness to an everyday task of their own choice. Finally, all participants are tasked with keeping a pleasant events journal (one or two entries), where they are encouraged to pay active attention to thoughts, feelings and physical sensations arising during pleasant moments.

Session/day 2 has the concept of acceptance as a key theme and integrates elements of MBSR's sessions two, three and four. In this session, the idea of experiential avoidance, variously named, is introduced. After the preliminaries, the session introduces a meditation on breath and body (a traditional seated meditation). After this, the homework is reviewed in small groups, eventually feeding back into the larger group—this typically elicits themes of awareness and heightened states of noticing, which tend to be appreciated but not always. After this, the instructor introduces movement practices such as chi kung or yoga postures. Prefaced with safety instructions, participants are invited to bring awareness to the body in stillness and motion. Eventually, participants are encouraged to hold a pose, for example, arms out, for as long as possible. The subsequent inquiry can help introduce themes of unpleasantness (aching arms from the posture or feeling bad for being the first to drop).

This exercise can provide a helpful segue into discussing habitual and automatic reactivity (fight/flight response) and more subtle forms of experiential avoidance. Once these ideas of escape, maladaptive coping and mood repair (experiential avoidance) are introduced, participants can be broken into groups to discuss some of the different ways in which they/or others use digital technology as a means of escaping, repairing or avoiding unpleasant states, such as anxiety, sadness and boredom. The session ends by introducing the homework, including everything from the previous session plus the breath-body meditation. However, the pleasant events journal is now substituted for an unpleasant events journal. The idea is to invite participants to bring attention (compassionate curiosity) to thoughts, feelings and physical sensations arising during unpleasant moments. This encourages accepting them, at least for a while, even if escape is possible.

Session/day 3 focuses on choice and responding intentionally. Integrating elements of MBSR's sessions five, six and seven, day 3 typically begins with a seated meditation before reviewing the homework. It is often advisable to encourage participants to draw their unpleasant event and discuss it in a way that preserves the anonymity of other people who may be involved in the event. The mood in the room often shifts noticeably after this activity. Key themes emerging from this exercise include noticing bodily sensations associated with unpleasant emotions and a heightened appreciation of the ephemerality and tolerability of unpleasant feelings.

Moving to the core theme of this session, a helpful activity to illustrate "choice" is the changing chairs exercise. In this task, participants are invited to switch chairs and move to an alternative seat, a place they suspect they will enjoy. After moving to their new place and sitting for a while, they are asked to choose a place/seat that they would find unpleasant. Finally, they return to their home seat. The inquiry after this exercise typically highlights ideas and insights around habits, expectations and the insights gained by trying out new things. Another exercise in this session, illustrating the same theme, involves mindful messaging. In this activity, participants are invited to use their phones either to respond to an unanswered message or to compose a message to a person of their choosing. The guidance for this practice emphasizes slowing down and making conscious choices, from selecting the target for one's message to choosing one's words carefully to craft a thoughtful and compassionate response/message. In this session, the links between awareness, acceptance, and choice are often discussed spontaneously.

The homework assigned at the end of this session includes meditative practices but also invites participants to occasionally bring mindful awareness to their phone-based activities, from photography to reading and sending messages. Participants are encouraged to apply principles such as intentionality, slowing down, mono-tasking, paying close attention, and compassion. Additionally, participants are invited to actively seek out an unpleasant event (something they would usually avoid) and bring awareness to the experience. The instructor always provides examples and additional guidance emphasizing safety.

Session/day 4 focuses on the post-program next steps, taking the learning, if any, forward. This integrates elements of MBSR's session eight. This session starts with the body scan meditation introduced in session one (slightly longer and with less guidance). People often make spontaneous comparisons with their day 1 experience of the body scan, frequently noting how it has become easier to stay focused or bring attention back during the practice. The homework is reviewed, and then participants are broken into small groups to share what, if anything, they have learned. This learning is then shared with the larger reconvened group. After a brief pause (a short meditative practice), participants are broken into small groups to discuss what, if anything, they will take away from the course and what changes, if any, they will attempt. This session usually throws up things like "continue with mindfulness practices," "spend more time in nature," and "remove apps that I see as harmful to my mental health." Such intentions are often carried out and sustained at least 3 months later, as detailed in our evaluative follow-up study [28]. Finally, we provide participants with information about mindfulness courses and direct them to the reducing digital distractions (ReDD) project, which offers many vetted tools for modifying one's digital environment to promote well-being. At this stage, there is typically a strong sense of camaraderie and group belonging, so the final session offers a social element, and the group typically continues online way beyond the physical program's end.

4. The retreat context

To date, all iterations (at the time of writing, there have been five) of the MBDB program have been offered as a retreat. This means that participants have been able to liberate themselves from their usual surroundings, environments and daily routines. We choose locations of natural beauty, green space and blue space. The choice to locate the retreat in nature is based on the idea that natural, bio-diverse environments have positive impacts on well-being and creativity [29–31]. Attention-restoration theory (ART) proposes that nature can provide a restorative environment, a space free from daily hassles, capable of engendering a sense of ease and appreciation [32].

At the time of writing, 1540 individuals have applied to participate in the retreat program, reflecting a wide interest from different age groups and backgrounds. Out of these 1540 participants, 108 have been selected to attend the previous six retreats, organized into groups of 14 to 24 individuals for each cohort. This small-group structure allows for more personalized attention and interaction among participants, fostering a supportive developmental environment.

The largest age demographic is individuals between 22 and 36 years who self-report technology-related challenges. Participants to date have been primarily from Saudi Arabia; however, there have been a significant number of participants from other countries, including Bahrain, Malaysia, Mexico, Oman, the United Kingdom, and the United States. This diversity enriched discussions and perspectives shared during the retreats.

Participant's motivations for joining included issues with social media, gaming, and messaging apps. For instance, one participant discussed how social media led to unrealistic self-assessments through social comparison. Another participant shared her struggle with excessive time on platforms, resulting in guilt and self-reproach.

These experiences underscored the psychological difficulties associated with technology use, highlighting the need for targeted interventions.

Once at the retreat, participants will typically have their own rooms within a hotel, with the hotel's function room doubling as the MBDB classroom. Beyond the official MBDB session, other retreat activities include walks in nature, Yoga and visits to cultural and historic sites. There is always a link between the classroom session and these extracurricular activities. For instance, mindful walking might be practiced on one of the nature walks, and at several of the meals (eating is always communal), a mindful eating table was available for participants to dine together, tech-free, and in silence. Participants were also repeatedly invited and encouraged to experiment with their technology use, for instance, leaving their phones behind or consciously deciding to take fewer but more thoughtful photos.

In the evaluation of MBDB [28], the natural environment was mentioned frequently and favorably. Several participants suggested that they now seek out the beauty of nature closer to home, taking walks and engaging in other outdoor activities. The retreat context also allowed the group to form deep interpersonal connections quickly. The participants also experienced this positively, leading to positive and enduring relationships.

One challenge of intensive retreat-type programs is ensuring that gains and changes can be sustained once participants return to their usual habitats and routines. Although we have evidence that the MBDB retreat leads to positive, sustained change, there is room to explore integrating additional elements and frameworks to enhance its effectiveness and the durability of the changes engendered by the MBDB retreat.

5. Sustaining changes with compassion: Lessons from recovering addicts

Whilst digital well-being retreats such as the MBDB retreat are not addiction-based in their theoretical positioning and ethos, they are uniquely positioned to adopt evidence-based practices from addiction recovery to foster sustained behavioral change. Studies indicate that strategies developed in addiction treatment, such as mindfulness-based relapse prevention and structured habit-formation frameworks, can be successfully adapted to address other compulsive behaviors, including technology use [33, 34].

This is particularly relevant given the similarities between digital habits and substance dependencies, both of which involve reward-based neural mechanisms that reinforce compulsive behavior [35, 36]. Neuroimaging studies show that both substance abuse and problematic technology use activate similar pathways in the brain's reward system, further underscoring the value of applying addiction recovery principles to this domain [37, 38]. Excessive technology use has been linked to behavioral addiction-like symptoms, such as loss of control, neglect of responsibilities, and mood regulation challenges [39]. Digital habits interfere with attention, well-being, and self-regulation in ways that mirror substance dependencies. Consequently, insights from addiction recovery—especially those focusing on maintaining behavioral changes in unsupportive real-world contexts—offer valuable guidance for structuring effective post-retreat strategies.

Addiction recovery programs provide robust frameworks designed to help individuals maintain behavioral changes beyond controlled environments. Principles such as self-compassion, curiosity-driven exploration, and gradual habit-building have demonstrated efficacy in equipping participants to navigate challenges and embed sustainable changes in their daily lives [40, 41]. Furthermore, individuals who choose structured behavioral interventions like retreats often display high motivation for change, which can be a double-edged sword. While their motivation may enhance initial commitment, it may also lead to heightened expectations, increasing the risk of disillusionment when habits are difficult to sustain post-retreat [33, 42].

In contrast to traditional detox models, which often emphasize strict abstinence, digital well-being retreats like this one adopt a non-detox, compassionate approach. This innovative framework prioritizes moderation and mindfulness, offering participants the opportunity to explore their habits in a low-pressure, supportive environment. Moderation-based interventions have been shown to reduce resistance and foster long-term adherence compared to rigid abstinence models, particularly in behaviors where complete avoidance is unrealistic [43, 44]. By integrating strategies from addiction recovery, such as sobriety sampling, retreats can enhance their ability to prepare attendees for long-term success. Sobriety sampling—an intervention encouraging intentional, temporary breaks from habits—has shown efficacy in helping individuals recalibrate their behaviors without the stress of rigid abstinence. For example, studies in alcohol moderation programs demonstrate that sobriety sampling helps individuals identify triggers, build self-awareness, and develop healthier coping strategies, all of which are critical for sustaining change [45–47]. For retreat participants, this approach not only fosters curiosity and self-awareness but also equips them with practical tools for maintaining progress post-retreat. By combining mindfulness principles with evidence-based relapse prevention strategies, this retreat offers an innovative model for addressing habitual behaviors in a holistic and sustainable way.

6. Reinforcing the non-detox philosophy: A framework for lifelong curiosity and optimization

A distinctive strength of digital well-being retreats such as this one is the non-detox philosophy, which provides a flexible, compassionate environment for participants to explore their relationship with technology. Unlike abstinence-based interventions, which often result in rebound behaviors and heightened resistance, the non-detox approach allows participants to maintain access to their devices while experimenting with moderation. Research supports this approach, showing that gradual, exploratory habit modification is more effective for long-term adherence than strict avoidance [48, 49]. This philosophy aligns with the concept of sobriety sampling, an evidence-based method widely used in addiction recovery. Sobriety sampling encourages individuals to take manageable, temporary breaks from substances or behaviors to observe their effects on well-being. It allows participants to reflect on their habits in a low-pressure environment, promoting self-awareness and intentionality without the stress of rigid abstinence.

Studies demonstrate that this approach is effective for behaviors requiring moderation rather than abstinence, such as alcohol consumption, sugar intake, and technology use [47, 48]. In the context of a retreat, the non-detox philosophy and sobriety sampling provide participants with a unique opportunity to experiment with small, intentional changes. For example, they might choose to leave their phone in another room during meals, silence notifications for a day, or set specific intentions before engaging with digital devices. These exercises are particularly valuable because they allow participants to notice immediate benefits, such as improved attention, reduced stress, and deeper interpersonal connections, which reinforce their motivation to sustain these behaviors post-retreat [34]. Furthermore, this approach fosters a mindset of curiosity and growth, encouraging participants to generalize the principles they learn during the retreat to other aspects of their lives. For instance, someone who experiments with reducing screen time during the retreat might later apply the same mindset to managing sugar cravings or building a morning mindfulness routine. Research shows that curiosity-driven frameworks promote self-efficacy and adaptability, key factors in sustaining long-term behavior change [49, 50]. Unlike detox-based models, which often emphasize avoidance and control, the retreat's philosophy empowers participants to embrace moderation and mindfulness as tools for self-optimization.

Technology is integral to modern life, and rigid abstinence can create unnecessary stress and disillusionment. By contrast, the retreat's approach aligns with evidence-based strategies that emphasize sustainable habit formation, making it particularly suited to participants seeking to recalibrate their relationship with technology while maintaining flexibility and agency [35, 51].

7. Integrating sobriety sampling into the retreat design for lasting change

Sobriety sampling, an approach widely recognized in addiction recovery, emphasizes intentional, time-limited breaks from behaviors or substances to foster self-awareness and explore the benefits of moderation. Unlike abstinence models, which require permanent elimination of behaviors, sobriety sampling provides a low-pressure opportunity for individuals to recalibrate their habits. Research shows that this method is effective for behaviors where abstinence is impractical, such as alcohol moderation and technology use [34]. This retreat already integrates sobriety sampling principles, offering participants the opportunity to experiment with reduced technology use in a supportive environment. For example, participants are encouraged to turn off notifications during meals, leave devices behind during nature walks, and engage in guided reflection on how these changes influence their mood and focus. These exercises mirror the strategies used in sobriety sampling by promoting incremental change and fostering curiosity about habit modification. Studies demonstrate that such gradual, exploratory approaches reduce resistance and increase the likelihood of sustained behavior change [33].

Technology use, unlike substances such as alcohol or drugs, is essential for daily functioning. The challenge lies in managing its use intentionally rather than eliminating it entirely. Sobriety sampling reduces the stress associated with all-or-nothing approaches by allowing participants to retain access to their devices while experimenting with small, manageable changes. For instance, a participant might allocate specific tech-free times during the day and reflect on the effects. This flexibility minimizes the sense of deprivation and rebellion that often undermines behavior change [43, 47]. Participants who engage in sobriety sampling often experience immediate benefits, such as improved clarity, reduced stress, or increased presence in social interactions. These positive outcomes serve as intrinsic motivators, reinforcing the desire to continue experimenting with reduced device use [34].

Sobriety sampling empowers participants to explore what works for them rather than adhering to prescriptive rules. This agency fosters a mindset of self-compassion and curiosity, which has been shown to enhance resilience and long-term commitment to behavior change [33, 48]. By encouraging participants to regularly check in on their habits and assess their alignment with personal values, sobriety sampling offers a transferable tool for managing not just technology use but other habitual behaviors. Participants can apply this framework to areas such as diet, work-life balance, and stress management, creating a ripple effect of intentional living across multiple domains [45].

8. Embedding sobriety sampling in retreat design

To maximize the impact of sobriety sampling, it is crucial to embed its principles more intentionally into the retreat's design and facilitation. This ensures that participants leave not only with the immediate benefits of reduced device use but also with the tools to sustain their progress in real-life contexts. Structured sampling periods can be introduced by designating specific retreat activities, such as meals, nature walks, or journaling sessions, as device-free zones. These breaks can be framed as opportunities to observe the effects of reduced device use rather than as obligations, helping participants engage with the experience in a positive and exploratory way. Participants can also be encouraged to adopt intentional scrolling practices by setting clear goals before using their devices, such as responding to an email, and assessing their focus and satisfaction afterward.

Reflection and feedback loops are essential for deepening participants' engagement with sobriety sampling. Facilitators can incorporate structured reflection exercises, such as journaling prompts that ask questions like, "How did you feel during the device-free period?" or "What did you notice about your attention and mood?" Group discussions can normalize diverse experiences, provide peer support, and reinforce a shared commitment to exploring new habits. It is equally important to frame lapses in reduced device use as learning opportunities rather than failures. Behavioral change can be presented as a process of continuous experimentation, where setbacks are a natural part of growth [42]. Finally, participants should leave the retreat with practical takeaway tools, such as a structured sobriety sampling guide that includes reflection prompts and suggestions for integrating device-free practices into their daily lives. Providing access to a digital or physical journal can help them track their progress and revisit their retreat learnings.

9. Why sobriety sampling is uniquely valuable for retreat participants

Retreat participants are often individuals motivated by self-improvement but prone to all-or-nothing thinking, which can undermine their ability to sustain behavioral changes. Sobriety sampling offers a compassionate alternative by encouraging exploration, curiosity, and flexibility. Unlike detox approaches, which often create a false sense of achievement during the retreat but fail to address real-world challenges, sobriety sampling equips participants with a practical, adaptable framework for intentional living. By embedding sobriety sampling into the retreat's core design, facilitators can ensure that participants leave with more than just temporary relief from digital overload. Instead, they gain a lifelong tool for auditing and managing their habits, fostering resilience and adaptability in an increasingly technology-driven world.

10. Sustaining retreat practices post-retreat: Evidence-based adaptations for everyday life

For digital well-being retreats to have a lasting impact, their interventions must be designed not only for the immersive retreat environment but also for practical application in participants' daily lives. Research underscores the importance of ensuring that practices learned in structured, controlled environments are adaptable to real-world contexts, where external demands, time constraints, and distractions are prevalent [42, 45]. Evidence-based adaptations can help participants continue benefiting from these practices in a sustainable, self-directed manner.

In daily life, mindful eating practices can be integrated by encouraging participants to pause briefly before meals to notice the texture of their first bite or reflect on gratitude for the meal. Even small practices like this can improve self-regulation, reduce emotional eating, and enhance the enjoyment of food [49]. Similarly, mindful walking, which participants practice during guided nature walks at the retreat, can be adapted to urban settings by engaging in "micro-nature" walks, such as short strolls in parks or observing greenery on the street. Even small doses of nature exposure have been shown to reduce stress, restore attention, and improve mood [50, 51].

Sitting meditation, another retreat practice can be performed through short meditations during transitions, such as before starting work or after a commute. Brief mindfulness sessions of just 2–5 minutes have been shown to reduce stress, improve focus, and enhance emotional regulation [52, 53]. Similarly, device-free challenges from the retreat can be adapted to daily life by designating specific times or spaces as tech-free zones, such as during meals or before bed. Structured, intentional, device-free periods reduce anxiety and improve focus, making them a valuable addition to participants' daily routines [34].

Reflection and journaling practices, which help participants explore their relationship with technology during the retreat, can be simplified into brief daily habits. For instance, writing down one positive moment or insight each evening can reinforce self-awareness, goals, and emotional resilience [54]. Intentional technology use, which participants practice by setting clear goals before engaging with devices, can also be structured into daily life. For example, participants might check notifications only at designated times or use devices exclusively for specific tasks, allowing them to retain control over their technology use.

By integrating these evidence-based adaptations into daily routines, participants can maintain and build upon the benefits of their retreat experiences. This ensures that the tools and practices developed during the retreat lead to long-term, sustainable changes in their relationship with technology and other areas of their lives.

11. Embedding real-life integration during the retreat

Integrating retreat practices into participants' everyday lives begins with embedding real-life applicability into the retreat itself. Daily real-life context reflections are essential, encouraging participants to journal with prompts like "How could I adapt this practice for my home routine?" These reflections help participants bridge the gap between retreat activities and the realities of their daily lives, fostering proactive consideration of practical integration. Personalized habit workshops can further support this process by facilitating sessions where participants experiment with shorter, real-world versions of retreat practices, such as mini-meditations or tech-free intervals. Immediate feedback during these sessions ensures that participants leave the retreat equipped with practical adjustments tailored to their unique challenges. To solidify these experiences, participants should receive structured takeaway tools, including guides, templates, and habit trackers. These resources provide continued support and accountability as they transition from the retreat environment to their everyday routines.

12. Relapse prevention and long-term self-management: Equipping participants for sustained change

For any behavioral intervention to achieve long-term success, it must equip participants to navigate challenges and sustain their progress independently. While retreats provide a supportive environment to explore and practice new habits, the transition back to daily life presents significant obstacles. Without intentional relapse prevention strategies and tools for self-management, even the most motivated participants may struggle to maintain the changes they have worked to establish. Relapse prevention, a cornerstone of addiction recovery programs, offers a valuable framework for addressing these challenges. By anticipating high-risk scenarios, fostering self-awareness, and providing practical tools, relapse prevention strategies empower individuals to sustain progress in less controlled environments [41]. Integrating these principles into digital well-being retreats ensures participants are equipped for sustained behavioral change.

Anticipating high-risk scenarios is a critical component of relapse prevention. Research highlights the importance of identifying and preparing for situations that may trigger lapses, whether external (e.g., time pressure and environmental distractions) or internal (e.g., stress and negative self-talk) [44]. In the context of technology use, participants often face high-risk scenarios such as work environments that demand constant connectivity, social settings that normalize device overuse, or emotional triggers like boredom and loneliness. During the retreat, participants can engage in scenario mapping exercises, brainstorming potential triggers they might encounter post-retreat and reflecting on strategies they have successfully employed during the retreat. Facilitators can also guide participants in developing pre-planned alternatives, such as engaging in physical activity, journaling, or practicing mindful breathing, to navigate high-risk moments effectively.

Building self-awareness through reflection is another foundational element of relapse prevention. Journaling and mindfulness exercises enable participants to recognize patterns, track progress, and identify barriers to change [51]. Developing self-awareness helps participants notice early signs of lapses, such as mindless scrolling or increased device dependency, and reflect on their emotional and behavioral triggers. Facilitators can emphasize reflective practices during the retreat by encouraging daily journaling. Prompts such as "What triggered my urge to check my device today?" and "What benefits did I notice from device-free time?" help participants gain deeper insights into their habits. Providing habit-tracking tools further supports this self-awareness by allowing participants to log behaviors and recognize patterns post-retreat.

Creating personal action plans ensures participants have clear, actionable strategies to maintain their progress. Research demonstrates that individuals with well-defined plans, including specific goals and timelines, are significantly more likely to sustain their changes [42]. Facilitators can dedicate sessions to guiding participants through the creation of these plans. Key elements include identifying priorities by choosing practices that resonate most, defining small and scalable goals, such as a 5-minute daily meditation or a single tech-free meal, and establishing checkpoints for progress evaluation, such as a 30-day or 90-day review. Tailored action plans help participants integrate retreat practices into their daily lives with clarity and confidence.

Fostering accountability and support significantly enhances long-term behavior change. Social support systems, whether through peer partnerships or group forums, have been shown to strengthen adherence to new habits [25]. Retreats can facilitate these connections by pairing participants with accountability partners to share progress and challenges or by organizing post-retreat virtual meetups or forums. These support networks provide encouragement, shared strategies, and a sense of community that helps participants navigate setbacks and stay motivated.

Finally, emphasizing self-compassion and resilience is vital for relapse prevention. Self-compassion allows individuals to recover from setbacks without excessive self-criticism, while resilience fosters a mindset that views lapses as opportunities for growth [55, 56]. Participants can approach lapses in mindful technology use with curiosity and forgiveness, asking, "What can I learn from this experience?" rather than focusing on self-blame. Facilitators can normalize lapses by highlighting their role in the learning process and providing examples of recalibration strategies. Curiosity-driven reflection, supported by prompts like "What triggered this behavior?" and "What can I try differently next time?" further reinforces a compassionate and growth-oriented perspective.

By embedding relapse prevention frameworks into the retreat's structure, facilitators ensure participants leave with the tools, self-awareness, and support needed to maintain their progress independently. These strategies empower participants to navigate the complexities of daily life with resilience, adaptability and sustained confidence in their ability to manage their digital habits effectively.

13. Embedding structured frameworks for lifelong digital well-being

While retreats offer transformative experiences, long-term behavioral change is best supported by structured frameworks that provide participants with tools for continuous self-management. In contexts such as substance use recovery, frameworks like the 12-step model have proven effective for guiding individuals through sustained self-regulation, offering a shared philosophy, clear practices, and community-based accountability [57, 58]. Applying a similar structured approach to digital well-being offers significant potential for equipping retreat participants to manage their relationship with technology long after the immersive environment ends.

14. A case for a taught structured framework

The retreat's existing design includes many of the core components necessary for an effective structured framework to support participants in achieving long-term digital well-being. Research underscores the importance of structured approaches in sustaining behavior change, as they provide clarity, consistency, and accountability—critical factors for success. A structured framework would formalize and integrate these existing components, enabling participants to translate retreat interventions into sustained, self-directed practices that extend beyond the immersive environment. Unlike ad hoc strategies, a framework offers a cohesive, adaptable roadmap for participants to navigate the complexities of modern digital habits with intention and self-compassion.

Structured frameworks have been demonstrated to reduce ambiguity, support gradual progress, and encourage self-regulation by guiding participants through incremental changes rather than overwhelming transformations. By leveraging the retreat's current strengths—such as sobriety sampling and mindfulness—the development of a formalized framework would further enhance the retreat's ability to meet participants' diverse needs, fostering both immediate impact and long-term adherence.

15. Building on existing strengths

The retreat already incorporates several foundational elements of an effective structured framework. Practices such as mindfulness exercises, device-free challenges, and guided reflection provide participants with tools to explore their digital habits in a safe, supportive environment. Similarly, the integration of sobriety sampling promotes a philosophy of moderation and exploration, encouraging participants to experiment with new behaviors in low-pressure settings. These components align with evidence-based approaches for sustainable behavior change and serve as a strong foundation for further development.

To formalize these elements into a structured framework, the retreat could further enhance its focus on guiding principles that emphasize self-compassion, curiosity, and intentionality. These principles would provide participants with an overarching philosophy for approaching their digital habits, fostering a mindset of growth. The framework could also offer practical tools, such as personalized habit-mapping exercises, tech-free rituals, and reflective journaling templates, enabling participants to adapt retreat practices to their unique routines and challenges.

16. Core components of the proposed framework

The proposed structured framework would include four key components designed to build on the retreat's current strengths:

1. *Guiding principles:* A set of foundational principles would underpin the framework, helping participants approach their digital habits with intentionality and balance. For example, principles such as "Intention Before Action," which encourages participants to pause and reflect before engaging with technology, and "Moderation Over Perfection," which emphasizes gradual, sustainable change, align seamlessly with the retreat's current philosophy.

2. *Personalized practices:* Participants would be encouraged to customize their engagement with the framework by selecting practices that resonate with their needs. These practices might include device-free rituals, mindful scrolling strategies, and the use of habit trackers to monitor progress. This personalization ensures that the framework is adaptable to diverse lifestyles and challenges.

3. *Social connection and accountability:* Building on the retreat's existing emphasis on peer support, the framework could incorporate structured opportunities for social connection, such as accountability partnerships or group check-ins. Research highlights the critical role of social support in sustaining behavior change, particularly in fostering motivation and resilience [54].

4. *Regular checkpoints for growth:* Periodic evaluations, such as 30-day and quarterly reflections, would allow participants to recalibrate their goals and refine their practices. These checkpoints provide an opportunity for participants to reflect on their progress, identify emerging challenges, and celebrate milestones, reinforcing a sense of accomplishment and forward momentum.

17. Integrating the framework into the retreat

To integrate the structured framework into the retreat, facilitators could incorporate sessions dedicated to habit mapping and framework orientation. These sessions would guide participants in identifying key practices, tailoring them to their routines, and understanding how the framework can support sustained progress. Additionally, resources such as digital well-being planners, guided reflection journals, and accountability group guides could serve as tangible tools for participants to continue engaging with the framework post-retreat.

Facilitators might also draw on case studies to illustrate the effectiveness of similar frameworks, such as the 12-step model or sobriety sampling, in fostering sustained change. Interactive workshops could further engage participants in brainstorming ways to apply the framework to their own lives, ensuring that the framework feels relevant and accessible to all.

18. Expected outcomes and advantages

Formalizing the retreat's existing components into a structured framework could yield several key benefits. First, it would enhance participants' ability to sustain behavior change by providing a clear and cohesive pathway for integrating retreat practices into daily life. Second, the framework's flexibility and scalability would allow participants to apply its principles beyond technology use, addressing other habitual behaviors such as overworking or excessive media consumption. Third, the emphasis on progress over perfection would align with the retreat's compassionate philosophy, empowering participants to approach their personal growth with self-compassion and adaptability.

The development of a structured framework represents a natural evolution for the MBDB retreat, building on its existing strengths to further enhance effectiveness. By formalizing its principles and practices into a cohesive system, the retreat can offer participants a transformative resource for lifelong growth. Grounded in the philosophy of progress over perfection, this framework would further empower participants to sustain their progress, adapt to new challenges, and continually optimize their relationship with technology in a realistic and compassionate way.

19. Conclusions

This chapter explored the growing concern that some of us can develop problematic relationships with digital technology. The idea that such problems can attain clinical significance is attested by the inclusion of gaming disorder within the WHO's diagnostic manual. Mindfulness-based approaches to problematic technology use and the fostering of adaptive relationships have demonstrated early promise. The Mindfulness-based digital balance retreat described within this chapter offers a blueprint for intervention and psycho-educational initiatives in this domain. There is further scope to improve such interventions by exploring structured frameworks to help sustain healthy relationships with digital technology.

Acknowledgements

We want to acknowledge Dh. Karunavira for his kind help and guidance in formulating MBDB.

Author details

Justin Thomas[1*], Nada Al Juraib[1] and Shahroo Izadi[2]

1 King Abdulaziz Center for World Culture (Ithra), Global Digital Wellbeing Program (Sync), Dhahran, Saudi Arabia

2 Roocovery, Uxbridge, UK

*Address all correspondence to: justin.thomas@aramco.com

References

[1] Fuchs C, Hofkirchner W, Schafranek M, Raffl C, Sandoval M, Bichler R. Theoretical foundations of the web: Cognition, communication, and co-operation. Towards an understanding of web 1.0, 2.0, 3.0. Future Internet. 2010;**2**(1):41-59

[2] Griffiths M. Technological addictions. Clinical Psychology Forum. 1995;**76**:14-19

[3] Young KS. Internet addiction: The emergence of a new clinical disorder. Cyberpsychology, Behavior and Social Networking. 1998;**1**:237-244

[4] American Psychiatric Association. Diagnostic and Statistical Manual of Mental Disorders 4th Edn Revised [DSM-IV]. Washington DC: American Psychiatric Press; 1994

[5] American Psychiatric Association. Diagnostic and Statistical Manual of Mental Disorders: DSM-5-TR. Arlington, VA: American Psychiatric Association; 2022

[6] van den Eijnden RJJM, Lemmens JS, Valkenburg PM. The social media disorder scale. Computers in Human Behavior. 2016;**61**:478-487

[7] World Health Organization. International Classification of Diseases for Mortality and Morbidity Statistics [11th Revision]. World Health Organization; 2018

[8] Lindenberg K, Kindt S, Szász-Janocha C. Effectiveness of cognitive behavioral therapy-based intervention in preventing gaming disorder and unspecified internet use disorder in adolescents: A cluster randomized clinical trial. JAMA Network Open. 2022;**5**(2):e2148995

[9] Brand M, Rumpf HJ, Demetrovics Z, Müller A, Stark R, King DL, et al. Which conditions should be considered as disorders in the International Classification of Diseases [ICD-11] designation of "other specified disorders due to addictive behaviors"? Journal of Behavioral Addictions. 2020;**11**(2):150-159

[10] Lan Y, Ding J-E, Li W, Li J, Zhang Y, Liu M, et al. A pilot study of a group mindfulness-based cognitive-behavioral intervention for smartphone addiction among university students. Journal of Behavioral Addictions. 2018;**7**(4):1171-1176

[11] Li W, Garland EL, McGovern P, O'Brien JE, Tronnier C, Howard MO. Mindfulness-oriented recovery enhancement for internet gaming disorder in U.S. adults: A stage I randomized controlled trial. Psychology of Addictive Behaviors. 2017;**31**(4):393-402

[12] Li W, Garland EL, Howard MO. Therapeutic mechanisms of Mindfulness-Oriented Recovery Enhancement for internet gaming disorder: Reducing craving and addictive behavior by targeting cognitive processes. Journal of Addictive Diseases. 2018;**37**(1-2):5-13

[13] Van Gordon W, Shonin E, Griffiths MD. Meditation awareness training for the treatment of sex addiction: A case study. Journal of Behavioral Addictions. 2016;**5**(2):363-372

[14] Chen P, Jindani F, Perry J, Turner NL. Mindfulness and problem gambling treatment. Asian Journal of Gambling Issues and Public Health. 2014;**4**(1):2

[15] Li W, Howard MO, Garland EL, McGovern P, Lazar M. Mindfulness treatment for substance misuse: A systematic review and meta-analysis. Journal of Substance Abuse Treatment. 2017;**75**:62-96

[16] Kabat-Zinn J. An outpatient program in behavioral medicine for chronic pain patients based on the practice of mindfulness meditation: Theoretical considerations and preliminary results. General Hospital Psychiatry. 1982;**4**:33-47

[17] Kabat-Zinn J. Wherever You Go, There You Are: Mindfulness Meditation in Everyday Life. New York: Hyperion; 1994

[18] Kabat-Zinn J. Some reflections on the origins of MBSR, skillful means, and the trouble with maps. Contemporary Buddhism. 2011;**12**(1)

[19] Segal ZV, Williams JMG, Teasdale JD. Mindfulness-Based Cognitive Therapy for Depression: A New Approach to Preventing Relapse. New York: Guilford Press; 2002

[20] Teasdale JD, Williams JMG, Soulsby JM, Segal ZV. Prevention of relapse/recurrence in major depression by mindfulness-based cognitive therapy. Journal of Consulting and Clinical Psychology. 2000;**68**(4):615-623

[21] Colder Carras M, Aljuboori D, Shi J, Date M, Karkoub F, García Ortiz K, et al. Prevention and health promotion interventions for young people in the context of digital well-being: Rapid systematic review. Journal of Medical Internet Research. 2024;**26**:e59968

[22] Hayes SC, Wilson KG, Gifford EV, Follette VM, Strosahl K. Experimental avoidance and behavioral disorders: A functional dimensional approach to diagnosis and treatment. Journal of Consulting and Clinical Psychology. 1996;**64**(6):1152-1168

[23] Crane R. Mindfulness-Based Cognitive Therapy. New York: Routledge; 2009

[24] Kim SS, Bae SM. Social anxiety and social networking service addiction proneness in university students: The mediating effects of experiential avoidance and interpersonal problems. Psychiatry Investigation. 2022;**19**(6):462-469

[25] Pontes HM, Griffiths MD. Measuring DSM-5 internet gaming disorder: Development and validation of a short psychometric scale. Computers in Human Behavior. 2015;**45**:137-143

[26] Ekşi F. The mediating role of social media disorder in the relationship of experiential avoidance with psychological symptoms. Addicta: The Turkish Journal on Addictions. 2019;**6**(3):497-509

[27] García-Oliva C, Piqueras JA. Experiential avoidance and technological addictions in adolescents. Journal of Behavioral Addictions. 2016;**5**(2):293-303

[28] Thomas J, AlJuraib N, Ashour L, Karunavira D. The mindfulness-based digital wellbeing retreat: An interpretative phenomenological analysis. Computers in Human Behaviour Reports. 2024;**14**:100408

[29] Yeh C-W, Hung S-H, Chang C-Y. The influence of natural environments on creativity. Frontiers in Psychiatry. 2022;**13**

[30] Bikomeye JC, Balza J, Beyer KM. The impact of schoolyard greening on children's physical activity and socioemotional health: A systematic

review of experimental studies. International Journal of Environmental Research and Public Health. 2021;**18**(2)

[31] Ulrich RS. View through a window may influence recovery from surgery. Science. 1984;**224**(4647):420-421

[32] Kaplan R, Kaplan S. The Experience of Nature: A Psychological Perspective. New York, NY, US: Cambridge University Press; 1989. xii, 340-xii p

[33] Bowen S, Chawla N, Marlatt GA. Mindfulness-Based Relapse Prevention for Addictive Behaviors: A Clinician's Guide. New York: Guilford Press; 2014. 224 p

[34] Wilcockson TDW, Pothos EM, Privitera C. Digital addiction: Increased engagement versus perceived disconnection. Computers in Human Behavior. 2019;**99**:54-64. DOI: 10.1016/j.chb.2019.04.019

[35] Volkow ND, Wang G-J, Fowler JS. Addiction: Decreased reward sensitivity and increased expectation sensitivity conspire to overwhelm the brain's control circuit. BioEssays. 2011;**33**(6):427-438. DOI: 10.1002/bies.201100031

[36] Andreassen CS. Online social network site addiction: A comprehensive review. Current Addiction Reports. 2015;**2**(2):175-184. DOI: 10.1007/s40429-015-0056-9

[37] Yuan K, Qin W, Wang G, et al. Microstructure abnormalities in adolescents with internet addiction disorder. PLoS ONE. 2011;**6**(6):e20708. DOI: 10.1371/journal.pone.0020708

[38] Brand M, Young KS, Laier C. Prefrontal control and internet addiction: A theoretical model and review of neuropsychological and neuroimaging findings. Frontiers in Human Neuroscience. 2016;**10**:314. DOI: 10.3389/fnhum.2016.00314

[39] Kuss DJ, Griffiths MD. Online social networking and addiction—A review of the psychological literature. International Journal of Environmental Research and Public Health. 2015;**8**(3):3528-3552. DOI: 10.3390/ijerph8033528

[40] Neff KD. Self-Compassion: The Proven Power of Being Kind to Yourself. New York: William Morrow; 2011. 320 p

[41] Marlatt GA, Donovan DM. Relapse Prevention: Maintenance Strategies in the Treatment of Addictive Behaviors. 2nd ed. New York: Guilford Press; 2005. 416 p

[42] Prochaska JO, DiClemente CC. Stages of change model and integration. Alcohol Research and Health. 1983;**2**(4):124-130

[43] Heather N, Rollnick S, Bell A. Moderation versus abstinence in the treatment of alcohol problems: A commentary on the research evidence. Addictive Behaviors. 2010;**35**(1):243-249. DOI: 10.1016/j.addbeh.2009.09.023

[44] Carey KB, Carey MP, Maisto SA. Pooled analyses of brief alcohol interventions for college drinkers. Psychology of Addictive Behaviors. 2007;**21**(3):322-335. DOI: 10.1037/0893-164X.21.3.322

[45] Marlatt GA, Witkiewitz K. Harm reduction approaches to alcohol use: Health promotion, prevention, and treatment. Addictive Behaviors. 2005;**30**(2):1179-1191. DOI: 10.1016/j.addbeh.2005.02.005

[46] Kashdan TB, Steger MF. Curiosity and pathways to well-being and meaning in life: Traits, states, and everyday behaviors. Motivation and

Emotion. 2007;**31**:159-173. DOI: 10.1007/s11031-007-9068-7

[47] Deci EL, Ryan RM. The 'what' and 'why' of goal pursuits: Human needs and the self-determination of behavior. Psychological Inquiry. 2000;**11**(4):227-268. DOI: 10.1207/S15327965PLI1104_01

[48] Kabat-Zinn J. Full Catastrophe Living: Using the Wisdom of Your Body and Mind to Face Stress, Pain, and Illness. New York: Delacorte Press; 2003. 650 p

[49] Prochaska JO, Velicer WF. The transtheoretical model of health behavior change. American Journal of Health Promotion. 1997;**12**(1):38-48. DOI: 10.4278/0890-1171-12.1.38

[50] Kristeller JL, Wolever RQ. Mindfulness-based eating awareness training for treating binge eating disorder: The conceptual foundation. Eating Disorders. 2011;**19**(1):49-61. DOI: 10.1080/10640266.2011.533605

[51] Kaplan S. The restorative benefits of nature: Toward an integrative framework. Journal of Environmental Psychology. 1995;**15**(3):169-182. DOI: 10.1016/0272-4944[95]90001-2

[52] Yin J, Zhu S, MacNaughton P. Systematic review of the association between residential greenness and human health. Environmental Research. 2022;**204**:111910. DOI: 10.1016/j.envres.2021.111910

[53] Tang YY, Hölzel BK, Posner MI. The neuroscience of mindfulness meditation. Nature Reviews Neuroscience. 2015;**16**(4):213-225. DOI: 10.1038/nrn3916

[54] Hölzel BK, Carmody J, Vangel M, et al. Mindfulness practice leads to increases in regional brain gray matter density. Psychiatry Research: Neuroimaging. 2011;**191**(1):36-43. DOI: 10.1016/j.pscychresns.2010.08.006

[55] Holt-Lunstad J, Smith TB, Layton JB. Social relationships and mortality risk: A meta-analytic review. PLoS Medicine 2010;**7**(7):e1000316. DOI: 10.1371/journal.pmed.1000316

[56] Neff KD, Germer CK. A pilot study and randomized controlled trial of the mindful self-compassion program. Journal of Clinical Psychology. 2013;**69**(1):28-44. DOI: 10.1002/jclp.21923

[57] Pennebaker JW, Chung CK. Expressive writing: Connections to physical and mental health. In: Friedman HS, editor. Encyclopedia of Mental Health. 2nd ed. Elsevier; 2011. pp. 145-152. DOI: 10.1016/B978-0-12-397045-9.00020-0

[58] Kelly JF, Humphreys K, Ferri M. Alcoholics anonymous and other 12-step programs for alcohol use disorder. Cochrane Database of Systematic Reviews. 2020;**3**:CD012880. DOI: 10.1002/14651858.CD012880.pub2

Chapter 3

Diverse Advanced Approaches of Transcranial Magnetic Stimulation in Obsessive-Compulsive Disorder

Xian-Jun Lan, Chaomeng Liu, Xin-Hu Yang and Wei Zheng

Abstract

Obsessive-Compulsive Disorder (OCD) significantly contributes to mental health morbidity. Empirical evidence supports the use of selective serotonin reuptake inhibitors (SSRIs) or cognitive-behavioral therapy (CBT) with exposure and response prevention (ERP) as primary treatment options. However, approximately 40–60% of patients do not achieve satisfactory results with these interventions. This result has led to the exploration of non-invasive brain stimulation alternatives, focusing on advanced repetitive transcranial magnetic stimulation (rTMS) paradigms. This chapter discusses these paradigms, including prolonged intermittent theta burst stimulation (piTBS), accelerated rTMS (aTMS), deep TMS (dTMS), priming TMS (pTMS), synchronized TMS (sTMS), various forms of theta burst stimulation (TBS) such as intermittent, continuation, and bilateral TBS, and magnetic seizure therapy (MST).

Keywords: rTMS, piTBS, aTMS, dTMS, pTMS, sTMS, TBS, MST

1. Introduction

Transcranial magnetic stimulation (TMS) was introduced as a neurophysiological tool in 1985, following the development of a portable device by Anthony Barker and colleagues. This innovation allowed for non-invasive stimulation of the cerebral cortex [1]. Subsequently, TMS has been widely used for assessing the motor system, examining the functionality of different brain regions, and investigating the pathophysiology of various neuropsychiatric disorders. Notably, TMS has been adopted as a therapeutic intervention for conditions including major depressive disorder (MDD) [2] and obsessive-compulsive disorder (OCD) [3, 4].

Repetitive TMS (rTMS), which involves rhythmic and repetitive application of TMS, was approved by the US Food and Drug Administration (FDA) in 2008 for treating medication-resistant depression [5]. rTMS is classified into high-frequency (HF) (≥5 Hz) and low-frequency (LF) (≤1 Hz) forms [3, 6]. HF-rTMS stimulates targeted areas, whereas LF-rTMS aims to inhibit stimulation [7]. Evidence from numerous studies supports the antidepressant effectiveness of HF-rTMS (such as 10 Hz) targeting the left dorsolateral prefrontal cortex (DLPFC) or LF-rTMS (such as 1 Hz) applied to the right DLPFC [8, 9].

OCD is a prevalent and chronic disorder that contributes significantly to global disability [10]. Consensus statements and treatment guidelines, grounded in empirical research, recommend the utilization of selective serotonin reuptake inhibitors (SSRIs, such as sertraline and fluvoxamine) or a combination of cognitive behavioral therapy (CBT) with exposure and response prevention (ERP) as primary therapeutic approaches [11, 12]. However, 40–60% of patients do not achieve satisfactory results with these interventions [13]. Multiple randomized controlled trials (RCTs) have examined the effects of rTMS on the cortico-striatal-thalamic-cortical (CSTC) circuits, which are implicated in OCD. These trials have specifically targeted brain regions such as the DLPFC, anterior cingulate cortex (ACC), supplementary motor area (SMA), orbitofrontal cortex (OFC), and medial prefrontal cortex [14–16]. For instance, LF-rTMS aimed at the SMA yielded significant benefits in some RCTs [15, 17]; however, this was not the case in all studies [18, 19]. Similarly, the outcomes of RCTs investigating rTMS targeting DLPFC in OCD have been inconsistent [20, 21]. Notably, a recent meta-analysis revealed that rTMS can be beneficial for patients with OCD who have not responded to previous SSRI therapy [3]. Therefore, it is crucial to explore novel rTMS paradigms to enhance response and remission rates and overall treatment outcomes in patients with OCD. In this chapter, English databases such as the Cochrane Library, PubMed, EMBASE and PsycINFO were systematically searched by three independent investigators (XJL, CML, and XHY) from inception to 10 November 2023, to identify relevant studies examining the efficacy and safety of various advanced rTMS paradigms [e.g., prolonged intermittent theta burst stimulation (piTBS), accelerated rTMS (aTMS), deep TMS (dTMS), priming TMS (pTMS), synchronized TMS (sTMS), theta burst stimulation (TBS) (including the intermittent, continuation, and bilateral forms of TBS), and magnetic seizure therapy (MST)] for patients with OCD.

2. TMS

2.1 rTMS

rTMS is a non-invasive neuromodulation method that administers a series of TMS pulses at a consistent frequency to modulate neuronal activity through a magnetic field pulse [22]. In 2018, rTMS received approval from the FDA for treating OCD [23], offering new treatment avenues for patients with this condition. Recent research indicates that the therapeutic efficacy of rTMS is influenced by various stimulation parameters, such as unilateral or bilateral, treatment frequency and intensity, and the targeted brain regions [24]. Both unilateral and bilateral rTMS have shown greater effectiveness than sham rTMS in treating OCD in clinical settings [24]. The frequency of stimulation in rTMS plays a critical role, where LF-rTMS at $\leq$1 Hz produces an inhibitory effect, and HF-rTMS at $\geq$5 Hz produces an excitatory effect on cortical excitability in targeted areas [25]. The choice of stimulation areas significantly affects rTMS outcomes [24]. The DLPFC, OFC, and SMA (or pre-supplementary motor area [pre-SMA]) are identified as the most effective stimulation sites. These regions are part of the CSTC, which is hypothesized to be associated with the pathophysiology of OCD [26]. Furthermore, rTMS may be able to alter cortical excitability and neuroplasticity in OCD patients. Over the past two decades, numerous studies have explored the effectiveness of rTMS in treating various psychiatric disorders [27], with a predominant focus on MDD [28].

However, established and comprehensive rTMS treatment approaches for OCD are still lacking. Further investigation is required to identify and optimize rTMS treatment strategies to achieve optimal clinical effectiveness for OCD.

Growing evidence indicates that rTMS is generally effective and safe for the treatment of OCD [29]. A pairwise meta-analysis of 21 RCTs involving 662 patients showed that rTMS for OCD is efficacious across all protocols [29]. Additionally, this meta-analysis reported several side effects associated with rTMS treatment in patients diagnosed with OCD [29], such as headache, sedation, concentration difficulties, scalp pain, weakness, fatigue, mood swings, memory impairment, dizziness, fainting, and facial nerve stimulation. However, all side effects were generally mild and transient, and rTMS was well-tolerated by most patients. Notably, this meta-analysis did not report any severe adverse events, such as cognitive dysfunction or seizures [29].

2.1.1 Unilateral rTMS

The initial clinical trial indicated that right prefrontal rTMS could affect prefrontal mechanisms associated with OCD [30]. In this trial, 12 patients diagnosed with OCD received rTMS at parameters of 80% motor threshold and 20 Hz for 2 seconds per minute, lasting 20 minutes. This intervention targeted the right lateral prefrontal and left lateral prefrontal regions on alternate days. The severity of symptoms was evaluated for 8 hours post-rTMS administration. All participants completed the study, and there was a significant reduction in compulsive urges for 8 hours following right lateral prefrontal rTMS. In another study by SEO et al., LF-rTMS (1 Hz) targeting the right DLPFC was used as a therapeutic intervention for OCD [31]. This study showed a substantial reduction in Yale-Brown Obsessive Compulsive Scale (Y-BOCS) scores, offering preliminary evidence for the effectiveness of rTMS stimulation of the right DLPFC in managing OCD. However, there is currently no consensus on the optimal frequency (low or high) for unilateral rTMS in OCD treatment.

Moreover, several randomized, double-blinded, sham-controlled studies examining the effects of rTMS on the left DLPFC at different frequencies did not report significant improvements in OCD symptoms. For instance, a research by Sachdev et al. [32] involved 18 participants and investigated the efficacy of a two-week rTMS course targeting the left DLPFC in treating treatment-resistant OCD. The rTMS protocol in one study employed a frequency of 10 Hz, set at 110% of the motor threshold, with 25-second intervals between trains and 1500 stimulations per session. In another study [33], 33 right-handed patients underwent LF-rTMS treatment at 1 Hz, set at 110% of the motor threshold. Post-treatment assessments using the Clinical Global Impression (CGI), Hamilton Anxiety Rating Scale (HAMA), Y-BOCS, and Beck Anxiety Inventory (BAI) revealed no significant differences in psychopathology scores between the active rTMS and sham rTMS groups.

Recent studies indicate that rTMS targeting the left OFC may significantly impact the OCD treatment [24]. A study involving 25 patients found that LF-rTMS applied to the left OFC led to a partial response in 13 patients (13/25, 52%) and a complete response in 11 (11/25, 44%) [34]. The Y-BOCS scores significantly decreased from the baseline after 20 rTMS sessions, with no significant changes during the subsequent 1-month follow-up. However, LF-rTMS to the right OFC showed only a 19% response rate, without symptom improvement after 1 month [35]. Research also suggests the importance of the number of OFC treatments, indicating that at least 20 rTMS sessions within the OFC are necessary for a significant impact [36].

2.1.2 Bilateral rTMS

Bilateral rTMS is gaining recognition as a promising therapeutic approach for individuals with OCD. In bilateral treatments, the primary focus is on stimulating the DLPFC and SMA. Recent meta-analyses have substantiated the efficacy of bilateral rTMS over sham stimulation in treating OCD [24, 29, 37]. A notable meta-analysis, which included six cortical targets (bilateral DLPFC, left DLPFC, right DLPFC, SMA, OFC, and medial prefrontal cortex [mPFC]) and analyzed 26 studies, identified bilateral DLPFC stimulation as a well-tolerated rTMS modality, demonstrating significant effects and emerging as the optimal approach [37]. Overall, rTMS exhibited a modest and substantial reduction in Y-BOCS scores. (Hedges' $g = 0.77$, $p < 0.0001$), with bilateral DLPFC targeting yielding the most considerable effect size (Hedges' $g = 1.04$, $p < 0.0001$). Both HF- and LF-rTMS yielded comparable results. Furthermore, studies with follow-up data indicated that the benefits of active rTMS were significantly more significant than sham treatment, even after 4 weeks.

The SMA is recognized as an effective target for rTMS in OCD treatment [38]. A multicenter study involving 27 treatment facilities across 10 countries revealed that 41.8% of these centers chose the SMA as the target for TMS in treating OCD [39]. In a 4-week double-blinded trial, 57 patients with untreated OCD were randomly assigned to receive either active or sham rTMS [40]. The participants received 1-Hz rTMS directed at the SMA daily, 5 days a week, over 4 weeks. Patients in the active rTMS group exhibited significantly lower Y-BOCS scores than those in the sham group. This research further revealed that the 5-Hydroxytryptamine Transporter Linked Polymorphic Region (5-HTTLPR) polymorphism in the SLC6A4 gene could be a reliable biomarker for predicting rTMS treatment response in patients with OCD. Furthermore, the SMA was identified as a prime target for rTMS due to its extensive connections with regions involved in cognitive processes and motor control [41].

A recent case report [42] introduced a novel approach to treating treatment-resistant OCD, combining rTMS and iTBS across three distinct brain areas (bilateral SMA, left and right DLPFC) within a single session. The case involved an 18-year-old female patient who showed significant symptom improvement after 6 weeks of treatment. The outcomes included a notable reduction in the duration of OCD symptoms, improved control over obsessions, and ameliorated depressive symptoms. The patient's Y-BOCS score reduced from 34 at baseline to 11 after 6 weeks, and the Hamilton Depression Rating Scale (HAMD-17) score decreased from 18 to eight in the same period. No clinically significant side effects were noted. These findings suggest that sequential treatment targeting different brain regions could be feasible and beneficial for those with treatment-resistant OCD. However, larger-scale studies are necessary to corroborate these results further.

2.1.3 Comparison of bilateral and unilateral rTMS

A recent systematic review and meta-analysis [43], encompassing 31 trials, compared bilateral rTMS with unilateral rTMS. The analysis assessed differences in effect sizes when stimulating the bilateral, left, and right DLPFC regions. Findings suggested that bilateral DLPFC stimulation may result in a more significant decrease in Y-BOCS scores compared to stimulating either the left DLPFC or right DLPFC (Hedge's $g = -0.85$, $p < 0.001$ vs. Hedge's $g = -0.17$, $p = 0.32$ vs. Hedge's $g = -0.64$, $p < 0.001$). Furthermore, the study explored variations in treatment efficacy in trials using rTMS targeted at the left DLPFC with either HF or LF; however, no significant effects were observed. A separate analysis for rTMS stimulation on the right DLPFC revealed a considerable impact for LF stimulation (Hedge's $g = -0.87$, $p < 0.001$). Regarding other specific brain regions, an open, sham-controlled trial involving 20 patients (10 in the experimental group) found no significant effects when comparing sham treatment with sequential 1 Hz stimulation (110% threshold) of the right DLPFC and bilateral pre-SMA [44]. Moreover, no significant changes in cognitive functioning were observed post-stimulation. However, it is crucial to customize treatment approaches according to each patient's unique needs and preferences, considering the diverse effects of different therapeutic interventions.

Currently, there is a notable gap in the literature regarding RCTs that directly compare the efficacy of bilateral rTMS and unilateral rTMS in treating OCD. The most effective dosing strategy for rTMS is yet to be determined, necessitating further research to assess the relative effectiveness of bilateral and unilateral rTMS.

2.1.4 Accelerated rTMS

aTMS represents a progression in the use of rTMS for OCD treatment. This approach involves increasing the frequency of daily stimulations and extending the treatment duration. Unlike the conventional rTMS protocol (which lasts approximately 38 minutes per day over 2–4 weeks), aTMS is more practical and time-saving. This advantage has contributed to its widespread adoption in treating MDD and its subsequent application in OCD treatment. However, evidence supporting the use of aTMS in OCD treatment is still limited, and it remains an experimental technique.

A case study focused on a 37-year-old woman diagnosed with OCD [45]. She received LF-rTMS (1 Hz) targeting the SMA, delivering 1600 pulses per session, twice daily, at least 5 days a week, for 42 sessions over 4 weeks. The rTMS was administered at 100% of the resting motor threshold. Upon completing the rTMS sessions, her Y-BOCS score reduced to 18 out of 40, indicating a significant improvement of approximately 49%. This improvement significantly enhanced the patient's quality of life and led to the complete resolution of her depressive symptoms. The patient reported no adverse effects during or after the rTMS therapy. She maintained stability on the exact dosage of escitalopram up to her second follow-up, 2 months post-hospital discharge.

In a recent study involving nine patients diagnosed with OCD [46], a unique approach was adopted, consisting of a one-week, magnetic resonance imaging-guided, individualized, double-daily rTMS protocol. The rTMS was delivered at a frequency of 1 Hz and an intensity of 110% of the resting motor threshold, amounting to 7200 pulses per day. Bilateral stimulation was applied to the SMA region. The study reported a significant 25% improvement in OCD symptoms after treatment, with the beneficial effects persisting up to 3 months post-treatment. The study further observed decreased connectivity between the SMA and subcortical brain regions. None of the participants reported any adverse effects. These findings suggest that the aTMS protocol used in this study is both safe and effective, offering substantial evidence for its potential as a viable treatment option for OCD.

In summary, rTMS serves as a tertiary modality in managing OCD, complementing pharmacological and psychological treatments, and has been clinically applied. Currently, there are no published direct comparative studies between bilateral and unilateral rTMS, and aTMS, in the treatment of OCD. Further research is required to identify this purpose's most effective stimulation paradigm.

2.2 dTMS

dTMS technology has evolved as an advanced version of traditional rTMS. The dTMS H7 Coil is specifically designed to target the medial prefrontal cortex (mPFC)-dACC (3 cm^3) and further stimulates other cortical regions, such as the OFC (8.4 cm^3), DLPFC (10.5 cm^3), and SMA (6.8 cm^3), at suprathreshold levels (>100 V/m) [47, 48]. The H-coil utilized in dTMS, distinct from traditional TMS coils, is part of a wearable helmet that the user securely wears. This H-coil comprises two layers, each with four elliptically shaped windings stacked above each other. Their major and minor axes vary between 70 and 130 mm and 55–105 mm, respectively [48]. The magnetic field from the H-coil diminishes more slowly, allowing stimulation of neurons across a broader and deeper region. The subdural depth and H-coil stimulation volume are approximately 3 cm and 40.3 cm^3, respectively [48].

In 2018, the FDA approved the dTMS H7 Coil for OCD treatment, following favorable outcomes from a pilot study and a multicenter RCT conducted by Carmi et al. [49, 50]. 2 years later, the D-B80 coil was approved by the FDA for therapeutic applications. The multicenter RCT involving 99 patients with OCD revealed that active 20 Hz dTMS treatment resulted in a significantly higher reduction in Y-BOCS scores compared to sham treatment, with reductions of 6.0 points and 3.3 points, respectively. Moreover, response rates were 38.1% and 11.1% in the active and sham treatment groups, respectively [50]. At the one-month follow-up, the active treatment group exhibited a response rate of 45.2%, while the sham group had a response rate of 17.8%. These findings highlighted significant differences between the two groups, which persisted during the follow-up. Safety-wise, the HF-dTMS using the H7 coil was well-tolerated, with no severe adverse events such as seizures reported. The most common side effect was a mild headache during or immediately after stimulation, consistent with findings from previous comprehensive reviews [6].

Beyond RCTs, real-world data analysis from 219 patients with OCD across 22 clinical sites using the H7 Coil revealed overall first and sustained response rates of 72.6% and 52.4%, respectively [51]. Furthermore, patients who underwent 29 dTMS sessions exhibited a response rate of 57.9%, surpassing the multicenter trial results [50]. The improved real-world outcomes might be attributed to the longer duration of dTMS neuromodulation and the flexibility to employ augmentation strategies, infrequently available options within the confines of an RCT design. Furthermore, Harmelech et al. [52] investigated the long-term efficacy of dTMS as a therapeutic intervention for OCD. The study included clinical centers from multicenter trials and those providing post-market data. Findings revealed that the average duration of dTMS effectiveness for OCD was approximately 1.98 years (standard deviation = 0.13) or longer, with 62% of patients maintaining this durability at the time of the survey. Symptomatic ratings did not determine this durability; it is defined pragmatically as the time elapsed from the conclusion of dTMS treatment to when a change in treatment was deemed necessary.

A recent network meta-analysis (NMA) identified ondansetron, dTMS, therapist-administered CBT, and aripiprazole as the top four treatments for OCD, based on the surface under the cumulative ranking percentage values (85.4%, 83.2%, 80.3%, and 67.9%, respectively) [53]. In sensitivity analyses, dTMS emerged as the most effective treatment strategy for treatment-resistant OCD. However, the NMA faced significant heterogeneity due to subject variations across studies, including differences in baseline treatment resistance levels and treatment modalities. This heterogeneity is a standard limitation in NMAs on treatment-resistant OCD [54]. Furthermore, Gregory et al. [55] assessed the cost-effectiveness of dTMS compared to established treatments such as antidepressant medication (ADM), ADM with antipsychotic augmentation, real-world cognitive-behavioral therapy (ADM + CBT Effectiveness), clinical trial CBT (ADM + CBT), and others, for individuals with treatment-refractory OCD. The study concluded that dTMS is cost-effective across different levels of care, from outpatient medication management and CBT to more intensive, facility-based treatments. Moreover, dTMS was suggested as a valuable, incremental strategy in scenarios where more intensive treatment options are inaccessible or financially impractical or when patients experience long wait times for access to these higher levels of care.

The neuroanatomical basis of dysfunction in OCD has been thoroughly researched and is known to involve the CSTC circuitry [56]. A recent study compared the two FDA-cleared coils for dTMS and suggested that while the H7 coil can stimulate certain OCD-specific prefrontal regions within the CSTC, the D-B80 coil may not have this capability [47]. Expanding on this research, a 2022 study by Tzirini et al. explored the characteristics of these coils' induced electric field [48]. They analyzed the field distribution by positioning the coils over the prefrontal cortex of a head phantom in a treatment setup for OCD. Furthermore, numerical simulations were conducted using eight models from the Population Head Model repository with two sets of conductivity values, three Virtual Population anatomical head models, and their homogeneous counterparts. The findings showed that the H7 coil produced significantly higher maximal electric fields and stimulated brain volumes two to five times larger than the other coil. Furthermore, the rate of electric field decay over distance was considerably slower for the H7 coil. Specifically, at the scalp level, the field strength with the D-B80 coil was 306% of that at a depth of 3 cm, whereas with the H7 coil, it was 155%. The H7 coil demonstrates a considerable capability to generate higher intensities within larger brain volumes, including specific regions implicated in OCD, such as the dACC, DLPFC, inferior frontal gyrus, OFC, and pre-SMA, in contrast to the D-B80 coil. Given the substantial disparities between these two coils, it is imperative to conduct separate assessments and validations of their clinical efficacy in future OCD treatment research.

Currently, there is a limited body of research elucidating the mechanisms through which dTMS operates in the treatment of OCD. Recently, Arıkan et al. [57] conducted a neurophysiological study to investigate the effects of dTMS using the H7 coil on both electrophysiological parameters and clinical outcomes in individuals with OCD. This retrospective, single-center study involved 29 patients with OCD, comprising 15 women and 14 men, who underwent 30 dTMS sessions. Baseline and endpoint measurements were obtained through quantitative electroencephalography (EEG) recordings and the Y-BOCS. The findings yielded positive treatment outcomes in all 29 patients, with a minimum 35% reduction in Y-BOCS scores. Analysis of quantitative EEG recordings indicated a significant decrease in theta, alpha, and beta rhythms. Furthermore, the reduction in the severity of OCD symptoms was associated with a specific decrease in beta activity within the left central region. Consequently, it can be inferred that the therapeutic response mechanism may be linked to the reduction in beta-band power induced by dTMS. However, the absence of a sham-control condition in the study raises questions about the specificity of the observed EEG alterations. Furthermore, the lack of changes in beta-EEG power among non-responders is a source of uncertainty, considering that all patients included in the study were responders. Therefore, these results should be considered preliminary and require validation in a prospective study.

In general, while the study involving the dTMS H7 coil provided evidence for the effectiveness of mPFC-dACC stimulation, the studies involving D-B80 and figure-8 coils, which were small and heterogeneous, did not identify definitive targets [47]. In the field of dTMS treatment for OCD, further exploration is necessary to improve its efficacy. This exploration includes and is not limited to (1) personalizing treatment based on promising evidence for predictors and moderators of response to mPFC-dACC stimulation; (2) investigating the underlying mechanisms of dTMS treatment for OCD using various methods such as neuroimaging and molecular biochemistry; (3) considering the relatively complex operation of dTMS, including the induction of moderate to severe discomfort in patients with OCD and the simultaneous inhibition of compulsive behavior during treatment; and (4) conducting a comprehensive clinician interview, which involves utilizing the Y-BOCS symptom checklist, assessing the Y-BOCS severity score, and establishing a personalized hierarchy of OCD triggers before initiating dTMS therapy. Moreover, it is imperative to engage in discussions with the TMS technician regarding the unique manifestations of the patient's OCD and regularly monitor the patient's progress using the Y-BOCS severity score every week. Furthermore, considering the potential improvement or alteration of symptoms during the treatment course for OCD, patients may develop increased resistance to provocation. Therefore, comprehensive technical operation guidelines should be formulated early to facilitate its broader application.

2.3 Priming TMS

Priming TMS, an innovative approach in rTMS, involves preconditioning LF stimulation trains with subthreshold stimulation at an HF [57]. Research has demonstrated its significant ability to enhance the neural response to the subsequent LF stimulation train [58]. Notably, it has been observed that a brief pretreatment with stimulation in the 5–6 Hz range substantially enhances the effectiveness of subsequent 1-Hz stimulation in inducing a reduction in synaptic efficacy [59]. Current research on pTMS has primarily centered on the field of depression [5], and there is a lack of large-sample RCTs to assess the efficacy of pTMS in patients with OCD systematically. Vidya et al. [60] conducted an RCT of a comparable nature to investigate the impact of adjunctive pTMS targeting the SMA in individuals with treatment-resistant OCD. The study comprised 30 patients with OCD who continued to experience symptoms despite a sufficient trial of SSRIs. These individuals were randomly assigned to one of two groups: the pTMS group, which received active priming stimulation (6-Hz rTMS at 80% of the resting motor threshold), followed by 1-Hz rTMS, or the rTMS-only group, which received sham stimulation followed by 1-Hz rTMS. Both groups underwent ten sessions of these interventions over 2 weeks. The study revealed significant enhancements in all aspects of psychopathology for both groups over time. Notably, the pTMS group demonstrated superior outcomes to the rTMS-only group, as evidenced by a reduction in the compulsion score of the Y-BOCS and reductions in scores on the HAMA and HAMD-17.

It is noteworthy that this study represents the first examination of pTMS in individuals diagnosed with OCD. However, the small size impacts the overall statistical power of the applied tests. It is imperative to integrate neuroimaging and neurophysiological techniques alongside clinical assessment in future studies to enhance our comprehension of the precise neuronal mechanisms of pTMS over the SMA and its correlation with clinical improvement. Incorporating a larger sample size in conjunction with these techniques would enable the identification of neural patterns associated with clinical improvement. This identification facilitates a more comprehensive understanding of the specific neuronal mechanisms underlying pTMS over the SMA.

2.4 Synchronized TMS

sTMS represents an innovative approach to non-invasive brain stimulation. Using a trio of rotating neodymium magnets, sTMS can deliver extremely low-energy, sinusoidal magnetic fields that synchronize with an individual's intrinsic alpha frequency (IAF). This approach offers the potential for a brain stimulation system that can be used conveniently at home [61]. Previous studies have shown promise in using sTMS to alleviate depressive symptoms in individuals with MDD [62]. However, there is a lack of scholarly investigations into applying sTMS in OCD. Given that OCD's primary neurobiological basis involves heightened activation within the CSTC, it is plausible that sTMS, which can modulate cortical oscillations selectively, could offer therapeutic benefits by regulating cortical activity within the IAF range [63, 64].

3. TBS

TBS is a patterned version of rTMS. It comprises continuous TBS (cTBS) and intermittent TBS (iTBS), both of which are novel neuromodulation techniques widely employed in clinical practice for the treatment of psychiatric disorders [65]. In contrast to conventional rTMS protocols, the standard TBS protocol involves delivering bursts of three 50 Hz pulses (or 20 Hz) at 5 Hz intervals. This protocol is hypothesized to exert a more rapid and longer-lasting influence on brain synaptic plasticity [66]. Specifically, cTBS applies an uninterrupted train of bursts, consisting of either 300 or 600 pulses, to reduce cortical excitability. In contrast, iTBS aims to increase cortical excitability and involves 20 trains of 10 bursts, where each burst comprises short bursts of three stimuli at 50 Hz, repeated at 5 Hz, and given at 8-second intervals, resulting in a total of 600 stimuli delivered over 200 seconds [65]. Previous meta-analyses [67] have demonstrated that iTBS exhibits antidepressant effects similar to those of HF-rTMS, with comparable safety profiles. However, as a relatively new modality of rTMS, there is still a lack of evidence regarding the efficacy and safety of TBS for OCD. Earlier studies have indicated that the potential mechanism of TBS in treating OCD involves the modulation of CSTC abnormal functioning, primarily through its impact on glutamatergic and γ-aminobutyric-acid (GABA) ergic interneurons [68]. Over the past decade, there has been a growing number of studies investigating the efficacy and safety of TBS in patients with OCD. These studies have utilized various TBS models, including iTBS, cTBS, and accelerated TBS, targeting different brain regions such as the DLPFC, OFC, and SMA. TBS offers advantages such as shorter treatment duration, lower stimulation intensity than traditional TMS, increased acceptability, tolerability, and greater cost-effectiveness, collectively enhancing its clinical utility in OCD treatment.

3.1 iTBS

In 2019, Naro et al. conducted the inaugural randomized crossover pilot study to investigate the efficacy and safety of adjunctive standard iTBS (600 pulses per session) at 80% of the active motor threshold (aMT) [65]. This study targeted the left DLPFC in treating ten patients with treatment-resistant OCD. Over 1 month, this prefrontal iTBS monotherapy observed significant reductions in OCD symptoms among the active iTBS groups at the treatment endpoint. The positive effects of the treatment were sustained for up to 3 months. No adverse effects were reported in the sham iTBS groups [69]. These findings provide preliminary evidence for iTBS as a promising protocol for alleviating OCD symptoms. Subsequently, Syed et al. introduced a novel iTBS protocol using a double cone coil (deep TMS) to target both the dmPFC and ACC. This open-labeled case series included 12 patients with treatment-resistant OCD, and their results indicated that 5/12 of them (41.7%) met the response criteria, defined as achieving a > 35% reduction in Y-BOCS scores [70]. Recently, a novel case study explored the use of combined rTMS/iTBS protocols, involving LF-rTMS applied to the right DLPFC and the bilateral SMA, followed by the iTBS targeting the left DLPFC in the treatment of a patient with treatment-resistant OCD. After 30 treatment sessions spanning a 6-week course of treatment, a significant reduction in the Y-BOCS score was observed (Baseline: 34; 6th week: 11), and no substantial side effects were reported [42]. However, further high-quality RCTs are needed to determine the optimum iTBS protocol for treating OCD.

3.2 cTBS

Prior research has shown that cTBS can reduce cortical excitability for up to 50 minutes after a 40-second stimulation, whereas a 20-second application of cTBS results in decreased cortical excitability lasting for 20 minutes [71, 72]. In 2006, Mantovani et al. identified that inhibiting the function of the SMA may be beneficial in improving OCD symptoms [73]. Based on this finding, Harika-Germaneau et al. conducted a robust, randomized, double-blinded, sham-controlled trial involving 30 participants in 2019. Their study investigated the efficacy and safety of adjunctive cTBS (600 pulses; stimulus intensity: 70% resting motor threshold [RMT]) over the SMA for patients with treatment-resistant OCD. However, following 30 sessions of cTBS, there were no significant group differences in terms of the predefined study response criteria (>25% reduction in Y-BOCS scores) between the active cTBS and sham groups at both the post-cTBS treatment assessment (21.4% vs. 35.7%, $p = 0.403$) and the 12-week follow-up evaluation (28.4% vs. 35.7%, $p = 0.69$) [74]. Moreover, a recent randomized single-blinded, sham-controlled study conducted in China last year aimed to assess the efficacy and safety of cTBS involving 1200 pulses at a stimulus intensity of 110% RMT applied to the bilateral SMA for 54 patients with OCD. The study found that active cTBS did not significantly reduce OCD symptoms compared to sham stimulation [75]. Notably, the variability in cTBS stimulation parameters, including treatment pulses (600–1200 pulses per session) and stimulation intensity (70–120% RMT), has led to some confusion in clinical practice. Interestingly, a recent preliminary open-label trial involving 29 participants employed an LF (1 Hz) cTBS protocol targeting the bilateral SMA in the treatment of patients with moderately drug-resistant OCD. This trial yielded a positive outcome with a response rate of 37.3% [76]. However, further high-quality RCTs are warranted to replicate these findings in future investigations. Overall, cTBS has demonstrated safety and good tolerability in the treatment of patients with OCD [74–76].

3.2.1 Accelerated and intensive cTBS

To the best of our knowledge, an entire course of traditional TMS treatment (typically lasting 4–6 weeks) may increase the daily transportation burden for outpatients and pose challenges for medical institutions [77]. Previous research has demonstrated that accelerated/ intensive cTBS protocols (2 sessions/day) can facilitate metaplasticity and offer the advantage of time efficiency [78]. In an initial study, Williams et al. [79] conducted a pilot investigation utilizing an accelerated cTBS protocol consisting of ten sessions per day, targeting the right frontal cortex, for the treatment of seven patients with OCD over a 5-day treatment period. This approach achieved a response rate of >1 time point in 71% of cases, with minimal side effects, providing preliminary evidence regarding the effectiveness and safety of accelerated cTBS for treatment-refractory OCD. Subsequently, a recent case report further supported this evidence [80]. However, research assessing the potential of accelerated cTBS to improve OCD symptoms in patients with treatment-resistant OCD has yielded inconsistent results. For instance, Dutta et al. [81] were the first to investigate accelerated cTBS protocols (two sessions per day, totaling 1200 pulses) targeting the left OFC in treating 33 patients with OCD. They observed a significant group-by-time interaction effect concerning obsessions and compulsions. Conversely, another study reported adverse outcomes for cTBS over the right OFC in patients with OCD [82]. In contrast to the OFC studies, a randomized sham-controlled study conducted last year examined the impact of adjunctive neuronavigation-guided accelerated cTBS protocols, consisting of two daily sessions totaling 1800 pulses over the SMA, in patients with OCD. This study found that the active TBS group achieved a more significant reduction in the Y-BOCS total score than the sham group [83]. Recently, a case series by Noda et al. reported promising results when using bilateral SMA-targeted cTBS administered twice daily in six patients with OCD. This approach achieved a response rate of 67% (4/6) without apparent adverse events, suggesting that bilateral cTBS could serve as a viable alternative for OCD treatment [84].

3.3 Bilateral TBS

To the best of our knowledge, there has been only one prior case study demonstrating the therapeutic potential of bilateral TBS (combining iTBS and cTBS) for OCD treatment [85]. In this study, researchers initially applied ten sessions of cTBS (1200 pulses per session) over the right DLPFC, followed by another ten sessions of iTBS (1200 pulses per session) targeting the left DLPFC in the treatment of a 33-year-old patient with OCD and comorbid depression. The patient's Y-BOCS score improved from 19 to 9 after the two stages of treatment with cTBS and iTBS [85]. However, cTBS and iTBS were administered in separate sessions. Currently, no published RCT has examined the effectiveness of bilateral TBS protocols that sequentially apply iTBS and cTBS for OCD treatment.

4. MST

MST is an innovative neuromodulation treatment that employs HF magnetic stimulation to induce generalized seizures [86]. In contrast to electroconvulsive therapy (ECT), MST minimizes its impact on deeper brain structures. It reduces adverse neurocognitive effects by specifically targeting localized brain regions and inducing seizures in superficial cortex areas [87]. Consequently, MST has been proposed as a potential substitute for ECT [88]. Recent meta-analysis findings indicate that MST offers shorter recovery times and results in lower levels of cognitive impairments in individuals with MDD compared to ECT [89]. Furthermore, emerging evidence supports the clinical efficacy of MST in MDD [90], bipolar depression [88], and schizophrenia [86] and suggests potential benefits in OCD.

MST has been considered as a potentially more effective option compared to rTMS. This notion is supported by studies demonstrating higher response rates in

ECT for MDD [91], where generalized seizure activity is hypothesized to be the underlying mechanism [92]. MST may offer the advantage of precise stimulation by targeting specific brain regions associated with OCD's pathophysiology. However, it is essential to note that no direct comparisons between MST and rTMS for OCD treatment have been published to date.

An open-label pilot study [93], which represents the initial report of using MST in a sample of participants (n = 10) diagnosed with OCD, revealed that only one participant who underwent frontal MST at 100 Hz experienced a clinically significant decrease in Y-BOCS scores. In contrast, the remaining participants did not observe any reduction in their OCD symptoms. Furthermore, no notable changes were observed in MDD, quality of life, or suicidality within the group. Consequently, additional research is necessary to thoroughly assess the efficacy of MST in individuals diagnosed with OCD.

5. Conclusion

Neurostimulation techniques, particularly rTMS, serve as a significant tertiary treatment alternative for OCD, complementing pharmacological and psychological interventions. The utilization of diverse advanced paradigms of TMS may be most effective in the initial stages of the stepped care pathway, potentially in conjunction with SSRIs or CBT. This approach has noteworthy implications for the development of clinical services, as diverse advanced paradigms of TMS, including conventional rTMS, are not commonly accessible as standard treatments for OCD within numerous healthcare systems [3]. A meta-analysis found that rTMS exhibits a minimal occurrence of adverse effects and is well-tolerated in the treatment of OCD [38]. Therefore, it could serve as a viable alternative to SSRIs or CBT in specific subsets of patients who are unsuitable candidates for or have contraindications to conventional first-line treatments.

This chapter provides an overview of contemporary variations of rTMS utilized in managing OCD, including piTBS, aTMS, dTMS, pTMS, sTMS, iTBS, cTBS, bilateral TBS, and MST. By identifying reliable early response indicators to rTMS in patients with OCD, such as patient characteristics or neurophysiological findings, appropriate stimulation protocols and modalities can be selected. For instance, potential predictors of poor response to rTMS in OCD treatment include a higher Y-BOCS score and comorbid depression [36]. The presence of an action-monitoring deficit is a fundamental trait of OCD [94]. The dACC, which plays a significant role in error monitoring and cognitive control, exhibits heightened activity in individuals with more severe OCD symptoms [95]. By enhancing rapid error monitoring, rTMS targeting the dACC in patients with OCD simultaneously improves real-time behavioral adjustment and clinical symptoms, suggesting a connection between errors monitoring impairment and the underlying pathophysiology of OCD [94]. Consequently, evaluating the impact of rTMS on error monitoring function can provide valuable insights into the mechanisms underlying the effective treatment of OCD with rTMS, thereby enhancing the therapeutic outcomes of this intervention. With increasing clarity in clinical effects and reliable prognostic indicators, it becomes essential to thoroughly examine the fundamental mechanisms associated with every novel TMS protocol, facilitating the exploration of personalized medicine. Furthermore, uncertainties persist regarding the optimal dosing strategy for each novel TMS protocol, necessitating further research to assess the neurophysiological effects and clinical implications of variables such as the number of daily sessions, total sessions, and intervals between sessions.

Disclosure/conflicts of interest

The authors declare no conflicts of interest in conducting this study or preparing the manuscript.

Financial support

This study was funded by the National Natural Science Foundation of China (82101609), China International Medical Exchange Foundation (Z-2018-2035-2002), the Science and Technology Program of Guangzhou (2023A03J0839 and 2023A03J0436), Science and Technology Planning Project of Liwan District of Guangzhou (202201012), The Natural Science Foundation Program of Guangdong (2023A1515011383), National Clinical Key specialty construction project [(2023) 33], Guangzhou Municipal Key Discipline in Medicine (2021–2023), Guangzhou High-level Clinical Key Specialty, Department of Emergency Medicine of National clinical key specialty, and Guangzhou Research-oriented Hospital. The funders had no role in study design, data collection and analysis, decision to publish, or preparation of the manuscript.

Abbreviations

5-HTTLPR	5-Hydroxytryptamine Transporter Linked Polymorphic Region
ACC	anterior cingulate cortex
ADM	antidepressant medication
aMT	active motor threshold
aTMS	accelerated rTMS
BAI	Beck Anxiety Inventory
CBT	cognitive-behavioral therapy
CGI	Clinical Global Impression
CSTC	cortico-striatal-thalamic-cortical
cTBS	continuous TBS
DLPFC	dorsolateral prefrontal cortex
dACC	dorsal anterior cingulate cortex
dTMS	deep transcranial magnetic stimulation
ECT	electroconvulsive therapy
EEG	electroencephalography
ERP	exposure and response prevention
FDA	Food and Drug Administration
HAMA	Hamilton Anxiety Rating Scale
HAMD-17	Hamilton Depression Rating Scale (17 items version)
HF	high-frequency
IAF	intrinsic alpha frequency
iTBS	intermittent TBS
LF	low-frequency
MDD	major depressive disorder
MST	magnetic seizure therapy
mPFC	medial prefrontal cortex

NMA	network meta-analysis
OCD	Obsessive-Compulsive Disorder
OFC	orbitofrontal cortex
piTBS	prolonged intermittent theta burst stimulation
pTMS	priming TMS
RCTs	randomized controlled trials
RMT	resting motor threshold
rTMS	repetitive transcranial magnetic stimulation
SMA	supplementary motor area
SSRIs	selective serotonin reuptake inhibitors
sTMS	synchronized TMS
TBS	theta burst stimulation
Y-BOCS	Yale-Brown Obsessive-Compulsive Scale.

Author details

Xian-Jun Lan[1], Chaomeng Liu[2,3], Xin-Hu Yang[4,5] and Wei Zheng[4,5]*

1 The Brain Hospital of Guangxi Zhuang Autonomous Region, LiuZhou, China

2 Beijing Key Laboratory of Mental Disorders, National Clinical Research Center for Mental Disorders and National Center for Mental Disorders, Beijing Anding Hospital, Capital Medical University, Beijing, China

3 Advanced Innovation Center for Human Brain Protection, Capital Medical University, Beijing, China

4 The Affiliated Brain Hospital of Guangzhou Medical University, Guangzhou, China

5 Key Laboratory of Neurogenetics and Channelopathies of Guangdong Province and the Ministry of Education of China, Guangzhou Medical University, Guangzhou

*Address all correspondence to: zhengwei0702@163.com

References

[1] Barker AT, Jalinous R, Freeston IL. Non-invasive magnetic stimulation of human motor cortex. Lancet. 1985;**1**(8437):1106-1107

[2] Perera T, George MS, Grammer G, Janicak PG, Pascual-Leone A, Wirecki TS. The clinical TMS society consensus review and treatment recommendations for TMS therapy for major depressive disorder. Brain Stimulation. 2016;**9**(3):336-346

[3] Pellegrini L, Garg K, Enara A, Gottlieb DS, Wellsted D, Albert U, et al. Repetitive transcranial magnetic stimulation (r-TMS) and selective serotonin reuptake inhibitor-resistance in obsessive-compulsive disorder: A meta-analysis and clinical implications. Comprehensive Psychiatry. 2022;**118**:152339

[4] Rapinesi C, Kotzalidis GD, Ferracuti S, Sani G, Girardi P, Del Casale A. Brain stimulation in obsessive-compulsive disorder (OCD): A systematic review. Current Neuropharmacology. 2019;**17**(8):787-807

[5] Cheng CM, Li CT, Tsai SJ. Current updates on newer forms of transcranial magnetic stimulation in major depression. Advances in Experimental Medicine and Biology. 2021;**1305**:333-349

[6] Lefaucheur JP, André-Obadia N, Antal A, Ayache SS, Baeken C, Benninger DH, et al. Evidence-based guidelines on the therapeutic use of repetitive transcranial magnetic stimulation (rTMS). Clinical Neurophysiology. 2014;**125**(11):2150-2206

[7] Martin JL, Barbanoj MJ, Pérez V, Sacristán M. Transcranial magnetic stimulation for the treatment of obsessive-compulsive disorder. Cochrane Database of Systematic Reviews. 2003;**2003**(3):CD003387

[8] McClintock SM, Reti IM, Carpenter LL, McDonald WM, Dubin M, Taylor SF, et al. Consensus recommendations for the clinical application of repetitive transcranial magnetic stimulation (rTMS) in the treatment of depression. The Journal of Clinical Psychiatry. 2018;**79**(1):16cs10905

[9] Mutz J, Vipulananthan V, Carter B, Hurlemann R, Fu CHY, Young AH. Comparative efficacy and acceptability of non-surgical brain stimulation for the acute treatment of major depressive episodes in adults: Systematic review and network meta-analysis. BMJ. 2019;**364**:l1079

[10] Stein DJ, Costa DLC, Lochner C, Miguel EC, Reddy YCJ, Shavitt RG, et al. Obsessive-compulsive disorder. Nature Reviews Disease Primers. 2019;**5**(1):52

[11] Baldwin DS, Anderson IM, Nutt DJ, Allgulander C, Bandelow B, den Boer JA, et al. Evidence-based pharmacological treatment of anxiety disorders, post-traumatic stress disorder and obsessive-compulsive disorder: A revision of the 2005 guidelines from the British Association for Psychopharmacology. Journal of Psychopharmacology. 2014;**28**(5):403-439

[12] Fineberg NA, Van Ameringen M, Drummond L, Hollander E, Stein DJ, Geller D, et al. How to manage obsessive-compulsive disorder (OCD) under COVID-19: A clinician's guide from the International College of Obsessive Compulsive Spectrum Disorders (ICOCS) and the obsessive-compulsive

and related disorders research network (OCRN) of the European College of Neuropsychopharmacology. Comprehensive Psychiatry. 2020b;**100**:152174

[13] Pallanti S, Quercioli L. Treatment-refractory obsessive-compulsive disorder: Methodological issues, operational definitions and therapeutic lines. Progress in Neuro-Psychopharmacology & Biological Psychiatry. 2006;**30**(3):400-412

[14] Fineberg NA, Hollander E, Pallanti S, Walitza S, Grünblatt E, Dell'Osso BM, et al. Clinical advances in obsessive-compulsive disorder: A position statement by the International College of Obsessive-Compulsive Spectrum Disorders. International Clinical Psychopharmacology. 2020a;**35**(4):173-193

[15] Gomes PV, Brasil-Neto JP, Allam N, Rodrigues de Souza E. A randomized, double-blind trial of repetitive transcranial magnetic stimulation in obsessive-compulsive disorder with three-month follow-up. The Journal of Neuropsychiatry and Clinical Neurosciences. 2012;**24**(4):437-443

[16] Milad MR, Rauch SL. Obsessive-compulsive disorder: Beyond segregated cortico-striatal pathways. Trends in Cognitive Sciences. 2012;**16**(1):43-51

[17] Mantovani A, Simpson HB, Fallon BA, Rossi S, Lisanby SH. Randomized sham-controlled trial of repetitive transcranial magnetic stimulation in treatment-resistant obsessive-compulsive disorder. The International Journal of Neuropsychopharmacology. 2010;**13**(2):217-227

[18] Arumugham SS, Subhasini VS, Madhuri HN, Vinay B, Sharma E, Thirthalli J, et al. Augmentation effect of low-frequency repetitive transcranial magnetic stimulation over Presupplementary motor area in obsessive-compulsive disorder: A randomized controlled trial. The Journal of ECT. 2018;**34**(4):253-257

[19] Pelissolo A, Harika-Germaneau G, Rachid F, Gaudeau-Bosma C, Tanguy ML, BenAdhira R, et al. Repetitive transcranial magnetic stimulation to supplementary motor area in refractory obsessive-compulsive disorder treatment: A sham-controlled trial. The International Journal of Neuropsychopharmacology. 2016;**19**(8):pyw025

[20] Elbeh KAM, Elserogy YMB, Khalifa HE, Ahmed MA, Hafez MH, Khedr EM. Repetitive transcranial magnetic stimulation in the treatment of obsessive-compulsive disorders: Double blind randomized clinical trial. Psychiatry Research. 2016;**238**:264-269

[21] Sarkhel S, Sinha VK, Praharaj SK. Adjunctive high-frequency right prefrontal repetitive transcranial magnetic stimulation (rTMS) was not effective in obsessive-compulsive disorder but improved secondary depression. Journal of Anxiety Disorders. 2010;**24**(5):535-539

[22] Blom RM, Figee M, Vulink N, Denys D. Update on repetitive transcranial magnetic stimulation in obsessive-compulsive disorder: Different targets. Current Psychiatry Reports. 2011;**13**(4):289-294

[23] George MS. Whither TMS: A one-trick pony or the beginning of a neuroscientific revolution? The American Journal of Psychiatry. 2019;**176**(11):904-910

[24] Liang K, Li H, Bu X, Li X, Cao L, Liu J, et al. Efficacy and tolerability of repetitive transcranial magnetic stimulation for

the treatment of obsessive-compulsive disorder in adults: A systematic review and network meta-analysis. Translational Psychiatry. 2021;**11**(1):332

[25] Berlim MT, Neufeld NH, Van den Eynde F. Repetitive transcranial magnetic stimulation (rTMS) for obsessive-compulsive disorder (OCD): An exploratory meta-analysis of randomized and sham-controlled trials. Journal of Psychiatric Research. 2013a;**47**(8):999-1006

[26] Gan J, Zhong M, Fan J, Liu W, Niu C, Cai S, et al. Abnormal white matter structural connectivity in adults with obsessive-compulsive disorder. Translational Psychiatry. 2017;**7**(3):e1062

[27] Lefaucheur J-P, Aleman A, Baeken C, Benninger DH, Brunelin J, Di Lazzaro V, et al. Evidence-based guidelines on the therapeutic use of repetitive transcranial magnetic stimulation (rTMS): An update (2014-2018). Clinical Neurophysiology: Official Journal of the International Federation of Clinical Neurophysiology. 2020;**131**(2):474-528

[28] Gogulski J, Ross JM, Talbot A, Cline CC, Donati FL, Munot S, et al. Personalized repetitive transcranial magnetic stimulation for depression. Biological Psychiatry: Cognitive Neuroscience and Neuroimaging. 2023;**8**(4):351-360

[29] Fitzsimmons SMDD, van der Werf YD, van Campen AD, Arns M, Sack AT, Hoogendoorn AW, et al. Repetitive transcranial magnetic stimulation for obsessive-compulsive disorder: A systematic review and pairwise/network meta-analysis. Journal of Affective Disorders. 2022;**302**:302-312

[30] Greenberg BD, George MS, Martin JD, Benjamin J, Schlaepfer TE, Altemus M, et al. Effect of prefrontal repetitive transcranial magnetic stimulation in obsessive-compulsive disorder: A preliminary study. The American Journal of Psychiatry. 1997;**154**(6):867-869

[31] Seo H-J, Jung Y-E, Lim HK, Um Y-H, Lee CU, Chae J-H. Adjunctive low-frequency repetitive transcranial magnetic stimulation over the right dorsolateral prefrontal cortex in patients with treatment-resistant obsessive-compulsive disorder: A randomized controlled trial. Clinical Psychopharmacology and Neuroscience: The Official Scientific Journal of the Korean College of Neuropsychopharmacology. 2016;**14**(2):153-160

[32] Sachdev PS, Loo CK, Mitchell PB, McFarquhar TF, Malhi GS. Repetitive transcranial magnetic stimulation for the treatment of obsessive compulsive disorder: A double-blind controlled investigation. Psychological Medicine. 2007;**37**(11):1645-1649

[33] Prasko J, Pasková B, Záleský R, Novák T, Kopecek M, Bares M, et al. The effect of repetitive transcranial magnetic stimulation (rTMS) on symptoms in obsessive compulsive disorder. A randomized, double blind, sham controlled study. Neuro Endocrinology Letters. 2006;**27**(3):327-332

[34] Kumar S, Singh S, Chadda RK, Verma R, Kumar N. The effect of low-frequency repetitive transcranial magnetic stimulation at orbitofrontal cortex in the treatment of patients with medication-refractory obsessive-compulsive disorder: A retrospective open study. The Journal of ECT. 2018;**34**(2):e16-e19

[35] Nauczyciel C, Le Jeune F, Naudet F, Douabin S, Esquevin A, Vérin M, et al. Repetitive transcranial magnetic

stimulation over the orbitofrontal cortex for obsessive-compulsive disorder: A double-blind, crossover study. Translational Psychiatry. 2014;**4**(9):e436

[36] Singh S, Kumar S, Gupta A, Verma R, Kumar N. Effectiveness and predictors of response to 1-Hz repetitive transcranial magnetic stimulation in patients with obsessive-compulsive disorder. The Journal of ECT. 2019a;**35**(1):61-66

[37] Perera MPN, Mallawaarachchi S, Miljevic A, Bailey NW, Herring SE, Fitzgerald PB. Repetitive transcranial magnetic stimulation for obsessive-compulsive disorder: A meta-analysis of randomized, sham-controlled trials. Biological Psychiatry: Cognitive Neuroscience and Neuroimaging. 2021;**6**(10):947-960

[38] Rehn S, Eslick GD, Brakoulias V. A meta-analysis of the effectiveness of different cortical targets used in repetitive transcranial magnetic stimulation (rTMS) for the treatment of obsessive-compulsive disorder (OCD). The Psychiatric Quarterly. 2018a;**89**(3):645-665

[39] Brakoulias V, Nguyen PHD, Lin D, Pham NDK. An international survey of different transcranial magnetic stimulation (TMS) protocols for patients with obsessive-compulsive disorder (OCD). Psychiatry Research. 2021;**298**:113765

[40] Zhang K, Fan X, Yuan J, Yin J, Su H, Hashimoto K, et al. Impact of serotonin transporter gene on rTMS augmentation of SSRIs for obsessive compulsive disorder. Neuropsychiatric Disease and Treatment. 2019;**15**:1771-1779

[41] Picard N, Strick PL. Imaging the premotor areas. Current Opinion in Neurobiology. 2001;**11**(6):663-672

[42] Chou P-H, Sack AT, Su K-P. Targeting three brain regions (bilateral SMA, left and right DLPFC) sequentially in one session using combined repetitive transcranial magnetic stimulation and intermittent theta-burst stimulation in treatment-refractory obsessive-compulsive disorder: A case report. Clinical Psychopharmacology and Neuroscience. 2022a;**20**(4):773-776

[43] Grassi G, Moradei C, Cecchelli C. Will transcranial magnetic stimulation improve the treatment of obsessive-compulsive disorder? A systematic review and meta-analysis of current targets and clinical evidence. Life (Basel). 2023;**13**(7):1494

[44] Kang JI, Kim C-H, Namkoong K, Lee C-I, Kim SJ. A randomized controlled study of sequentially applied repetitive transcranial magnetic stimulation in obsessive-compulsive disorder. The Journal of Clinical Psychiatry. 2009;**70**(12):1645-1651

[45] Kar SK, Choudhary P, Agarwal V, Dalal PK. Fusion of extended and accelerated protocol of rTMS in management of OCD: A case study. Asian Journal of Psychiatry. 2020;**48**:101917

[46] Mantovani A, Neri F, D'Urso G, Mencarelli L, Tatti E, Momi D, et al. Functional connectivity changes and symptoms improvement after personalized, double-daily dosing, repetitive transcranial magnetic stimulation in obsessive-compulsive disorder: A pilot study. Journal of Psychiatric Research. 2021;**136**:560-570

[47] Tzirini M, Roth Y, Harmelech T, Zibman S, Pell GS, Kimiskidis V, et al. Electrical field measurements and simulations of the H7 and D-B80 coils: Non-equivalence of the TMS coils for obsessive compulsive disorder. Brain Stimulation. 2021;**14**(6):1525-1527

[48] Tzirini M, Roth Y, Harmelech T, Zibman S, Pell GS, Kimiskidis VK, et al. Detailed measurements and simulations of electric field distribution of two TMS coils cleared for obsessive compulsive disorder in the brain and in specific regions associated with OCD. PLoS One. 2022;**17**(8):e0263145

[49] Carmi L, Alyagon U, Barnea-Ygael N, Zohar J, Dar R, Zangen A. Clinical and electrophysiological outcomes of deep TMS over the medial prefrontal and anterior cingulate cortices in OCD patients. Brain Stimulation. 2018;**11**(1):158-165

[50] Carmi L, Tendler A, Bystritsky A, Hollander E, Blumberger DM, Daskalakis J, et al. Efficacy and safety of deep transcranial magnetic stimulation for obsessive-compulsive disorder: A prospective Multicenter randomized double-blind placebo-controlled trial. The American Journal of Psychiatry. 2019;**176**(11):931-938

[51] Roth Y, Tendler A, Arikan MK, Vidrine R, Kent D, Muir O, et al. Real-world efficacy of deep TMS for obsessive-compulsive disorder: Post-marketing data collected from twenty-two clinical sites. Journal of Psychiatric Research. 2021;**137**:667-672

[52] Harmelech T, Tendler A, Arikan MK, Çetin HL, Esmeray MT, Ilhan R, et al. Long-term outcomes of a course of deep TMS for treatment-resistant OCD. Brain Stimulation. 2022;**15**(1):226-228

[53] Suhas S, Malo PK, Kumar V, Issac TG, Chithra NK, Bhaskarapillai B, et al. Treatment strategies for serotonin reuptake inhibitor-resistant obsessive-compulsive disorder: A network meta-analysis of randomised controlled trials. The World Journal of Biological Psychiatry. 2023;**24**(2):162-177

[54] Zhou DD, Zhou XX, Lv Z, Chen XR, Wang W, Wang GM, et al. Comparative efficacy and tolerability of antipsychotics as augmentations in adults with treatment-resistant obsessive-compulsive disorder: A network meta-analysis. Journal of Psychiatric Research. 2019;**111**:51-58

[55] Gregory ST, Goodman WK, Kay B, Riemann B, Storch EA. Cost-effectiveness analysis of deep transcranial magnetic stimulation relative to evidence-based strategies for treatment-refractory obsessive-compulsive disorder. Journal of Psychiatric Research. 2022;**146**:50-54

[56] Harmelech T, Roth Y, Tendler A. Transcranial magnetic stimulation in obsessive-compulsive disorder. The Psychiatric Clinics of North America. 2023;**46**(1):133-166

[57] Arıkan MK, İlhan R, Esmeray T, Laçin Çetin H, Aytar EK, Aktas H, et al. Deep transcranial magnetic stimulation effects on the electrophysiological parameters in obsessive-compulsive disorder. Clinical EEG and Neuroscience. 2022;**53**(6):484-490

[58] Abraham WC, Bear MF. Metaplasticity: The plasticity of synaptic plasticity. Trends in Neurosciences. 1996;**19**(4):126-130

[59] Abraham WC, Tate WP. Metaplasticity: A new vista across the field of synaptic plasticity. Progress in Neurobiology. 1997;**52**(4):303-323

[60] Vidya KL, Rao PG, Goyal N. Adjuvant priming repetitive transcranial magnetic stimulation for treatment-resistant obsessive-compulsive disorder: In search of a new paradigm! The Journal of ECT. 2022;**38**(1):e1-e8

[61] Philip NS, Leuchter AF, Cook IA, Massaro J, Goethe JW, Carpenter LL.

Predictors of response to synchronized transcranial magnetic stimulation for major depressive disorder. Depression and Anxiety. 2019;**36**(3):278-285

[62] Leuchter AF, Cook IA, Feifel D, Goethe JW, Husain M, Carpenter LL, et al. Efficacy and safety of low-field synchronized transcranial magnetic stimulation (sTMS) for treatment of major depression. Brain Stimulation. 2015a;**8**(4):787-794

[63] Fuggetta G, Noh NA. A neurophysiological insight into the potential link between transcranial magnetic stimulation, thalamocortical dysrhythmia and neuropsychiatric disorders. Experimental Neurology. 2013;**245**:87-95

[64] Leuchter AF, Hunter AM, Krantz DE, Cook IA. Rhythms and blues: Modulation of oscillatory synchrony and the mechanism of action of antidepressant treatments. Annals of the New York Academy of Sciences. 2015b;**1344**(1):78-91

[65] Huang YZ, Edwards MJ, Rounis E, Bhatia KP, Rothwell JC. Theta burst stimulation of the human motor cortex. Neuron. 2005;**45**(2):201-206

[66] Rachid F. Safety and efficacy of theta-burst stimulation in the treatment of psychiatric disorders: A review of the literature. The Journal of Nervous and Mental Disease. 2017;**205**(11):823-839

[67] Lan XJ, Yang XH, Qin ZJ, Cai DB, Liu QM, Mai JX, et al. Efficacy and safety of intermittent theta burst stimulation versus high-frequency repetitive transcranial magnetic stimulation for patients with treatment-resistant depression: A systematic review. Frontiers in Psychiatry. 2023;**14**:1244289

[68] Suppa A, Huang YZ, Funke K, Ridding MC, Cheeran B, Di Lazzaro V, et al. Ten years of theta burst stimulation in humans: Established knowledge, Unknowns and Prospects. Brain Stimulation. 2016;**9**(3):323-335

[69] Naro A, Billeri L, Cannavò A, De Luca R, Portaro S, Bramanti P, et al. Theta burst stimulation for the treatment of obsessive-compulsive disorder: A pilot study. Journal of Neural Transmission (Vienna). 2019;**126**(12):1667-1677

[70] Syed FA, Naik SS, Arumugham SS, Mehta UM, Thirthalli J, Reddy YCJ. Adjuvant intermittent theta burst stimulation over dorsomedial prefrontal cortex in treatment-resistant obsessive-compulsive disorder type: Letter to the editor. Brain Stimulation. 2021;**14**(1):74-76

[71] Huang YZ, Rothwell JC, Chen RS, Lu CS, Chuang WL. The theoretical model of theta burst form of repetitive transcranial magnetic stimulation. Clinical Neurophysiology. 2011;**122**(5):1011-1018

[72] Wischnewski M, Schutter DJ. Efficacy and time course of theta burst stimulation in healthy humans. Brain Stimulation. 2015;**8**(4):685-692

[73] Mantovani A, Lisanby SH, Pieraccini F, Ulivelli M, Castrogiovanni P, Rossi S. Repetitive transcranial magnetic stimulation (rTMS) in the treatment of obsessive-compulsive disorder (OCD) and Tourette's syndrome (TS). The International Journal of Neuropsychopharmacology. 2006;**9**(1):95-100

[74] Harika-Germaneau G, Rachid F, Chatard A, Lafay-Chebassier C, Solinas M, Thirioux B, et al. Continuous theta burst stimulation over the supplementary motor area in refractory obsessive-compulsive disorder treatment: A randomized sham-controlled trial. Brain Stimulation. 2019;**12**(6):1565-1571

[75] Guo Q, Wang K, Han H, Li P, Cheng J, Zhu J, et al. Continuous theta burst stimulation over the bilateral supplementary motor area in obsessive-compulsive disorder treatment: A clinical randomized single-blind sham-controlled trial. European Psychiatry. 2022;**65**(1):e64

[76] Li P, Cheng J, Fan Q, Lin L, Zhou S, Gao J, et al. The functional connectivity predictor of therapeutic effect of continuous theta burst stimulation on obsessive-compulsive disorder: A preliminary study. Journal of Affective Disorders. 2022;**311**:231-238

[77] Frey J, Najib U, Lilly C, Adcock A. Novel TMS for stroke and depression (NoTSAD): Accelerated repetitive transcranial magnetic stimulation as a safe and effective treatment for Post-stroke depression. Frontiers in Neurology. 2020;**11**:788

[78] Thomson AC, Sack AT. How to design optimal accelerated rTMS protocols capable of promoting therapeutically beneficial Metaplasticity. Frontiers in Neurology. 2020;**11**:599918

[79] Williams NR, Sudheimer KD, Cole EJ, Varias AD, Goldstein-Piekarski AN, Stetz P, et al. Accelerated neuromodulation therapy for obsessive-compulsive disorder. Brain Stimulation. 2021;**14**(2):435-437

[80] Joseph JT, Jammigumpula A, Praharaj SK, Purohit AN, Shenoy S. Tolerability of accelerated theta burst stimulation for treatment-resistant obsessive-compulsive disorder: A case report. The Journal of ECT. 2023;**39**(3):e1-e2

[81] Dutta P, Dhyani M, Garg S, Tikka SK, Khattri S, Mehta S, et al. Efficacy of intensive orbitofrontal continuous theta burst stimulation (iOFcTBS) in obsessive compulsive disorder: A randomized placebo controlled study. Psychiatry Research. 2021;**298**:113784

[82] Liu W, Shao H, Liao J, Yang D, Ma M, Yang J. Continuous theta-burst stimulation over the right orbitofrontal cortex in treatment-resistant obsessive-compulsive disorder treatment: A randomized sham-controlled trial. International Journal of Generalized Medicine. 2021;**14**:3109-3118

[83] Mukherjee A, Kumre P, Goyal N, Khanra S. Adjunctive neuronavigated accelerated continuous theta-burst stimulation (cTBS) in obsessive-compulsive disorder: A randomized sham-controlled study. CNS Spectrums. 5 Sep 2022:1-10

[84] Noda Y, Fujii K, Tokura F, Nakajima S, Kitahata R. A case series of continuous theta burst stimulation treatment for the supplementary motor area twice a day in patients with obsessive-compulsive disorder: A real world TMS registry study in Japan. Journal of Personalized Medicine. 2023;**13**(5):875

[85] Wu CC, Tsai CH, Lu MK, Chen CM, Shen WC, Su KP. Theta-burst repetitive transcranial magnetic stimulation for treatment-resistant obsessive-compulsive disorder with concomitant depression. The Journal of Clinical Psychiatry. 2010;**71**(4):504-506

[86] Zhang X-Y, Chen H-D, Liang W-N, Yang X-H, Cai D-B, Huang X, et al. Adjunctive magnetic seizure therapy for schizophrenia: A systematic review. Frontiers in Psychiatry. 2021;**12**:813590

[87] Deng Z-D, Lisanby SH, Peterchev AV. Electric field strength and focality in electroconvulsive therapy and magnetic seizure therapy: A finite element simulation study. Journal of Neural Engineering. 2011;**8**(1):016007

[88] Tang VM, Blumberger DM, Throop A, McClintock SM, Voineskos D, Downar J, et al. Continuation magnetic seizure therapy for treatment-resistant ynipolar or bipolar depression. The Journal of Clinical Psychiatry. 2021a;**82**(6):20m13677

[89] Chen M, Yang X, Liu C, Li J, Wang X, Yang C, et al. Comparative efficacy and cognitive function of magnetic seizure therapy vs. electroconvulsive therapy for major depressive disorder: A systematic review and meta-analysis. Translational. Psychiatry. 2021;**11**(1):437

[90] Daskalakis ZJ, Dimitrova J, McClintock SM, Sun Y, Voineskos D, Rajji TK, et al. Magnetic seizure therapy (MST) for major depressive disorder. Neuropsychopharmacology. 2020;**45**(2):276-282

[91] Berlim MT, Van den Eynde F, Daskalakis ZJ. Efficacy and acceptability of high frequency repetitive transcranial magnetic stimulation (rTMS) versus electroconvulsive therapy (ECT) for major depression: A systematic review and meta-analysis of randomized trials. Depression and Anxiety. 2013b;**30**(7):614-623

[92] Bolwig TG. How does electroconvulsive therapy work? Theories on its mechanism. Canadian Journal of Psychiatry. Revue Canadienne de Psychiatrie. 2011;**56**(1):13-18

[93] Tang VM, Blumberger DM, Weissman CR, Dimitrova J, Throop A, McClintock SM, et al. A pilot study of magnetic seizure therapy for treatment-resistant obsessive-compulsive disorder. Depression and Anxiety. 2021b;**38**(2):161-171

[94] Meek BP, Fotros A, Abo Aoun M, Modirrousta M. Improvements in error-monitoring and symptoms following low-frequency rTMS of dorsal anterior cingulate cortex in obsessive compulsive disorder; a randomized, sham-controlled study. Brain and Cognition. 2021;**154**:105809

[95] Modirrousta M, Fellows LK. Dorsal medial prefrontal cortex plays a necessary role in rapid error prediction in humans. The Journal of Neuroscience. 2008;**28**(51):14000-14005

Section 2

What's New in Bipolar Disorder?

Chapter 4

Suicidal Behavior in Mania and Hypomania

Didem Bostan Bendas and Cicek Hocaoglu

Abstract

Bipolar disorder is a chronic, episodic illness that can cause functional impairment and has a variable course. Compared to other psychiatric disorders, bipolar disorder is linked to a more elevated risk of suicide. The incidence of fatal suicide methods was shown to be higher in these patients compared to the general population. Severe, pure, or mixed depression episodes are most commonly linked to thoughts and behavior of suicide. However, it is less prevalent in episodes of dysphoric mania and seldom during episodes of euphoric mania or euthymia. Various factors have been studied as risk factors for suicide in bipolar disorder. These include gender, history of suicide attempts, suicidal thought, family history of suicide, mood episodes, rapid cycling illness, age of onset, attack polarity, drug use, and personality traits. Lithium therapy is known to dramatically lower rates of self-harm and suicide behavior in patients with unipolar and bipolar depression. ECT has an effect on the prevention of suicide in unipolar and bipolar depression. Identifying protective factors is as important as identifying risk factors. Adaptive coping mechanisms and social support seem to have protective effects. It is crucial to remember that treatment and a good response to treatment are protective against suicide.

Keywords: suicidal behavior, mania, hypomania, risk factors, treatment

1. Introduction

Approximately 800,000 deaths worldwide occur each year due to suicide. Therefore, suicide is considered a significant public health problem [1–3]. Bipolar disorder is an episodic, lifelong mood disorder in which manic/hypomanic or depressive episodes occur, sometimes separately and sometimes together and can also lead to functional impairment [4–6]. The all-cause mortality rate in bipolar disorder is twice as high as in the general population. Of the specific causes, the risk is highest in suicide. Patients with bipolar disorder have approximately 20–30 times higher suicide risk than the general population [7, 8].

Patients with bipolar disorder have been observed to have more lethal suicide attempts and methods compared to the general population [9]. Bipolar disorder carries the highest risk of suicide among other psychiatric disorders [10–12]. They are also at higher risk of completing suicide than both the general population and those with other mental illnesses [13]. Approximately one-third to one-half of patients with bipolar disorder attempt suicide at least once during their lifetime. Approximately 15–20% of patients die by suicide [14–17]. Patients with bipolar disorder who have previously attempted suicide have a significantly impaired quality of life, even if they are clinically euthymic [12, 18, 19]. A history of previous suicide attempts is the strongest predictor of completed suicide [20].

There is evidence to suggest that completed suicides tend to occur disproportionately in depressive, dysphoric, and mixed episodes compared to manic or hypomanic episodes [21]. Bipolar disorder-II (BD-II) is associated with a comparatively elevated risk of suicide in comparison to bipolar disorder-I (BD-I). This disparity may be attributed to the longer duration of depressive episodes experienced by individuals with BD-II [8, 22]. Multiple studies have also shown comparatively elevated rates of completed suicide among BD-II compared to those with BD-I, therefore disproving the assertion that BD-II is a less severe form of bipolar disorder [23]. Reconsolidating the current data on suicide risk in BD-I and BD-II might enhance clinical evaluation, care planning, and therapy choices for individuals with bipolar illness [24].

This chapter is about suicidal behavior in patients with bipolar disorder. In particular, the relationship between suicidal behavior and hypomanic and manic episodes of bipolar disorder has been investigated. The history, epidemiology, risk factors, treatment and preventive approaches of suicidal behavior have been mentioned. It has been written in order to contribute to the literature by reviewing the studies on suicidal behavior in bipolar disorder. Suicidal behavior in bipolar disorder was first investigated by scanning the articles of the last 10 years in PubMed and Google Scholar. Since the resources on suicidal behavior in mania and hypomania were limited, the year criterion was removed and the search was expanded. In screening (1) bipolar disorder, (2) suicide, (3) suicidal behavior, (4) hypomania, (5) mania, (6) lithium, (7) ECT keywords were used. The reviewed articles and the sources of the articles were evaluated and the appropriate ones for this study were taken into consideration.

2. Definition and history of suicidal behavior

Although there are several different definitions of suicide that mean the same thing, I think the definition that best explains it is "any death that is the direct or indirect result of a positive or negative action taken by a person knowing that it will result in death" by French sociologist Emile Durkheim [25]. Throughout human history, actions and views on suicide have changed. When we look at the history of suicide, some societies have called suicide the work of the devil and an attempt that would attract the wrath of the Gods.

In the past, some societies burned the houses of individuals who committed suicide and prevented their bodies from being buried [26]. The provision in the Attic Laws in Ancient Greece, which required a person wishing to end her life to notify the state in advance of her/his action, stating her/his reasons, shows that the State controlled the action rather than prohibiting suicide. In Roman society, society consisted of various classes and each class was subject to its own laws. Therefore, the treatment given to freemen, slaves, and soldiers differed from each other in terms of suicide. Free people who attempted suicide were punished severely, while slaves were deprived of all their rights. Many slaves were seen to commit suicide due to overwork and the behavior of their masters. A slave who attempted suicide was considered an immoral person. Later, the Romans, who learned the maxims of the Stoics and Greek philosophy, accepted suicide as a pleasant way to end one's life [27, 28]. In the military, a soldier who ended his life due to fear or laziness was considered a dishonorable person. Since a soldier who was assigned to protect his country was obliged to serve his state in this capacity, the act of suicide was considered desertion from the army [27].

According to the Christian religion, suicide is not tolerated and there is a belief that the individual cannot voluntarily take the life given by God. Suicide is not tolerated in Islam too, and there is an opinion that no individual should kill himself/herself [28]. On the other hand, Buddha and Brahman religions do not see suicide as a sin [26].

The prosecution of the act of suicide, which was not tolerated and was punished severely, declined toward the end of the eighteenth century, particularly under the influence of Beccaria, Montesquieu and Voltaire [27]. In England, people who attempted suicide were punished until 1955. In six tribes living in Nigeria, Uganda and Kenya, it is believed that touching individuals who have committed suicide will bring bad luck. In contrast, in Trikopia, some types of suicide acts are respected and admired [26].

There are many approaches to explaining suicidal behavior from a psychosocial perspective [29]. One of the most important theories on suicide is Emile Durkheim's socially oriented theory. Durkheim argued that suicide stems from conflicts between individuals and society and irregularities in the individual's relationship with society. As the level of social integration increases in a society, suicide decreases. He stated that the suicide rates of those who cannot identify with social groups are higher than those who are committed to society. He explained that this rate is lower in married people than in single, separated, or divorced people, and lower in religious people than in non-religious people. He stated that suicide rates increase even more when there is a deterioration in social values such as a war defeat or economic depression. Durkheim seems to have concluded that the weakening of the bonds of individuals with the social groups they identify with is the main factor in suicidal behavior [27]. His theory is successful in explaining the distribution of suicide rates across societies and countries. In theories that focus on the relationship between suicide and internal factors, such as psychodynamic theories, which define suicide as "the desire to kill oneself as a result of directing one's anger at others," suicide is expressed as a means of communication, providing help, remorse, confession, threat, or revenge [29].

A behavioral process that begins with thought and ends in death is defined as "suicidal behavior." The National Institute of Mental Health has identified three main concepts related to suicide. The first of these is completed suicide, which is a voluntary, self-directed behavior that results in death [30]. The second is called a suicide attempt. It describes behaviors that aim to end a person's life but do not result in death [28, 30]. This term encompasses behaviors classified as nonfatal acts, such as incomplete suicide, failed suicide, suicide declaration, and contradictory attempt. Individuals who attempt suicide are known to attempt suicide multiple times later in life [30]. The last one is suicidal ideation. It is defined as the person constantly thinking about suicide, making plans in this direction, openly threatening to kill himself, openly expressing a desire to die but not having any observable behavior [30, 31].

3. Epidemiology of suicide

Annually, approximately 800,000 fatalities occur globally due to suicide, underscoring its significance as a public health concern [1]. Suicide ranks among the top 10 leading causes of death worldwide, and in certain countries, it is the second most prevalent cause of death for individuals aged 15–34. This issue presents substantial challenges to both medical practitioners and society at large [32]. Notably, suicide rates exhibit geographical and national variations, influenced by factors such as age, gender, socioeconomic status, chosen methods, and access to healthcare services. While the incidence of suicide attempts is notably higher among women, completed suicides occur three times more frequently among men. Overall, suicide attempts are estimated to be 30 times more prevalent than completed suicides, with repeated attempts serving as significant predictors of eventual completion. The most common methods of suicide include hanging, chemical poisoning, and firearms [33].

Psychiatric disorders are identified as the primary contributors to the majority of suicides [33]. The mortality rate associated with suicide in patients with major affective disorders is estimated to be between 15% and 20% [17]. Furthermore, it is believed that this mortality rate may exceed 20% in patients with bipolar disorder [15]. Studies indicate that nearly 50% of these patients will have at least one suicide attempt. Bipolar disorder is recognized as one of the most prevalent mental disorders associated with suicidal behavior, with the risk of suicide mortality approximately 30 times higher than in the general population [12]. Bipolar disorder is one of the most common mental disorders that lead to suicidal behavior. Suicide mortality risk in bipolar disorder is approximately 30 times higher than in the general population [8, 34, 35]. Suicide attempters with bipolar disorder use more lethal methods than patients with unipolar depression. This may partly explain why bipolar disorder is frequently mentioned in completed suicides [36].

The correlation between bipolar disorder and the risk of suicidal behavior is well established. Some studies have indicated that rates of suicidal ideation among patients with bipolar disorder may be higher, comparable, or lower than those observed in individuals with major depression, suggesting challenges in distinguishing the relative risk of suicidal behavior between these disorders [34, 37].

Moreover, the literature reveals difficulty in determining whether specific subtypes of bipolar disorder (BD-I or BD-II) correlate with higher levels of suicidal ideation [8, 35, 37, 38]. Nevertheless, a consensus exists in many studies that individuals diagnosed with bipolar disorder, particularly those with the BD-II subtype, are at an increased risk for both suicide attempts and completion. This heightened risk in BD-II may be attributed to the increased prevalence of agitated depression and anxiety disorders within this subgroup compared to BD-I [24, 39–41].

4. The relationship between suicide and mental disorders

A diagnosis of mental disorder is present in 95% of all individuals exhibiting suicidal behavior [42]. Depression, drug use, psychosis are the primary risk factors [43] and other conditions including anxiety disorders, eating disorders, trauma-related disorders, personality disorders, and organic mental disorders [44]. Depressive disorder accounts for 80% of these mental disorders. For both males and females, the psychiatric diagnosis that carries the greatest risk of suicide is mood disorders. Depressed men are more likely to attempt suicide [42].

Approximately 10% of patients with schizophrenia die by suicide. These patients are affected by social isolation and stigma. Suicide in schizophrenia is often due to depressed mood. Hallucinations influence suicidal behavior in a small percentage of patients with schizophrenia. Although the suicide rate among patients with schizophrenia is quite low throughout their inpatient treatment, 50% of suicides happen during the first weeks and months after their release from the hospital [42].

Suicidal behavior is seen in 15% of patients with alcohol dependence. Approximately 80% of these are male. Personality disorders, difficulties in relationships and social adaptation, excessive negative life events, decreased ability to cope with discomfort, conflicts with people around them such as family members and healthcare personnel, depressive disorder, and alcohol addiction may lead to suicidal tendencies. In addition, approximately 20% of completed suicide attempts were made by patients with panic disorder and social phobia [42].

5. The relationship between mania and suicidal behavior

Data in the literature on suicidal behavior in mania are limited. Studies have shown that suicidal behavior is more common in mixed mania than in pure mania [45–48]. A total of 26–55% of patients with mixed mania have suicidal ideation, compared with only 2–7% in patients with pure mania [49]. In patients with bipolar disorder, suicidal behavior occurs most frequently during severe, pure, or mixed depressive episodes. It is less common during dysphoric mania and very uncommon during euphoric mania or euthymia [50–53]. Suicidality in mania is unclear if it is a categorical phenomena indicating dysphoria without major depression or whether it arises from many simultaneous depressed symptoms. The analysis of clinical and demographic features of dysphoric manic patients with and without suicidality revealed a notable increase in suicidal thoughts among individuals with a previous suicide attempt, those who had taken antidepressants in the week leading up to hospitalization, those with a history of alcohol abuse, and who were Caucasian. Suicidal thoughts occurred in approximately 50% manic patients whose concurrent depressive symptoms were not sufficient to constitute major depression. Suicidality is a clinically significant concern in most dysphoric manic patients. Dysphoric mania alone and no single emotional symptom or symptom pattern usefully distinguishes suicidal from nonsuicidal manic patients [45].

A hypothesis has been proposed that the higher prevalence of suicidal thoughts in Caucasians may be due to the higher rate of dysphoric mania in Caucasians compared to non-Caucasians [47]. There is an opinion that dysphoric manic patients who take antidepressants immediately before admission may have more severe psychopathology or depression than those who do not take antidepressants. This may be one reason why dysphoric manic patients who take antidepressants immediately before admission are approximately four times more likely to commit suicide than those who do not take antidepressants. Another possible explanation is that antidepressants may cause increased agitation in some dysphoric manic patients, which may lead to increased suicidal thoughts [45].

Mixed depression is a major risk factor for suicide, and mixed depression is especially linked to BD-II [50]. Mixed depression is three times more common in BD-II than in unipolar depression, and this may partially explain the higher suicide risk seen in BD-II compared to unipolar depression [54, 55]. Every manic patient displaying significant depressive symptoms should undergo a thorough assessment for suicidal tendencies. Current findings support that suicide is fairly prevalent in dysphoric mania and is often concurrently two additional depressed symptoms [45]. Additionally, the risk of suicide may increase due to the patient's delusions during a manic episode [56]. There is one study that found that symptoms of mania and anxiety during a depressive episode do not increase the risk of suicidal behavior in patients with bipolar disorder and at least moderate depressive symptoms. However, it is unclear whether symptoms of mania and anxiety during a depressive episode increase suicidal behavior in patients with bipolar disorder [57].

Bipolar disorder patients who have previously attempted suicide also exhibit traits such as increased severity of mania, more frequent occurrence of suicidal ideation during manic or depressive episodes, and higher prevalence of medical illnesses [58].

6. Suicidal behavior in hypomania

As with mania, there is limited data in the literature on suicidal behavior in hypomania. It is known that 8–55% of patients with major depression have subthreshold hypomanic symptoms. Several studies have shown an association between subthreshold bipolarity and elevated levels of suicidality. This shows that patients with major depression who have subthreshold hypomanic symptoms have some differences from patients with major depression who do not have subthreshold hypomanic symptoms [59–61]. The limited data on hypomania and the little known effect on suicide risk may indicate the need for further studies on this subject.

7. Risk factors and warning signs

Although common suicide risk factors are applicable to patients with bipolar disorder, there exist distinct risk factors that are unique to the pathology. Characterizing the risk factors unique to bipolar disorder patients for suicide has been challenging. Research examining suicide risk factors in bipolar disorder over the last few decades has produced mixed findings. Gender, mood episodes, rapid cycling illness, age of initiation, episode polarity, polarity of initial emotional episode, familial suicide history, previous suicide attempts, suicidal thoughts, personality disorders, personality traits, traumatic experiences, and substance abuse have been examined as risk factors for suicide in bipolar disorder. These factors are listed in **Table 1** [16, 38, 62]. Results on gender are contradictory. Research shows that women attempt suicide at a higher rate, especially at a younger age, while men have a higher rate of completed suicide [9, 53, 63]. However, there are also studies that show no significant difference between men and women [17, 51, 58, 63, 64].

In patients with bipolar disorder, having previously attempted suicide increases the likelihood of suicide by 37 times [65]. At least 50% of all suicides are seen in people who have previously attempted suicide [66, 67]. Suicidal thought is linked to despair, mixed depression, severe depression, psychotic symptoms, prior suicide attempts, alcohol use, symptoms of panic disorder, and an early onset [16, 68, 69].

In bipolar disorder, major depression episodes by themselves are an important risk factor for suicide, with the majority of suicide attempts and committed suicides taking place during depressed periods. Additionally, if the initial mood episode was of a predominantly depressive polarity, there was an eightfold increased risk for a suicide attempt. An elevated incidence of suicide actions and suicide attempts is linked to the prevalence of dominant depressive polarity in future episodes [15, 70, 71]. Suicidal thoughts and behaviors are quite common in mixed episodes and dysphoric mania. Specifically, suicidal thoughts are present in 26–55% of patients with dysphoric mania, but only in 2–7% of patients with pure mania [16, 49, 64]. However, patients

Sociodemographic factors	• Men have higher rates of completed suicide • Women have higher rates of attempted suicide • Caucasian • Marital status (single, widowed, divorced) • Living alone • No children • Younger age (<35 years), elderly age (>75 years) • Unemployment
Clinical history	• Prior suicide attempt/ideation (especially violent/highly lethal methods) • Family history of attempted or completed suicide • Family history of mood disorders in first and second degree relatives • Suicidal ideation • Predominant depressive polarity • Major depressive episode • Phase of illness: depression > mixed > dysphoric mania > pure mania > euthymia • Rapid cycling subtype • Earlier age of onset • Earlier stage of illness course • Longer duration of untreated illness • Number of previous depressive episodes • Previous hospitalizations • Concurrent medical comorbidity • Mood-incongruent psychotic symptoms • Rapid cycling course • Acute psychosocial stressors • Permanent adverse life situations
Psychiatric comorbidity	• Personality disorders: borderline, antisocial, histrionic, narcissistic
Genetic factors	• Noncoding RNA LOC105374524 • Serotonin-related genes: 5-HTT, 5-HT1–7, TPH1, TPH2 • Other genes: AKT1, AKT1P, ADRA2, BDNF, COMT, CREB1, GSK3B, FOX03A and MAPK1
Other	• Alcohol and drug use disorders • Early negative life events (separation, emotional, physical and sexual abuse, neglect) • Cyclothymic temperament • Aggressive or impulsive behavior • Higher altitude • Dysfunctional personality traits • Poor social support

Table 1.
Risk factors of suicidal behavior in bipolar disorder patients.

with bipolar disorder tend to make suicide attempts most commonly (78–80%) during severe pure or mixed episodes, less often (11–20%) during mixed affective episodes or dysphoric mania, and quite rarely (0–7%) during euphoric mania or euthymia [16, 72]. Suicide attempts have also been linked to the bipolar disorder subtype known as rapid cycling [73, 74].

The onset of a first depressive episode, the early phases of illness, untreated illness, the frequency of past depressive episodes, prior hospitalizations, and concurrent medical comorbidities have all been related to suicide in mood disorders [75]. Furthermore, there is a correlation between the development of mood-incompatible psychotic symptoms and a higher likelihood of suicide [76]. Bipolar disorder onset age has been linked to the likelihood of suicide attempts; a lower diagnostic age corresponds to a greater risk [51, 73]. Borderline, antisocial, histrionic, and narcissistic types of comorbid personality disorders significantly increase the risk of suicide. These personality disorders are associated with greater impulsivity, aggressiveness, and raised levels of severe mood episodes [16].

There is insufficient evidence to conclude that drug, alcohol, or nicotine use problems increase the risk of suicide in people with bipolar disorder [16]. A number of risk variables, including childhood abuse and neglect [75], higher altitude [77], dysfunctional personality characteristics [78, 79], being single, widowed, or divorced, inadequate social support, spirituality, and religiosity [12] have not been well explored but are believed to play a role in suicide.

Studies consistently demonstrate that a past history of suicide attempts [16, 63, 73, 80, 81] and a family history of attempted or completed suicide [64], especially in first-degree relatives [63, 73] are the most dependable and potent risk factors for suicide attempts and completed suicide in bipolar disorder patients. This may be partially attributed to the inherent heredity of bipolar illness (40%) and the intra-family transfer of suicidal tendencies [82]. As shown in primary research and other twins, family and adoption studies, there is evidence that genetic risk factors contribute significantly to suicide in patients with bipolar disorder [38, 66, 76]. Strong associations were found between the risk of suicidal behavior and the serotonin-related genes 5-HT1–7 and 5-HTT, as well as the tryptophan hydroxylase genes TPH1 and TPH2. Suicidal attempts have been associated with several genes, such as AKT1, AKT1P, ADRA2, BDNF, COMT, CREB1, GSK3B, FOX03A, and MAPK1 [8, 83–85]. Three major genes linked to a higher risk of suicide attempt were identified in the biggest genome-wide association study (GWAS) conducted so far. Bipolar disorder has been linked to an intronic variation of non-coding RNA LOC105374524, an insertion-deletion polymorphism on chromosome 4 [86]. Genetic studies on suicide may guide us in determining the underlying biological mechanisms, developing suicide prevention strategies, and taking precautions against suicidal behavior in the future.

There exists data indicating that the presence of white matter hyperintensities in the brains of patients with bipolar disorder may raise the risk of suicide [87–89]. Nevertheless, the expansion of white matter hyperintensity volume in bipolar disorder may be associated with disease burden and may not have a direct connection to the risk of suicide [90]. Suicidal behavior in bipolar disorder has been linked to disruption of the hypothalamic-pituitary-adrenal (HPA) axis, according to evidence [91]. Nevertheless, a lot of studies on how the HPA axis functions in bipolar illness have not specifically looked at how it can affect suicidal behavior. Furthermore, there is presently no clinical evidence to support the use of salivary/plasma cortisol level testing or dexamethasone suppression testing in the assessment of suicide risk in bipolar disorder patients [92–94].

8. Diagnosis of suicidal behavior

The assessment of suicide risk in people with bipolar disorder should be conducted by direct clinical questioning. Insufficient attention given to psychiatric emergencies in overcrowded institutions and the failure to routinely assess bipolar disorder patients may have adverse consequences for instances involving suicidal thoughts or suicide attempts. A thorough psychiatric assessment should be carried out while evaluating suicide, including analyzing the patient's mood, irritability, presence or absence of psychosis, and suicidal thoughts. Particular attention should be given to ascertaining the duration of suicidal thoughts, the presence of a detailed plan, the intended method of death, the characteristics and severity of prior suicide attempts, and the availability of deadly methods [95]. An analysis of the patient's emotional temperament (depressed, hyperthymic, cyclothymic, irritable, anxious) and personality characteristics may provide a more precise assessment of suicide risk [51].

There are no suicide risk assessment tools that have been specially developed and validated for bipolar disorder. However, there are general risk assessment methods that can help clinicians to detect patients at high risk of suicide and effectively begin treatment. These should, of course, not be used as a substitute for comprehensive clinical assessment, but rather as a guide. Columbia Suicide Severity Rating Scale (C-SSRS) [96], Columbia Classification Algorithm of Suicide Assessment (C-CASA) [97], The Tool for Assessment of Suicide Risk (TASR) [98], the Oxford Mental Illness and Suicide tool (OxMIS) [99] or the Modular Assessment of Risk for Imminent Suicide (MARIS) [100] may be used for this assessment.

9. Therapeutic approaches

The best treatment method for bipolar disorder patients who have attempted suicide is to hospitalize them in a psychiatric clinic. In this way, these patients are both protected and treated. Knowing the patient's medication history and compliance with treatment contributes to treatment planning. Obtaining information from family members and/or close friends during the initial evaluation may be important for treatment planning, follow-up and prevention. For outpatients at high risk of suicide, follow-up evaluations should be performed at regular intervals after the initial evaluation, and any alteration in clinical status should be closely monitored [8].

The clinician should not hesitate to ask about suicide because of concerns that it may trigger suicidal behavior or because of personal concerns about the idea. Because patients with suicidal ideation often have had suicidal thoughts for a long time, most patients are open to discussing these thoughts. It is important to note that a significant number of individuals who complete suicide (regardless of diagnosis) have had contact with mental health services in the months leading up to their death. It is estimated that 75–83% of individuals who commit suicide have had contact with a physician in the past year. In the month leading up to the death, only 46% of these individuals have visited a mental health professional, and 36% have done so in the week prior to death. Therefore, it is important to discuss suicide with patients. The most effective way to prevent suicide in patients with bipolar disorder is to recognize clinical and demographic risk factors [62].

9.1 Pharmacotherapy

Initially, the initial stage in managing bipolar disorder involves verifying the diagnosis and assessing the present condition of the patient. Treatment varies depending on the episode. Mood stabilizers and antipsychotics are the primary therapeutic regimen for managing mania and depression [5, 38]. Clinical experience spanning decades, many randomized controlled trials, and meta-analyses have consistently shown that lithium significantly decreases suicidal and self-harm behaviors in patients with bipolar and unipolar depression [16, 101, 102]. Lithium is a prophylaxis against suicidal behavior, not an acute intervention. Furthermore, lithium overdose can be fatal. The long-term usage of lithium decreases the mortality risk by 60–80% [101, 103]. Noncompliance with lithium increases the risk of suicide [104]. Early intervention with suicide-preventive drugs like lithium, along with vigilant monitoring and regular follow-up, is the most effective approach to decreasing suicide rates [62]. The Food and Drug Administration reported an increased risk of suicide after reviewing clinical trials of carbamazepine, divalproex, felbamate, gabapentin, lamotrigine, levetiracetam, oxcarbazepine, pregabalin, tiagabine, topiramate, and zonisamide, but this report has been extensively reviewed over the past 15 years, showing that these drugs do not increase the risk of suicide in bipolar disorder [105, 106]. In addition, valproate, lamotrigine, and carbamazepine have been shown to have a suicide prevention effect, although less than that reported for lithium [107].

Antipsychotic drugs recommended for bipolar depression include quetiapine, lurasidone, and olanzapine (in combination with fluoxetine). Atypical antipsychotics, such as aripiprazole, olanzapine, and quetiapine, may have antidepressant effects and long-term mood-stabilizing effects in patients with bipolar disorder. However, there is no specific evidence for a suicide prevention effect [8, 108]. Clinical evidence indicates that clozapine decreases suicide attempts and hospitalizations for suicidal behavior in patients with schizophrenia. Although not well researched, it has preventive benefits against suicide in bipolar disorder [109].

Despite the substantial reduction in suicide risk among depressed individuals with prolonged therapy, no antidepressant drug has been shown to prevent suicide [110, 111]. There are concerns that antidepressant medications may worsen the course of the illness by causing agitation during mixed episodes or by triggering transitions to hypomanic or manic states and may contribute to suicidal behavior [112]. In addition, some studies have even suggested that antidepressant treatment may increase suicidality in a subgroup of bipolar disorder [75]. However, the International Society on Bipolar Disorders has recognized that some patients with bipolar disorder may benefit from antidepressant medications and that the risk of transition is minimal when bupropion is prescribed in addition to mood stabilizers [113]. Several studies suggest that intravenous and intranasal ketamine may expedite the treatment of suicidal tendencies in bipolar disorder. However, the availability of ketamine is limited [114–116].

9.2 Electroconvulsive therapy (ECT) and transcranial magnetic stimulation (TMS)

ECT is effective in reducing the acute risk of suicide in severely depressed and suicidal adult patients [103, 117]. ECT has been shown to provide better suicide prevention outcomes than current pharmacological treatments in both unipolar and bipolar depression [118]. Nevertheless, the enduring impact of ECT on the management of suicidal tendencies in individuals diagnosed with bipolar disorder remains uncertain [51].

TMS is an approved treatment for treatment-resistant major depression. It may have a short-term potential reduction in suicide risk. However, TMS is not currently FDA-approved for bipolar depression. Although TMS and rTMS (repetitive transcranial magnetic stimulation) have been shown to have potential benefits for bipolar depression, there is a theoretical risk of transitioning to hypomania or mania [119–121].

9.3 Psychotherapy

There are few studies investigating the effects of psychological treatment on suicidal ideation in patients with bipolar disorder [8, 103]. In general, psychotherapy and other psychological approaches are used in addition to pharmacotherapy in the treatment of patients with suicidal ideation [103]. The problem of compliance with treatment for suicidal patients is the biggest obstacle in treatment [122]. While depression itself may cause problems with treatment compliance, other diagnoses such as lack of motivation and personality disorders and hopelessness about treatment may also be effective [122, 123]. Once the patient has attended the first therapy session, measures such as fixing the therapist and meeting times and calling the patient when he/she does not show up will increase compliance [124].

Psychotherapeutic techniques based on problem-solving, cognitive and behavioral methods may limit the risk of suicide in relatively mildly depressed patients [125]. A systematic review of observational studies investigating the effects of psychotherapeutic programs in preventing suicidal behaviors found that cognitive behavioral therapy (CBT) and dialectical behavioral therapy (DBT) were the most commonly used and effective psychotherapeutic interventions, even in the short term, for patients with suicidal ideation or suicide attempts [126].

Problem-solving therapy is based on the idea that individuals who encounter problems do not have sufficient problem-solving skills and therefore try to solve them through inappropriate means, such as suicide [127].

After identifying the problem, it leads to finding more functional ways to solve this problem. The therapist should discuss the patient's way of thinking, expose them to the factors that cause negative emotions in a controlled manner, accompany the patient while producing new solutions, and help the patient evaluate himself/herself positively when he/she can produce healthy solutions [128].

Cognitive therapy used in suicidal behavior, although it originated from cognitive therapies used in the treatment of depression, shares many common techniques with problem-solving therapy. It states that thoughts and interpretations related to the event affect emotions and behavior. The thoughts and cognitive distortions that the individual automatically produces reveal unhelpful adaptive behaviors, including suicide. The patient's basic beliefs include distortions about the outside world and himself. These basic beliefs affect cognitive content and processes. The therapist tries to change the patient's suicidal behavior by focusing on the patient's cognitive content and processes [129].

A brief intervention addressing suicidal behavior disorder with Acceptance and Commitment Therapy has shown a reduction in both the frequency and intensity of suicidal ideation [130].

Alongside these findings, there are also opinions that psychological interventions have little or no apparent benefit in bipolar disorder [8, 17, 103, 125, 131].

10. Preventing suicidal behavior

Identifying protective factors is as important as identifying risk factors [8]. Prospective studies suggest that suicide attempts in bipolar disorder are predicted by long duration of untreated illness [132], smoking [133], rapid cycling [134], early onset of bipolar disorder [135], previous suicide attempts [80], severity of depression [110], alcohol or other substance abuse [136] and feelings of hopelessness [137]. Strong social support, good family structure, and the use of adaptive coping mechanisms may provide protective benefits. In addition, a hyperthymic temperament and a strong sense of perceived meaning in life are also protective elements [34, 138, 139]. It has been revealed that religiosity may play a protective role, but the results are not yet conclusive [12, 140, 141]. It is crucial to emphasize that treatment, and particularly a positive response to treatment, is protective against suicide. Given that treatment can reduce the risk of increased suicidality, it is not surprising that most suicides are untreated [8, 34, 142].

Pharmacologically speaking, lithium has the most potential to prevent suicide in patients with bipolar disorder [101, 143, 144]. Lithium treatment is likely to benefit suicide prevention by reducing impulsivity and aggression seen in depression or dysphoric-agitated, mixed states, which are especially linked to suicidal behavior [101, 145]. Some results suggest that lithium may contribute to suicide prevention even in patients with bipolar disorder who show limited or moderate response to its preventive properties. This finding may suggest that in a patient with a high risk of suicide who does not show improvement with lithium, the physician should either maintain lithium, even at a reduced dosage, or add it to another mood stabilizer instead of switching to a different mood stabilizer [143].

The International College of Neuropsychopharmacology clinical guidelines recommended ketamine as a fourth-line therapy for bipolar depression, only when used in combination with a mood stabilizer. The effects of ketamine on patients with bipolar depression have been the subject of few research. These investigations indicate that ketamine has antidepressant effects similar to those seen in unipolar depression [146–148].

Apart from its antidepressant properties, ECT is also regarded as a potent antisuicidal intervention. It has comparable effectiveness in treating bipolar depression to MDD. According to certain research, ECT has shown greater efficacy in treating bipolar depression compared to unipolar depression. Its antisuicidal effects are comparable to the psychopharmacological effects seen in bipolar mixed states and mania [8, 118, 143, 149].

11. Conclusions

Among mental diseases, bipolar disorder has the greatest association with suicide mortality. Predicting suicide is difficult, but some risk factors may be used to evaluate the risk of suicide in bipolar disorder. These include previous suicide attempts, family history of suicide, and a dominant depressive polarity. In order to reduce suicide in bipolar disorder patients, regular psychiatric controls, early intervention and treatment during attack periods, and close observation and follow-up are effective ways. Lithium's effect in reducing the risk of suicidal behavior may be advantageous in treatment. In addition, ECT may be a prompt and efficient method to treat suicidal tendencies in bipolar disorder. Supportive social environments and psychological support may also provide further benefits.

Author details

Didem Bostan Bendas[1] and Cicek Hocaoglu[2]*

1 Sivas Cumhuriyet University, Sivas, Turkey

2 Recep Tayyip Erdoğan University, Rize, Turkey

*Address all correspondence to: cicekh@gmail.com

References

[1] Suicide Worldwide in 2019. World Health Organization 2021. Available from: https://www.who.int/publications/i/item/9789240026643

[2] World Health Organization. Preventing Suicide: A Global Imperative. World Health Organization; 2014. Available from: https://iris.who.int/handle/10665/131056

[3] Turecki G, Brent DA. Suicide and suicidal behaviour. Lancet. 2016;**387**(10024):1227-1239

[4] American Psychiatric Association. Diagnostic and Statistical Manual of Mental Disorders. 5th ed. Arlington, VA: American Psychiatric Association; 2013

[5] Grande I, Berk M, Birmaher B, Vieta E. Bipolar disorder. Lancet. 2016;**387**(10027):1561-1572

[6] Martinez-Aran A, Vieta E, Torrent C, Sanchez-Moreno J, Goikolea JM, Salamero M, et al. Functional outcome in bipolar disorder: The role of clinical and cognitive factors. Bipolar Disorders. 2007;**9**(1-2):103-113

[7] Biazus TB, Beraldi GH, Tokeshi L, de Siqueira Rotenberg L, Dragioti E, Carvalho AF, et al. All-cause and cause-specific mortality among people with bipolar disorder: A large-scale systematic review and meta-analysis. Molecular Psychiatry. 2023;**28**(6):2508-2524

[8] Plans L, Barrot C, Nieto E, Rios J, Schulze TG, Papiol S, et al. Association between completed suicide and bipolar disorder: A systematic review of the literature. Journal of Affective Disorders. 2019;**242**:111-122

[9] Simon GE, Hunkeler E, Fireman B, Lee JY, Savarino J. Risk of suicide attempt and suicide death in patients treated for bipolar disorder. Bipolar Disorders. 2007;**9**(5):526-530

[10] Brown GK, Beck AT, Steer RA, Grisham JR. Risk factors for suicide in psychiatric outpatients: A 20-year prospective study. Journal of Consulting and Clinical Psychology. 2000;**68**(3):371-377

[11] Goldstein TR, Ha W, Axelson DA, Goldstein BI, Liao F, Gill MK, et al. Predictors of prospectively examined suicide attempts among youth with bipolar disorder. Archives of General Psychiatry. 2012;**69**(11):1113-1122

[12] da Silva Costa L, Alencar ÁP, Neto PJN, do Socorro Vieira dos Santos M, da Silva CGL, de França Lacerda Pinheiro S, et al. Risk factors for suicide in bipolar disorder: A systematic review. Journal of Affective Disorders. 2015;**170**:237-254

[13] Chesney E, Goodwin GM, Fazel S. Risks of all-cause and suicide mortality in mental disorders: A meta-review. World Psychiatry. 2014;**13**(2):153-160

[14] Nierenberg AA, Agustini B, Köhler-Forsberg O, Cusin C, Katz D, Sylvia LG, et al. Diagnosis and treatment of bipolar disorder: A review. Journal of the American Medical Association. 2023;**330**(14):1370-1380

[15] Baldessarini RJ, Undurraga J, Vázquez GH, Tondo L, Salvatore P, Ha K, et al. Predominant recurrence polarity among 928 adult international bipolar I disorder patients. Acta Psychiatrica Scandinavica. 2012;**125**(4):293-302

[16] Gonda X, Pompili M, Serafini G, Montebovi F, Campi S, Dome P, et al.

Suicidal behavior in bipolar disorder: Epidemiology, characteristics and major risk factors. Journal of Affective Disorders. 2012;**143**(1-3):16-26

[17] Tondo L, Isacsson G, Baldessarini RJ. Suicidal behaviour in bipolar disorder: Risk and prevention. CNS Drugs. 2003;**17**(7):491-511

[18] De Abreu LN, Nery FG, Harkavy-Friedman JM, De Almeida KM, Gomes BC, Oquendo MA, et al. Suicide attempts are associated with worse quality of life in patients with bipolar disorder type I. Comprehensive Psychiatry. 2012;**53**(2):125-129

[19] Michalak EE, Yatham LN, Kolesar S, Lam RW. Bipolar disorder and quality of life: A patient-centered perspective. Quality of Life Research. 2006;**15**(1):25-37

[20] Antypa N, Antonioli M, Serretti A. Clinical, psychological and environmental predictors of prospective suicide events in patients with bipolar disorder. Journal of Psychiatric Research. 2013;**47**(11):1800-1808

[21] Persons JE, Coryell WH, Solomon DA, Keller MB, Endicott J, Fiedorowicz JG. Mixed state and suicide: Is the effect of mixed state on suicidal behavior more than the sum of its parts? Bipolar Disorders. 2018;**20**(1):35-41

[22] Phillips ML, Kupfer DJ. Bipolar disorder 2—Bipolar disorder diagnosis: Challenges and future directions. The Lancet. 2013;**381**(9878):1663-1671

[23] Sani G, Tondo L, Koukopoulos A, Reginaldi D, Kotzalidis GD, Koukopoulos AE, et al. Suicide in a large population of former psychiatric inpatients. Psychiatry and Clinical Neurosciences. 2011;**65**(3):286-295

[24] Dev DA, Le GH, Kwan ATH, Wong S, Arulmozhi A, Ceban F, et al. Comparing suicide completion rates in bipolar I versus bipolar II disorder: A systematic review and meta-analysis. Journal of Affective Disorders. 2024;**361**:480-488

[25] Durkheim E. İntihar (Toplumsal bir inceleme). İstanbul: Cem Yayıncılık; 2002. 25 p

[26] Odağ C. İntihar (Özyıkım): Tanım-Kuram-Sağaltım. İzmir: Ege Üniversitesi Basımevi; 1995

[27] Odağ C. İntihar (Özkıyım)-Tanım, Kuram, Sağaltım. İzmir: Psikiyatri Derneği Yayınları; 1985. 5-95 pp

[28] Bulut E, Küçüker H, Bulut N. İntiharın kısa tarihçesinden sebep ve yöntemlerine genel bir bakış. Cumhuriyet Medical Journal. 2012;**34**(1):128-137

[29] Bryson CN, Cramer RJ, Schmidt AT. Need for affect, interpersonal psychological theory of suicide, and suicide proneness. Archives of Suicide Research. 2019;**23**(4):634-647

[30] Klonsky ED, May AM, Saffer BY. Suicide, suicide attempts, and suicidal ideation. Annual Review of Clinical Psychology. 2016;**12**:307-330

[31] Haydeh FARAJİ, Eylül Doğa DAĞ. Kumar bağimliliği ve intihar arasindaki ilişkinin değerlendirilmesi. Current Research and Reviews in Psychology and Psychiatry. 2022;**2**(2):184-200

[32] Pompili M, Gonda X, Serafini G, Innamorati M, Sher L, Amore M, et al. Epidemiology of suicide in bipolar disorders: A systematic review of the literature. Bipolar Disorders. 2013;**15**(5):457-490

[33] Wan Q, Ding X, Hu D, an Y, Wang S, Liu Y, et al. A study of the

epidemiology and risk factors for attempted suicide and suicide among non-psychiatric inpatients in 48 general hospitals in Hubei province, China, 2015-2017. General Hospital Psychiatry. 2020;**63**:21-29

[34] Malhi GS, Outhred T, Das P, Morris G, Hamilton A, Mannie Z. Modeling suicide in bipolar disorders. Bipolar Disorders. 2018;**20**(4):334-348

[35] Vieta E, Berk M, Schulze TG, Carvalho AF, Suppes T, Calabrese JR, et al. Bipolar disorders. Nature Reviews. Disease Primers. 2018;**4**:1-16

[36] Raja M, Azzoni A. Suicide attempts: Differences between unipolar and bipolar patients and among groups with different lethality risk. Journal of Affective Disorders. 2004;**82**(3):437-442

[37] Suicidal IE. Behaviour in mood disorders-who, when, and why? Canadian Journal of Psychiatry. 2014;**59**(3):120-130. Available from: www.TheCJP.ca

[38] Schaffer A, Isometsä ET, Tondo L, Moreno DH, Turecki G, Reis C, et al. International Society for Bipolar Disorders Task Force on Suicide: Meta-analyses and meta-regression of correlates of suicide attempts and suicide deaths in bipolar disorder. Bipolar Disorders. 2015;**17**(1):16

[39] Rihmer Z, Szadoczky E, Furedi J, Kiss K, Papp Z. Anxiety disorders comorbidity in bipolar I, bipolar II and unipolar major depression: Results from a population-based study in Hungary. Journal of Affective Disorders. 2001;**67**(1-3):175-179

[40] Henry C, Van den Bulke D, Bellivier F, Etain B, Leboyer M. Anxiety disorders in 318 bipolar patients: Prevalence and impact on illness severity and response to mood stabilizer. The Journal of Clinical Psychiatry. 2003;**64**(3):331-335

[41] Benazzi F, Koukopoulos A, Akiskal HS. Toward a validation of a new definition of agitated depression as a bipolar mixed state (mixed depression). European Psychiatry. 2004;**19**(2):85-90

[42] Sadock BJ, Ruiz P, Sadock VA. Kaplan & Sadock Psikiyatri Davranış Bilimleri/Klinik Psikiyatri. 11th ed. Ankara: Güneş Tıp Kıtapevleri; 2016. 764-766 pp

[43] Bachmann S. Epidemiology of suicide and the psychiatric perspective. International Journal of Environmental Research and Public Health. 2018;**15**(7):1425

[44] Cleare S, Wetherall K, Clark A, Ryan C, Kirtley OJ, Smith M, et al. Adverse childhood experiences and hospital-treated self-harm. International Journal of Environmental Research and Public Health. 2018;**15**(6):1235

[45] Goldberg JF, Garno JL, Portera L, Leon AC, Kocsis JH, Whiteside JE. Correlates of suicidal ideation in dysphoric mania. Journal of Affective Disorders. 1999;**56**(1):75-81

[46] Goldberg JF, Garno JL, Leon AC, Kocsis JH, Portera L. Association of recurrent suicidal ideation with nonremission from acute mixed mania. The American Journal of Psychiatry. 1998;**155**(12):1753-1755

[47] Dilsaver SC, Chen YW, Swann AC, Shoaib AM, Krajewski KJ. Suicidality in patients with pure and depressive mania. The American Journal of Psychiatry. 1994;**151**(9):1312-1315

[48] Strakowski SM, McElroy SL, Keck PE, West SA. Suicidality among patients with mixed and manic bipolar

disorder. The American Journal of Psychiatry. 1996;**153**(5):674-676

[49] Baldessarini RJ, Pompili M, Tondo L. Suicide in bipolar disorder: Risks and management. CNS Spectrums. 2006;**11**(6):465-471

[50] Rihmer Z. Suicide risk in mood disorders. Current Opinion in Psychiatry. 2007;**20**(1):17-22

[51] Pompili M, Rihmer Z, Innamorati M, Lester D, Girardi P, Tatarelli R. Assessment and treatment of suicide risk in bipolar disorders. Expert Review of Neurotherapeutics. 2009;**9**(1):109-136

[52] Baldessarini RJ, Tondo L, Davis P, Pompili M, Goodwin FK, Hennen J. Decreased risk of suicides and attempts during long-term lithium treatment: A meta-analytic review. Bipolar Disorders. 2006;**8**(5 Pt 2):625-639

[53] Valtonen M, Laaksonen DE, Tolmunen T, Viinamäki H, Nyyssönen K, Kauhanen J, et al. Hopelessness—Novel facet of the metabolic syndrome in men. Scandinavian Journal of Public Health. 2008;**36**(8):795-802

[54] Balázs J, Benazzi F, Rihmer Z, Rihmer A, Akiskal KK, Akiskal HS. The close link between suicide attempts and mixed (bipolar) depression: Implications for suicide prevention. Journal of Affective Disorders. 2006;**91**(2-3):133-138

[55] Benazzi F. Bipolar II depressive mixed state: Finding a useful definition. Comprehensive Psychiatry. 2003;**44**(1):21-27

[56] Wierzbiński P, Zdanowicz A, Klekowska J, Broniarczyk-Czarniak M, Zboralski K. The epidemiology of suicide in bipolar disorder in the manic episode—Preliminary reports. Polski Merkuriusz Lekarski. 2014;**36**(214):254-256

[57] Persons JE, Lodder P, Coryell WH, Nurnberger JI, Fiedorowicz JG. Symptoms of mania and anxiety do not contribute to suicidal ideation or behavior in the presence of bipolar depression. Psychiatry Research. 2022;**307**(6):1-21

[58] Leverich GS, Altshuler LL, Frye MA, Suppes T, Keck PE, McElroy SL, et al. Factors associated with suicide attempts in 648 patients with bipolar disorder in the Stanley Foundation Bipolar Network. The Journal of Clinical Psychiatry. 2003;**64**(5):506-515

[59] Park YM, Lee BH. Treatment response in relation to subthreshold bipolarity in patients with major depressive disorder receiving antidepressant monotherapy: A post hoc data analysis (KOMDD study). Neuropsychiatric Disease and Treatment. 2016;**12**:1227

[60] Koirala P, Hu B, Altinay M, Li M, DiVita AL, Bryant KA, et al. Sub-threshold bipolar disorder in medication-free young subjects with major depression: Clinical characteristics and antidepressant treatment response. Journal of Psychiatric Research. 2019;**110**:1-8

[61] Dome P, Gonda X, Rihmer Z. Effects of smoking on health outcomes in bipolar disorder with a special focus on suicidal behavior. Neuropsychiatry. 2012;**2**(5):429-441

[62] Miller JN, Black DW. Bipolar disorder and suicide: A review. Current Psychiatry Reports. 2020;**22**(2):6

[63] Cassidy F. Risk factors of attempted suicide in bipolar disorder.

Suicide & Life-Threatening Behavior. 2011;**41**(1):6-11

[64] Angst J, Angst F, Gerber-Werder R, Gamma A. Suicide in 406 mood-disorder patients with and without long-term medication: A 40 to 44 years' follow-up. Archives of Suicide Research. 2005;**9**(3):279-300

[65] Harris EC, Barraclough B. Suicide as an outcome for mental disorders. A meta-analysis. The British Journal of Psychiatry. 1997;**170**:205-228

[66] Dennehy EB, Marangell LB, Allen MH, Chessick C, Wisniewski SR, Thase ME. Suicide and suicide attempts in the systematic treatment enhancement program for bipolar disorder. Journal of Affective Disorders. 2011;**133**(3):427

[67] Owen R, Gooding P, Dempsey R, Jones S. A qualitative investigation into the relationships between social factors and suicidal thoughts and acts experienced by people with a bipolar disorder diagnosis. Journal of Affective Disorders. 2015;**176**:133-140

[68] Bottlender R, Jäger M, Strauß A, Möller HJ. Suicidality in bipolar compared to unipolar depressed inpatients. European Archives of Psychiatry and Clinical Neuroscience. 2000;**250**(5):257-261

[69] Johnson SL, McMurrich SL, Yates M. Suicidality in bipolar I disorder. Suicide & Life-Threatening Behavior. 2005;**35**(6):681-689

[70] Colom F, Vieta E, Daban C, Pacchiarotti I, Sánchez-Moreno J. Clinical and therapeutic implications of predominant polarity in bipolar disorder. Journal of Affective Disorders. 2006;**93**(1-3):13-17

[71] Carvalho AF, Quevedo J, McIntyre RS, Soeiro-De-Souza MG, Fountoulakis KN, Berk M, et al. Treatment implications of predominant polarity and the polarity index: A comprehensive review. The International Journal of Neuropsychopharmacology. 2014;**18**(2):1-11

[72] Black DW, Winokur G, Nasrallah A. Suicide in subtypes of major affective disorder. A comparison with general population suicide mortality. Archives of General Psychiatry. 1987;**44**(10):878-880

[73] Hawton K, Sutton L, Haw C, Sinclair J, Harriss L. Suicide and attempted suicide in bipolar disorder: A systematic review of risk factors. The Journal of Clinical Psychiatry. 2005;**66**(6):693-704

[74] Coryell W, Solomon D, Turvey C, Keller M, Leon AC, Endicott J, et al. The long-term course of rapid-cycling bipolar disorder. Archives of General Psychiatry. 2003;**60**(9):914-920

[75] McIntyre RS, Muzina DJ, Kemp DE, Blank D, Woldeyohannes HO, Lofchy J, et al. Bipolar disorder and suicide: Research synthesis and clinical translation. Current Psychiatry Reports. 2008;**10**(1):66-72

[76] Tsai SYM, Kuo CJ, Chen CC, Lee HC. Risk factors for completed suicide in bipolar disorder. The Journal of Clinical Psychiatry. 2002;**63**(6):469-476

[77] Huber RS, Coon H, Kim N, Renshaw PF, Kondo DG. Altitude is a risk factor for completed suicide in bipolar disorder. Medical Hypotheses. 2014;**82**(3):377-381

[78] Pompili M, Rihmer Z, Akiskal HS, Innamorati M, Iliceto P, Akiskal KK, et al. Temperament and personality dimensions in suicidal and nonsuicidal psychiatric inpatients. Psychopathology. 2008;**41**(5):313-321

[79] Rihmer A, Rozsa S, Rihmer Z, Gonda X, Akiskal KK, Akiskal HS. Affective temperaments, as measured by TEMPS-A, among nonviolent suicide attempters. Journal of Affective Disorders. 2009;**116**(1-2):18-22

[80] Coryell W, Kriener A, Butcher B, Nurnberger J, McMahon F, Berrettini W, et al. Risk factors for suicide in bipolar I disorder in two prospectively studied cohorts. Journal of Affective Disorders. 2016;**190**:1-5

[81] Marangell LB, Bauer MS, Dennehy EB, Wisniewski SR, Allen MH, Miklowitz DJ, et al. Prospective predictors of suicide and suicide attempts in 1,556 patients with bipolar disorders followed for up to 2 years. Bipolar Disorders. 2006;**8**(5 Pt 2):566-575

[82] McGuffin P, Perroud N, Uher R, Butler A, Aitchison KJ, Craig I, et al. The genetics of affective disorder and suicide. European Psychiatry. 2010;**25**(5):275-277

[83] Magno LAV, Santana CVN, Sacramento ÉK, Rezende VB, Cardoso MV, Maurício-Da-Silva L, et al. Genetic variations in FOXO3A are associated with Bipolar Disorder without confering vulnerability for suicidal behavior. Journal of Affective Disorders. 2011;**133**(3):633-637

[84] Magno LAV, Miranda DM, Neves FS, Pimenta GJ, Mello MP, De Marco LA, et al. Association between AKT1 but not AKTIP genetic variants and increased risk for suicidal behavior in bipolar patients. Genes, Brain, and Behavior. 2010;**9**(4):411-418

[85] Mirkovic B, Laurent C, Podlipski MA, Frebourg T, Cohen D, Gerardin P. Genetic association studies of suicidal behavior: A review of the past 10 years, progress, limitations, and future directions. Frontiers in Psychiatry. 2016;7:158

[86] Mullins N, Bigdeli TB, Børglum AD, Coleman JRI, Demontis D, Mehta D, et al. GWAS of suicide attempt in psychiatric disorders and association with major depression polygenic risk scores. The American Journal of Psychiatry. 2019;**176**(8):651-660

[87] Taylor WD, Payne ME, Krishnan KRR, Wagner HR, Provenzale JM, Steffens DC, et al. Evidence of white matter tract disruption in MRI hyperintensities. Biological Psychiatry. 2001;**50**(3):179-183

[88] Pompili M, Innamorati M, Mann JJ, Oquendo MA, Lester D, Del Casale A, et al. Periventricular white matter hyperintensities as predictors of suicide attempts in bipolar disorders and unipolar depression. Progress in Neuro-Psychopharmacology & Biological Psychiatry. 2008;**32**(6):1501-1507

[89] Grangeon MC, Seixas C, Quarantini LC, Miranda-Scippa A, Pompili M, Steffens DC, et al. White matter hyperintensities and their association with suicidality in major affective disorders: A meta-analysis of magnetic resonance imaging studies. CNS Spectrums. 2010;**15**(6):375-381

[90] Tighe SK, Reading SA, Rivkin P, Caffo B, Schweizer B, Pearlson G, et al. Total white matter hyperintensity volume in bipolar disorder patients and their healthy relatives. Bipolar Disorders. 2012;**14**(8):888

[91] Belvederi Murri M, Prestia D, Mondelli V, Pariante C, Patti S, Olivieri B, et al. The HPA axis in bipolar disorder: Systematic review and meta-analysis. Psychoneuroendocrinology. 2016;**63**:327-342

[92] Kamali M, Saunders EFH, Prossin AR, Brucksch CB, Harrington GJ, Langenecker SA, et al. Associations

between suicide attempts and elevated bedtime salivary cortisol levels in bipolar disorder. Journal of Affective Disorders. 2012;**136**(3):358

[93] Black DW, Monahan PO, Winokur G. The relationship between DST results and suicidal behavior. Annals of Clinical Psychiatry. 2002;**14**(2):83-88

[94] Daban C, Vieta E, Mackin P, Young AH. Hypothalamic-pituitary-adrenal axis and bipolar disorder. The Psychiatric Clinics of North America. 2005;**28**(2):469-480

[95] Saunders KEA, Hawton K. Clinical assessment and crisis intervention for the suicidal bipolar disorder patient. Bipolar Disorders. 2013;**15**(5):575-583

[96] Posner K, Brown GK, Stanley B, Brent DA, Yershova KV, Oquendo MA, et al. The Columbia-Suicide Severity Rating Scale: Initial validity and internal consistency findings from three multisite studies with adolescents and adults. The American Journal of Psychiatry. 2011;**168**(12):1266-1277

[97] Posner K, Oquendo MA, Gould M, Stanley B, Davies M. Columbia classification algorithm of suicide assessment (C-CASA): Classification of suicidal events in the FDA's pediatric suicidal risk analysis of antidepressants. The American Journal of Psychiatry. 2007;**164**(7):1043

[98] Sonia C, Kutcher SP. Suicide Risk Management: A Manual for Health Professionals. 2nd ed. Maiden, MA: Wiley-Blackwell; 2012. 164 p

[99] Fazel S, Wolf A, Larsson H, Mallett S, Fanshawe TR. The prediction of suicide in severe mental illness: Development and validation of a clinical prediction rule (OxMIS). Translational Psychiatry. 2019;**9**(1):98

[100] Hawes M, Yaseen Z, Briggs J, Galynker I. The Modular Assessment of Risk for Imminent Suicide (MARIS): A proof of concept for a multi-informant tool for evaluation of short-term suicide risk. Comprehensive Psychiatry. 2017;**72**:88-96

[101] Cipriani A, Hawton K, Stockton S, Geddes JR. Lithium in the prevention of suicide in mood disorders: Updated systematic review and meta-analysis. BMJ. 2013;**346**:1-13

[102] Song J, Sjölander A, Joas E, Bergen SE, Runeson B, Larsson H, et al. Suicidal behavior during lithium and valproate treatment: A within-individual 8-year prospective study of 50,000 patients with bipolar disorder. The American Journal of Psychiatry. 2017;**174**(8):795-802

[103] Wasserman D, Rihmer Z, Rujescu D, Sarchiapone M, Sokolowski M, Titelman D, et al. The European Psychiatric Association (EPA) guidance on suicide treatment and prevention. European Psychiatry. 2012;**27**(2):129-141

[104] Gonzalez-Pinto A, Mosquera F, Alonso M, López P, Ramírez F, Vieta E, et al. Suicidal risk in bipolar I disorder patients and adherence to long-term lithium treatment. Bipolar Disorders. 2006;**8**(5 Pt 2):618-624

[105] Gibbons RD, Hur K, Brown CH, Mann JJ. Relationship between antiepileptic drugs and suicide attempts in patients with bipolar disorder. Archives of General Psychiatry. 2009;**66**(12):1354-1360

[106] Leon AC, Solomon DA, Li C, Fiedorowicz JG, Coryell WH, Endicott J, et al. Antiepileptic drugs for bipolar disorder and the risk of suicidal behavior: A 30-year observational study.

The American Journal of Psychiatry. 2012;**169**(3):291

[107] Patorno E, Bohn RL, Wahl PM, Avorn J, Patrick AR, Liu J, et al. Anticonvulsant medications and the risk of suicide, attempted suicide, or violent death. Journal of the American Medical Association. 2010;**303**(14):1401-1409

[108] Yatham LN, Kennedy SH, Schaffer A, Parikh SV, Beaulieu S, O'Donovan C, et al. Canadian Network for Mood and Anxiety Treatments (CANMAT) and International Society for Bipolar Disorders (ISBD) collaborative update of CANMAT guidelines for the management of patients with bipolar disorder: Update 2009. Bipolar Disorders. 2009;**11**(3):225-255

[109] Yerevanian BI, Koek RJ, Mintz J. Bipolar pharmacotherapy and suicidal behavior Part 3: Impact of antipsychotics. Journal of Affective Disorders. 2007;**103**(1-3):23-28

[110] Angst F, Stassen HH, Clayton PJ, Angst J. Mortality of patients with mood disorders: Follow-up over 34-38 years. Journal of Affective Disorders. 2002;**68**(2-3):167-181

[111] Gibbons RD, Brown CH, Hur K, Marcus SM, Bhaumik DK, Mann JJ. Relationship between antidepressants and suicide attempts: An analysis of the Veterans Health Administration data sets. The American Journal of Psychiatry. 2007;**164**(7):1044-1049

[112] Musil R, Zill P, Seemüller F, Bondy B, Meyer S, Spellmann I, et al. Genetics of emergent suicidality during antidepressive treatment—Data from a naturalistic study on a large sample of inpatients with a major depressive episode. European Neuropsychopharmacology. 2013;**23**(7):663-674

[113] Pacchiarotti I, Bond DJ, Baldessarini RJ, Nolen WA, Grunze H, Licht RW, et al. The International Society for Bipolar Disorders (ISBD) task force report on antidepressant use in bipolar disorders. The American Journal of Psychiatry. 2013;**170**(11):1249-1262

[114] Wilkinson ST, Ballard ED, Bloch MH, Mathew SJ, Murrough JW, Feder A, et al. The effect of a single dose of intravenous ketamine on suicidal ideation: A systematic review and individual participant data meta-analysis. The American Journal of Psychiatry. 2018;**175**(2):158

[115] Zhan Y, Zhang B, Zhou Y, Zheng W, Liu W, Wang C, et al. A preliminary study of anti-suicidal efficacy of repeated ketamine infusions in depression with suicidal ideation. Journal of Affective Disorders. 2019;**251**:205-212

[116] Ballard ED, Yarrington JS, Farmer CA, Richards E, Machado-Vieira R, Kadriu B, et al. Characterizing the course of suicidal ideation response to ketamine. Journal of Affective Disorders. 2018;**241**:86-93

[117] Fink M, Kellner CH, McCall WV. The role of ECT in suicide prevention. The Journal of ECT. 2014;**30**(1):5-9

[118] Liang CS, Chung CH, Ho PS, Tsai CK, Chien WC. Superior anti-suicidal effects of electroconvulsive therapy in unipolar disorder and bipolar depression. Bipolar Disorders. 2018;**20**(6):539-546

[119] Dell'Osso B, Mundo E, D'Urso N, Pozzoli S, Buoli M, Ciabatti MT, et al. Augmentative repetitive navigated transcranial magnetic stimulation (rTMS) in drug-resistant bipolar depression. Bipolar Disorders. 2009;**11**(1):76-81

[120] Tamas RL, Menkes D, El-Mallakh RS. Stimulating research: A prospective, randomized, double-blind, sham-controlled study of slow transcranial magnetic stimulation in depressed bipolar patients. The Journal of Neuropsychiatry and Clinical Neurosciences. 2007;**19**(2):198-199

[121] Carnell BL, Clarke P, Gill S, Galletly CA. How effective is repetitive transcranial magnetic stimulation for bipolar depression? Journal of Affective Disorders. 2017;**209**:270-272

[122] Kennedy SH, Milev R, Giacobbe P, Ramasubbu R, Lam RW, Parikh SV, et al. Canadian Network for Mood and Anxiety Treatments (CANMAT) clinical guidelines fort he management of majör depressive disorder in adults: IV. Neurostimulation therapies. Journal of Affective Disorders. 2009;**117**:44-53

[123] Hawton K, McKeown S, Day A, Martin P, O'Connor M, Yule J. Evaluation of out-patient counselling compared with general practitioner care following overdoses. Psychological Medicine. 1987;**17**(3):751-761

[124] Allard R, Marshall M, Plante MC. Intensive follow-up does not decrease the risk of repeat suicide attempts. Suicide & Life-Threatening Behavior. 1992;**22**(3):303-314

[125] Egan MP. Contracting for safety: A concept analysis. Crisis. 1997;**18**(1):17-23

[126] Méndez-Bustos P, Calati R, Rubio-Ramírez F, Olié E, Courtet P, Lopez-Castroman J. Effectiveness of psychotherapy on Suicidal risk: A systematic review of observational studies. Frontiers in Psychology. 2019;**10**:277

[127] Brown GK, Ten Have T, Henriques GR, Xie SX, Hollander JE, Beck AT. Cognitive therapy for the prevention of suicide attempts: A randomized controlled trial. Journal of the American Medical Association. 2005;**294**(5):563-570

[128] Pollock LR, Williams JMG. Effective problem solving in suicide attempters depends on specific autobiographical recall. Suicide & Life-Threatening Behavior. 2001;**31**(4):386-396

[129] Aydemir Ç. Treatment strategies and suicide prevention in suicidal behavior. Update in Psychiatry. 2017;7(1):41

[130] Ducasse D, René E, Béziat S, Guillaume S, Courtet P, Olié E. Acceptance and commitment therapy for management of suicidal patients: A pilot study. Psychotherapy and Psychosomatics. 2014;**83**(6):374-376

[131] Gray SM, Otto MW. Psychosocial approaches to suicide prevention: Applications to patients with bipolar disorder. The Journal of Clinical Psychiatry. 2001;**62**(suppl. 25):56-64

[132] Altamura AC, Dell'Osso B, Berlin HA, Buoli M, Bassetti R, Mundo E. Duration of untreated illness and suicide in bipolar disorder: A naturalistic study. European Archives of Psychiatry and Clinical Neuroscience. 2010;**260**:385-391

[133] Ostacher MJ, LeBeau RT, Perlis RH, Nierenberg AA, Lund HG, Moshier SJ, et al. Cigarette smoking is associated with suicidality in bipolar disorder. Bipolar Disorders. 2009;**11**:766-771

[134] Garcia-Amador M, Colom F, Valenti M, Horga G, Vieta E. Suicide risk in rapid cycling bipolar patients. Journal of Affective Disorders. 2009;**117**(1-2):74-78

[135] Coryell W, Fiedorowicz J, Leon AC, Endicott J, Keller MB. Age of onset and

the prospectively observed course of illness in bipolar disorder. Journal of Affective Disorders. 2013;**146**(1):34-38

[136] Preuss UW, Schuckit MA, Smith TL, Danko GP, Bucholz KK, Hesselbrock MN, et al. Predictors and correlates of suicide attempts over 5 years in 1,237 alcohol-dependent men and women. American Journal of Psychiatry. 2003;**160**(1):56-63

[137] Maser JD, Akiskal HS, Schettler P, Scheftner W, Mueller T, Endicott J, et al. Can temperament identify affectively ill patients who engage in lethal or near-lethal suicidal behavior? A 14-year prospective study. Suicide & Life-Threatening Behavior. 2002;**32**(1):10-32

[138] Latalova K, Kamaradova D, Prasko J. Suicide in bipolar disorder: A review. Psychiatria Danubina. 2014;**26**(2):108-114

[139] Vázquez GH, Gonda XMA, Lolich M, Tondo L, Baldessarini RJ. Suicidal risk and affective temperaments, evaluated with the TEMPS-A scale: A systematic review. Harvard Review of Psychiatry. 2018;**26**(1):8-18

[140] Caribé AC, Studart P, Bezerra-Filho S, Brietzke E, Nunes Noto M, Vianna-Sulzbach M, et al. Is religiosity a protective factor against suicidal behavior in bipolar I outpatients? Journal of Affective Disorders. 2015;**186**:156-161

[141] Gearing RE, Alonzo D. Religion and suicide: New findings. Journal of Religion and Health. 2018;**57**(6):2478-2499

[142] Schaffer A, Isometsä ET, Tondo L, Moreno DH, Sinyor M, Lars Vedel K, et al. Epidemiology, neurobiology and pharmacological interventions related to suicide deaths and suicide attempts in bipolar disorder: Part I of a report of the International Society for Bipolar Disorders Task Force on Suicide in Bipolar Disorder. The Australian and New Zealand Journal of Psychiatry. 2015;**49**(9):802

[143] Tondo L, Baldessarini RJ. Antisuicidal effects in mood disorders: Are they unique to lithium? Pharmacopsychiatry. 2018;**51**(5):177-188

[144] Smith KA, Cipriani A. Lithium and suicide in mood disorders: Updated meta-review of the scientific literature. Bipolar Disorders. 2017;**19**(7):575-586

[145] Tondo L, Baldessarini RJ. Long-term lithium treatment in the prevention of suicidal behavior in bipolar disorder patients. Epidemiologia e Psichiatria Sociale. 2009;**18**(3):179-183

[146] Alberich S, Martínez-Cengotitabengoa M, López P, Zorrilla I, Núñez N, Vieta E, et al. Efficacy and safety of ketamine in bipolar depression: A systematic review. Revista de Psiquiatria y Salud Mental. 2017;**10**(2):104-112

[147] Andrade C. Ketamine for depression, 6: Effects on suicidal ideation and possible use as crisis intervention in patients at suicide risk. The Journal of Clinical Psychiatry. 2018;**79**(2):18f12242

[148] López-Díaz Á, Fernández-González JL, Luján-Jiménez JE, Galiano-Rus S, Gutiérrez-Rojas L. Use of repeated intravenous ketamine therapy in treatment-resistant bipolar depression with suicidal behaviour: A case report from Spain. Therapeutic Advances in Psychopharmacology. 2017;**7**(4):140

[149] Bahji A, Hawken ER, Sepehry AA, Cabrera CA, Vazquez G. ECT beyond unipolar major depression: Systematic review and meta-analysis of electroconvulsive therapy in bipolar depression. Acta Psychiatrica Scandinavica. 2019;**139**(3):214-226

Chapter 5

Recognizing Symptom Evolution in Bipolar Disorder in Aging Individuals

Pınar Harmancı

Abstract

This chapter explains the evolution of the symptoms of aging individuals diagnosed with bipolar disorder (BD). It is believed that understanding the common organic outcomes of aging individuals diagnosed with BD, especially their symptoms differentiating along with their neuroprogression, in addition to their age, sex, and other personal characteristics, will not only play a positive role in the development of treatment options and algorithms but also contribute to care processes. It is also worth noting that the literature is far from being interested in this topic, and certain research groups have focused on the neuroprogression of BD and changes in brain structures on structural changes. However, in a few decades, we may encounter transformations in the symptoms of aging individuals with BD and treatment options that can no longer keep up with these changes. It does not seem possible to understand a process like BD, which is characterized by fluctuations in mood, merely based on organic outcomes. Nevertheless, understanding how the brain experiences the effects of BD with aging and being able to distinguish this situation from the typical developmental aging process may help us manage the symptoms of individuals with BD, whose numbers are expected to increase in aging societies.

Keywords: bipolar disorder, older individuals, symptoms of bipolar disorder, symptom evolution, diagnosis and care in bipolar disorder

1. Introduction

The diagnosis of bipolar disorder (BD) is seen at a rate of 4.5% in society. More than 50% of individuals diagnosed with BD are diagnosed before the age of 25. At first glance, reports showing that the life expectancy of individuals with BD is well below (by approximately 20 years) the general average life expectancy do not raise curiosity about the transformation of the symptoms of aging individuals with BD after their diagnosis. However, 25% of aging individuals diagnosed with mood disorders have a diagnosis of BD. It is also seen that the episodes of this disorder, which has a chronic course, can persist even after the age of 70 [1–6]. Brain imaging studies conducted with individuals diagnosed with BD show that fundamental structural changes in the brain and differences that emerge in the functional sense indicate a gradual evolution. These changes, of course, contribute to the formation of guiding hypotheses regarding changing symptoms. Considering that the diagnosis of BD in the aging population was reported to increase by 1–11% from 1980 to 1998, it is important to collect more evidence about the BD symptoms and their outcomes that are expected to be faced in the next few decades. It is also thought that DSM-5 diagnostic criteria may need to be revised based on changing symptom indicators [1–12].

Although changes occurring in symptoms depend on several factors (e.g., sex, age of disease onset, frequency-severity of manic or depressive episodes, IQ, and comorbidities) [2–7, 13, 14], it is believed that understanding the common results of brain imaging studies indicating certain changes will help organize the main and auxiliary targets of treatment. Identifying the general and patient-specific changes created by the processes effective in the progression of aging [1, 15, 16] in symptoms related to the diagnosis of BD and knowing the effectiveness of these changes in the evolution of symptoms will shed light on all steps of treatment. For instance, the process that develops as a result of a decrease in hormone concentrations with aging and is considered to be within the scope of the developmental physiology of aging probably shows more pathologic progress along with the increasing cortisol and decreasing melatonin levels in individuals diagnosed with BD. After all, the shortening of sleep durations connected with aging changes the course of manic and depressive episodes in individuals diagnosed with BD [17–19]. Additionally, the co-occurrence of the effects of this process and those of BD on brain structures brings about another challenging issue for aging individuals diagnosed with BD: "Cognitive Impairment."

In light of all these considerations, it is believed that understanding the organic and psychosocial changes/transformations created by BD, in addition to the physiological changes experienced by healthy aging in the brain, will pave the way for establishing an environment that is more clinically convenient.

This chapter is specially designed to recognize the organic bases of the symptoms of BD, to predict how these bases change due to aging, and to draw attention to the fact that the symptoms of BD change with the aging process. In addition, this chapter is presented in order to explain how the cognitive changes that individuals experience in the normal process of aging evolve with the diagnosis of BD and to understand how this change is observed externally in the symptoms of the elderly individual with BD. This chapter offers the opportunity to observe the symptom course and the causes of these changes in the elderly with a total perspective for BD, whose organic and psychosocial symptom changes are tried to be revealed in the literature. Physicians, psychiatric nurses, psychologists, and other professionals working in the field of psychiatry will find out what kind of circulation is related to the symptom process in elderly individuals diagnosed with BD and how they can observe this change in diagnosis, treatment, and care. The chapter tried to offer a different perspective to the literature in terms of trying to explain what the literature on organic results tells us from a psychosocial point of view. We wanted to draw attention to this issue, considering that studies on elderly individuals diagnosed with BD would lead to overlooking the chronic (physical) diseases that will come with both the diagnosis of BD and the biological consequences of aging, and this would lead to a more disorganized course of BD disorder symptoms.

2. Brain imaging studies in the aging process in bipolar disorder

2.1 Gray matter and white matter imaging

The global prevalence of BD is 2.4%, and individuals are usually diagnosed before the age of 25. The mean life expectancy of individuals diagnosed with BD was reported to be 51.1 ± 12.5 years [1, 2]. In addition to this, in comparison to young samples diagnosed with BD, older adults (over 65 years of age) diagnosed with BD are observed to experience higher rates of depression. BD affects the aging process and, therefore, the functionality and structures of the brain [3–6]. Considering their average life expectancy, one may see that a significant proportion of individuals diagnosed with BD cannot reach the age of 65. The literature shows a decrease in the mass of white matter (WM) and gray matter (GM) structures starting at around the age of 40, even in individuals who led healthy lives [7, 8]. Although this striking hypothesis explains the inclusion of individuals diagnosed with BD in neuroimaging studies, neuroimaging results for such individuals over the age of 65 seem insufficient. At this point, there are some questions that need to be asked. Does BD accelerate the negative course of WM and GM, which already lose their volume through aging? How much are the volume, cortices, surface area, and thickness of WM and GM affected by BD? Can changes observed in the neuroimaging of these parameters indicate an aging process accelerated by BD? If the aging process is accelerated, how do BD symptoms evolve? In this context, the literature mostly offers studies focusing on GM volume. Current findings suggest that the early onset of changes in the volume and thickness of GM can be associated with the effects of BD such that low amounts of GM are observed in the amygdala of individuals diagnosed with BD, even if they are adolescents or young adults [9–11]. Low amounts of cortical GM have been reported in ventral prefrontal areas in the progressive course of BD, and this points to the neurodevelopmental pathophysiology of BD that evolves over time. Some studies have shown that emotion processing and regulation activities are influenced by reductions in GM volume in the dorsolateral and ventromedial prefrontal cortex, hippocampus, amygdala, and striatal regions of individuals under the age of 40 diagnosed with BD. The lack of sufficient information in the literature on changes in GM in old age in the context of emotional processes may be explained by the fact that cognitive parameters are the variables that are usually studied in older or aging individuals diagnosed with BD. Likewise, in older individuals diagnosed with frontotemporal dementia and BD, it is seen that the accelerating effect of BD on GM changes (volume loss) raises the risk of dementia as individuals with BD age [20–23].

The hyperintensity that develops in WM in both young and older individuals diagnosed with BD has been known for a long time. Additionally, deficits in WM have been found to be effective in the aging-related evolution of BD and symptom changes. Fractional anisotropy (FA) studies show that water diffusion in deep WM structures is limited. This situation is seen to be particularly more effective in the frontotemporal emotion regulation system. Although studies conducted on WM have revealed that hyperintensity is seen more prevalently in young individuals and that the emotion regulation system is expected to work more problematically in this group, in aging or older individuals diagnosed with BD, aging-related cognitive decline may lead to much lower quality of life, uncontrolled mixed symptoms, and severe functional loss in the rest of their lives [6, 24, 25].

2.2 Aging-related changes in biological processes in BD

Aging is defined as the functioning of some biological processes. These processes are listed as follows: (1) shorter telomere structures, (2) higher oxidative stress levels, and (3) reduced numbers of mitochondrial DNA replications. However, while it is argued that a fundamental biological difference associated with BD cannot be explained by the typical natural aging process, the extent and mechanism of the effects of BD on cognitive decline in the aging process are unknown. The changes to be brought about by the age of onset of the disorder as the person ages are also unclear. About half of the individuals with BD are diagnosed before the age of 25. In this case, studies on the imaging of brain structures to examine aging- and BD-related pathologies need to be supported by data to be obtained through long-term observations with a longitudinal methodology. Looking at the literature in this sense, the shorter life expectancy in BD cases compared to the neurotypical population and the early age of onset of the disorder indicate a clear path to the explanation of the evolution of BD symptoms [1, 15, 16]. As another striking issue, cortical thinning seems to be almost nonexistent in individuals older than middle-aged diagnosed with BD who do not have manic episodes. Aging-related cortical thickening is also not seen in these individuals [15, 16, 26].

2.3 Evolution of BD symptoms created by biological changes

To understand the aging-related evolution of symptoms in BD, it is needed to examine the symptoms observed before and during the diagnosis process. Studies have shown that mixed-type episodes become more dominant when the age of onset of BD corresponds to puberty. The subclinical symptoms emerging in these stages of development are considered precursors of major depressive attacks. It is needed to carefully consider whether the symptoms emerging in these periods belong to another mental illness, whether there is a comorbidity of BD, or whether these periods correspond to a particularly vulnerable stage of life [27]. After the diagnosis, the evolution of symptoms becomes inevitable as the individual starts using medication; their depressive periods (including suicide attempts) lower their average life expectancy, and the inflammatory process led by episodes of insomnia in manic periods accelerates aging [28]. It is contemplated that cognitive impairments start from this stage on, but it is not likely to understand whether these cognitive problems occur independently of BD. The success of neurocognitive assessment may be reduced by the initiation of the medication treatment of BD-diagnosed individuals, the probability of previous attacks having led to neuroanatomical changes, and the presence of subsyndromal symptoms [29]. Dhingra and Rabins reported deteriorating cognitive performance outcomes within 7 years following manic attacks in at least 1/3 of older individuals diagnosed with BD [30]. The association of findings of expanding ventricles and cortical thinning with manic periods suggests that we are facing a neuroprogressive illness that evolves with aging (**Figure 1**) [26].

In addition to all these biological changes and unexplained areas, there are hypotheses that individuals diagnosed with BD may have stages of symptom evolution. Accordingly, while transitioning to the older developmental period, the two poles may become more distinct, and the course of the condition may differ between men and women. Moreover, even though two individuals are the same age, the evolution of BD symptoms may differ between one who is diagnosed early and ages after this diagnosis and the other who is diagnosed with an older age of onset. Coryel et al. [32]

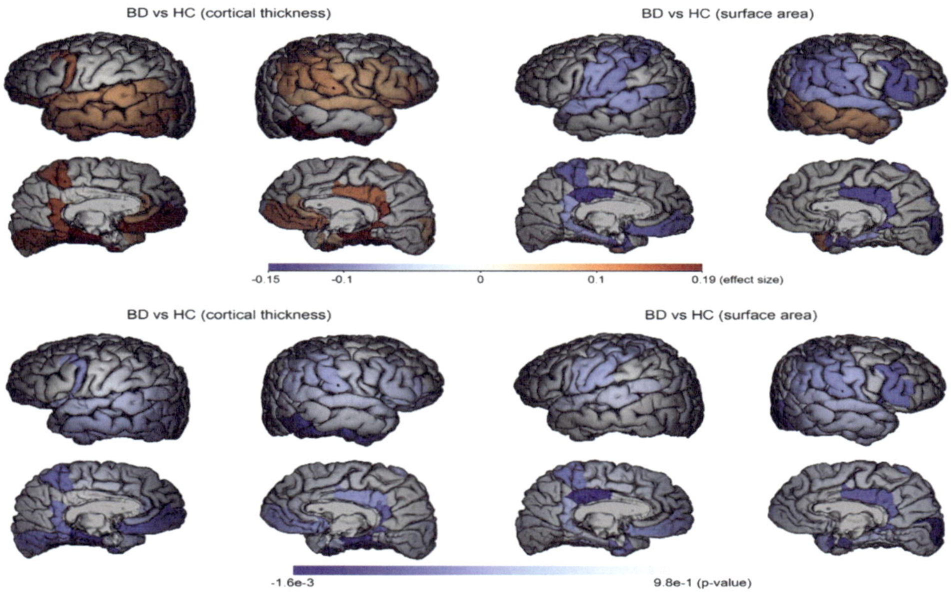

Figure 1.
Right and left areas with cortical thickness differences between older individuals diagnosed with BD and healthy counterparts. Positive effect sizes (warm red colors) represent BD > HC patterns (a more rapid decline in HC). Negative effect sizes (cool blue colors) represent BD < HC patterns (a more rapid decline in BD) HC: healthy counterpart [31].

reported that the prevalence and severity of depression increased in young and middle-aged adults, whereas these levels significantly decreased in the older group. In the same study, it was emphasized that the frequency and severity of depression decreased with age (over 65), and it was seen that the number and frequency of manic periods stayed almost the same after the middle-aged period. Accordingly, while an early age of onset was an indicator of poor prognosis in the middle-aged period, this fact also disappeared in older individuals [32].

In comparison to the typical older population, the memory, executive functions, attention, and operational speed of older individuals with BD are highly deteriorated. It is suggested that there may be a relationship between the disruption of the cognitive process and the higher frequency of psychotic symptoms with age [33]. In 2022, Montejo et al. [34] stated that there was significantly more deterioration in the cognitive symptoms of older individuals with BD.

From another point of view, the identification of BD-diagnosed individuals as "older individuals diagnosed with BD" refers to their current diagnosis involving an early or late onset (**Figure 2**). This group may also provide the opportunity to study the neuropathology and pathogenesis of BD. Notwithstanding, as a known outcome, which is important, therapeutic approaches are less effective in older individuals diagnosed with BD [6, 35]. To understand this situation, the neuroprogression hypothesis should be understood better (**Figure 3**).

Studies of age in the context of the etiology of BD, symptom changes, and the causes of outcomes that we see in symptom changes have highlighted that an increase in the concentration of cortisol, which is a stress hormone, and its toxic effect on specific brain regions are effective in the symptom change process [36–38]. Furthermore, while the specific changes in these areas that are supported by GM volume decline and microstructural alterations make the hypothesis stronger, there is still a need to study it further, considering that there are still several outcomes that are unexplained [38, 39].

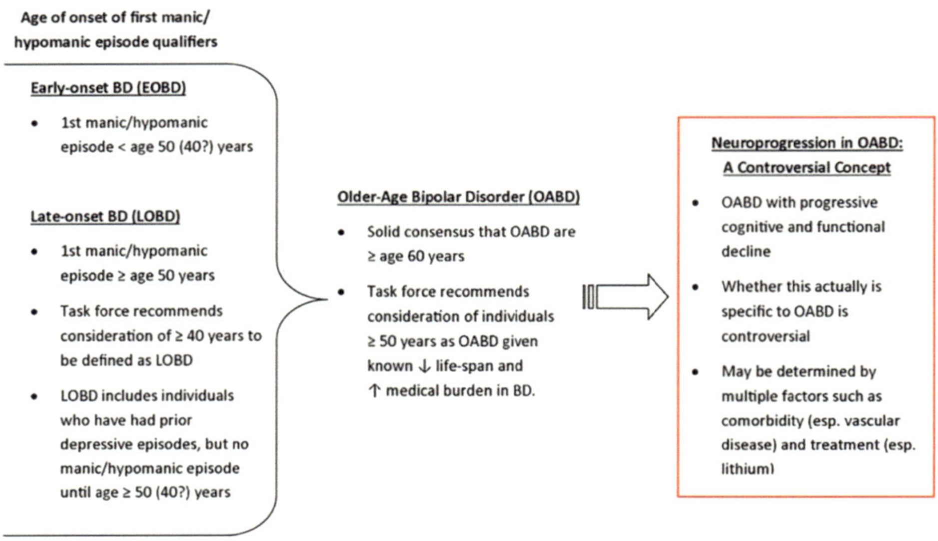

Figure 2.
Age of disease onset and conflicting neuroprogression outcomes in BD cases in the older population [6].

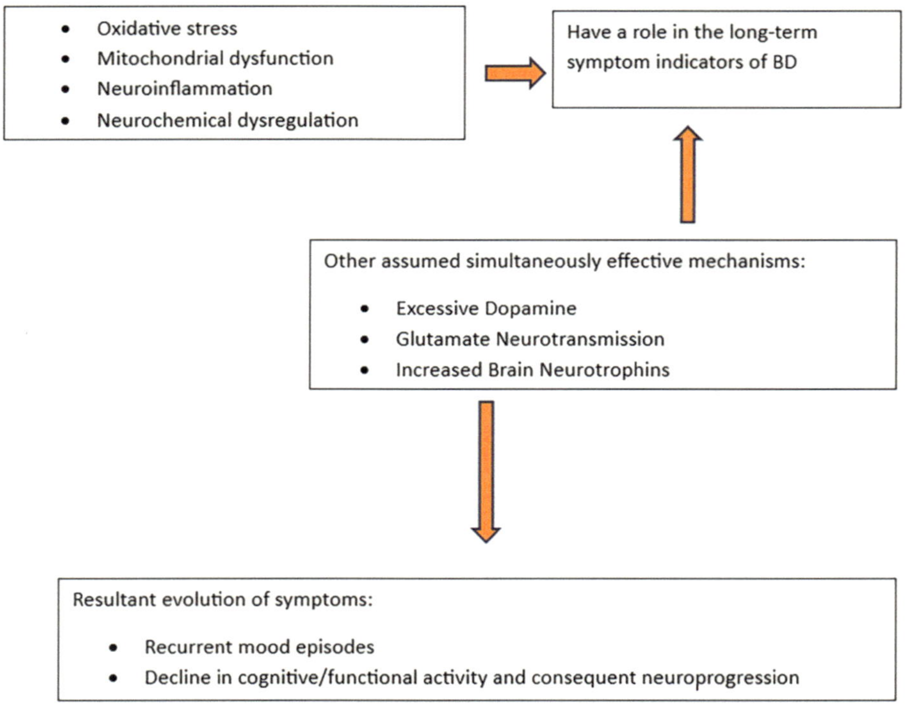

Figure 3.
Foundations of the neuroprogression hypothesis.

3. The effect of chronic diseases on symptom evolution in elderly individuals with BD

Individuals diagnosed with BD have been reported to have a mortality rate two times higher than that of the general population [40, 41]. In parallel, it is emphasized that cardiovascular diseases, metabolic diseases, and endocrine diseases are observed together in the part of individuals diagnosed with BD with a higher mortality rate. We know that the probability of occurrence of these diseases increases with the biological changes that develop due to aging [42]. However, how does the presence of a BD diagnosis before or after these diseases affect symptom change in elderly individuals? It is seen that we do not have sufficient information on this subject. It is reported that type 2 diabetes is seen in 10% of individuals who have been diagnosed with BD before being diagnosed with a chronic (physical) disease and who have been using psychotic agents for many years (this is two times higher than the general population) and hyperlipidemia develops in 15% of the same group. Although it is understood that individuals diagnosed with BD have a much higher risk of cardiovascular diseases and type 2 diabetes than the general population average, the lack of careful screening and regular records makes it difficult to see the real picture. Understanding the symptom evolution becomes more difficult with the accompaniment of these chronic diseases in the elderly [43–45]. For example, increased serum sodium and thyroxine levels in coronary heart disorders in elderly individuals with a diagnosis of BD are associated with acute effectiveness. In another example, it has been reported that increased serum sodium and thyroxine levels trigger acute effective phases and are highly responsible for acute hospitalizations in coronary heart disorders in elderly individuals diagnosed with BD [46]. Individuals diagnosed with type 2 diabetes mellitus with high insulin resistance as well as BD diagnoses are reported to have smaller hippocampal area and cortical gray matter volume compared to the general population. In addition, lower prefrontal N-acetyl aspartate (neuronal marker) is observed in these individuals. For this reason, elderly individuals diagnosed with BD should be monitored more closely. Antidiabetics are recommended for diabetes symptoms of these individuals to prevent the worsening of organic outcomes in these individuals. Treatment of type 2 diabetes ensures the preservation of brain gray matter and insulin sensitizers such as pioglitazone improve symptoms of depression in unipolar or bipolar disorders. Delaying the diagnosis and skipping treatment is not only a risk for worsening the symptoms of type 2 diabetes but also leads to worsening of the symptoms of BD [47].

Cognitive problems and other chronic (physical) disorders accompanying cognitive problems that may occur in elderly individuals with BD may lead to changes in the hippocampal area of the brain, white and gray matter, and serum levels of some biomarkers. This situation may lead to more negative outcomes of BD symptoms and increased hospitalizations.

4. Changes in bipolar disorder symptoms at old age and their reflections in care with therapeutic interventions

Considering that BD cases constitute 5–19% of mood disorders in older individuals, it is needed to redefine BD symptoms toward the end of life, set a better roadmap regarding how symptoms develop, conduct more studies examining cognitive outcomes, and develop interventions against declining functionality according to the results of these studies [6].

In addition to medication treatments provided to individuals diagnosed with BD, other therapeutic interventions also provide important outputs [48]. It is expected that knowing the organic changes in the brain structures of individuals diagnosed with BD, understanding the changes in neurotransmitters occurring as a result of changes in their brain structures, and recognizing the onset age- and individual-specific symptom cycle of BD will pave the way for therapeutic interventions. For example, the observation of cortical thinning along with aging in individuals with more intense numbers and severity of manic periods will provide a good justification for individual intervention programs. Another important concern involves the medications taken by individuals diagnosed with BD and the evolution of the usage of these medications following the moment they are diagnosed. In particular, the organic changes created by lithium usage should be investigated side by side with the evolution of the disorder. Non-pharmacological therapeutic interventions must be made depending on these organic processes in the context of the evolution of the symptoms of the older individual diagnosed with BD. A part of this symptom evolution process is the usage of mood-regulating antiepileptics, antidepressants, and antipsychotics [13, 49]. Studies on brain structures conducted throughout the process or publications explaining symptom changes should not be considered independent of the medications or psychotherapeutic interventions provided to the individual diagnosed with BD. It should be kept in mind that despite their organic outcomes, individuals diagnosed with BD who have different courses of symptom evolution may have different functionalities.

Nonmedical treatments in recent years have usually been about functionality, treatment adherence, quality of life, and reduction of hospitalization rates, which are areas that make life easier and increase adjustment [50–53]. However, although these publications make the lives of individuals diagnosed with BD easier, they have not asked about the extent to which these interventions contribute to the organic process in symptom evolution [13, 48–53]. Yet, in the literature, it is clearly known that cognitive-behavioral interventions and psychoeducation programs organized on this basis reveal various organic changes [54, 55]. Understanding which organic contributions will be made of symptom evolution in individuals diagnosed with BD by cognitive psychosocial interventions will inform the selection of interventions in commonly observed changes and medications to be given in addition to these interventions.
It is known that therapeutic interventions in which cognitive-behavioral therapy methods are used or integrated are more effective, especially when implemented with combinations of medications. It is observed that individuals diagnosed with BD 1 who receive these treatments experience fewer relapses compared to those diagnosed with BD 2 who receive them, and longer-lasting (90–120 minutes) cognitive-behavioral intervention sessions are more effective than shorter ones. While this situation is defined as "adjustment," it would also surely create a change in behaviors and cognitive schemas [14, 56, 57]. Therefore, the ordinary adjustment of the individual should not be the only factor used to explain this process that involves a change in schemas, the formation of new schemas, the acquisition of certain information, and the alteration of behaviors. It is needed to identify the potential structural and functional changes created in the brain by this situation and distinguish it from changes linked to symptom differentiations. The understanding of these changes and the planning of individualized treatments should be established as the basic needs of older individuals diagnosed with BD whose care needs in clinics increase. Indeed, due to the cognitive impairments that develop throughout the aging-related evolution of symptoms of the

individual diagnosed with BD, the increase in the quality of life, treatment adherence, and symptom evaluation of the individual should be reevaluated for this age group.

Outcomes related to changes that occur in the brain are also influenced by factors such as sex and whether the diagnosis of BD is made after the age of 40 or before the age of 25. This situation may differentiate the needs of a BD-diagnosed individual who is in their aging process and an individual who gets the diagnosis of BD in their aging period. Although processes developing in relation to the cortical differences or prefrontal cortex changes of older individuals diagnosed with BD in whom manic episodes are intense may suggest similar interventions and treatment methods, the needs of individuals may differ. For instance, in addition to changes in secretions in the physiology of aging, such as cortisol, melatonin, thyroid-stimulating hormone, or catecholamines, specific mania/hypomania episodes accompanied by periods of insomnia may initiate neuroinflammatory processes depending on elevated cortisol levels caused by excessive stress. Knowing this situation will reveal when a worsening cognitive state will be a BD pathology and how the direction of the intervention should change (neuroprogression hypothesis) [12, 17–19, 36–39]. Understanding the symptom cycle of older individuals diagnosed with BD and evaluating all aspects of this cycle in terms of treatments will be an important step in developing interventions.

In studies on the care of older individuals diagnosed with BD, it was found that motivational interviews improved treatment compliance [58], and programs based on positive psychology increased hope for the future and self-confidence [59]. Despite the positive outputs of studies on treatment protocols and care, an individual diagnosed with BD who is at the late stage of their life may state that "the process is very challenging, and they have lost their friends whom they need most in old age and their company." Understanding older individuals diagnosed with BD will not only determine the direction of interventions but also potentially change the course of their social lives. Psychosocial interventions have brought about several positive outcomes, whereas the necessary care should be paid to these individuals who have developed cognitive impairments over the age of 65, experienced several episodes over the years, and felt the burden of being someone who occasionally affected the social and psychological statuses of their family and friends negatively in order to resolve these challenges in their lives [51].

5. Conclusion

It is expected that identifying the evolution of symptoms in older individuals diagnosed with BD will allow us to (1) understand the organic changes in their brain structures and the effects of these changes on clinical developments, (2) comprehend the outcomes of cognitive-behavioral treatments (as well as other psychosocial treatments), in particular, and their effects on organic processes, (3) learn about the outcomes of these interventions that can be generalized to BD and those that are individual-specific, (4) reevaluate treatment protocols and standard diagnostic criteria in line with this knowledge, and (5) to understand the place of chronic (physical) disorders in symptom evolution and the importance of treatment in elderly individuals diagnosed with BD.

In conclusion, this study has some specific aims; although the main aim was to understand how BD symptoms evolve with aging, some of the important aims of this chapter were to draw attention to the fact that aging will bring chronic diseases and this will affect BD symptoms, to draw attention to the fact that organic changes will accompany the aging process in brain imaging and understanding this will contribute to treatment management in elderly people with BD, to emphasize that symptom evolution is important in diagnosis/treatment and care stages, and to explain the psychosocial outcomes of biological and organic changes. The literature shows that elderly individuals with BD have been neglected in many aspects, and the changing symptoms of BD in these individuals have not been recognized. It seems important to conduct adequate experimental and qualitative studies and to bring their results to the world literature at the level of evidence. In addition, it is also noticeable that symptom assessment studies on individuals diagnosed with BD over the age of 50 years are contradictory with the increasing life expectancy. For this reason, it is recommended to conduct evidence-level studies that can examine the recognition of BD and aging in every dimension.

Author details

Pınar Harmancı
Department of Nursing, Kahramanmaraş İstiklal University, Kahramanmaraş, Turkey

*Address all correspondence to: forzapinar@hotmail.com

References

[1] Rajashekar N, Blumberg HP, Villa LM. Neuroimaging studies of brain structure in older adults with bipolar disorder: A review. Journal of Psychiatry and Brain Science. 2022;7(4):e220006. DOI: 10.20900/jpbs.20220006

[2] Cansız A, İnce B, Altınbaş K, Kurt E. Evaluation of mortality causes among patients with bipolar disorder in a specialized mood clinic. Turkish Journal of Clinical Psychiatry. 2018;**21**(4):389-396

[3] Aizenberg D, Olmer A, Barak Y. Suicide attempts amongst elderly bipolar patients. Journal of Affective Disorders. 2006;**91**(1):91-94. DOI: 10.1016/j.jad.2005.12.013

[4] Kessing LV. Diagnostic subtypes of bipolar disorder in older versus younger adults. Bipolar Disorders. 2006;**8**(1):56-64. DOI: 10.1111/j.1399-5618.2006.00278.x

[5] Angst J, Preisig M. Course of a clinical cohort of unipolar, bipolar and schizoaffective patients. Results of a prospective study from 1959 to 1985. Schweizer Archiv für Neurologie und Psychiatrie. 1995;**146**(1):5-16

[6] Sajatovic M, Strejilevich SA, Gildengers AG, Dols A, Al Jurdi RK, Forester BP, et al. A report on older-age bipolar disorder from the International Society for Bipolar Disorders Task Force. Bipolar Disorders. 2015;**17**(7):689-704. DOI: 10.1111/bdi.12331

[7] Bartzokis G, Lu PH, Heydari P, Couvrette A, Lee GJ, Kalashyan G, et al. Multimodal magnetic resonance imaging assessment of white matter aging trajectories over the lifespan of healthy individuals. Biological Psychiatry. 2012;**72**(12):1026-1034. DOI: 10.1016/j.biopsych.2012.07.010

[8] Bartzokis G, Beckson M, Lu PH, Nuechterlein KH, Edwards N, Mintz J. Age-related changes in frontal and temporal lobe volumes in men: A magnetic resonance imaging study. Archives of General Psychiatry. 2001;**58**(5):461-465. DOI: 10.1001/archpsyc.58.5.461

[9] Blumberg HP, Kaufman J, Martin A, Whiteman R, Zhang JH, Gore JC, et al. Amygdala and hippocampal volumes in adolescents and adults with bipolar disorder. Archives of General Psychiatry. 2003;**60**(12):1201-1208. DOI: 10.1001/archpsyc.60.12.1201

[10] Hibar DP, Westlye LT, Van Erp TGM, Rasmussen J, Leonardo CD, Faskowitz J, et al. Subcortical volumetric abnormalities in bipolar disorder. Molecular Psychiatry. 2016;**21**(12):1710-1716. DOI: 10.1038/mp.2015.227

[11] Sato J, Hirano Y, Hirakawa N, Takahashi J, Oribe N, Kuga H, et al. Lower hippocampal volume in patients with schizophrenia and bipolar disorder: A quantitative MRI study. Journal of Personalized Medicine. 2021;**11**(2):1-14. DOI: 10.3390/JPM11020121

[12] Tampi RR, Joshi P, Bhattacharya G, Gupta S. Evaluation and treatment of older-age bipolar disorder: A narrative review. Drugs in Context. 2021;**10**:2021-1-8. DOI: 10.7573/dic.2021-1-8

[13] Gitlin MJ, Miklowitz DJ. The difficult lives of individuals with bipolar disorder: A review of functional outcomes and their implications for treatment. Journal of Affective Disorders. 2017;**209**:147-154

[14] Strakowski SM, Adler CM, Almeida J, Altshuler LL, Blumberg HP, Chang KD, et al. The functional neuroanatomy of bipolar disorder: A consensus model. Bipolar Disorders. 2012;**14**(4):313-325

[15] Sarrazin S, Cachia A, Hozer F, McDonald C, Emsell L, Cannon DM, et al. Neurodevelopmental subtypes of bipolar disorder are related to cortical folding patterns: An international multicenter study. Bipolar Disorders. 2018;**20**(8):721-732

[16] Penttilä J, Cachia A, Martinot JL, Ringuenet D, Wessa M, Houenou J, et al. Cortical folding difference between patients with early-onset and patients with intermediate-onset bipolar disorder. Bipolar Disorders. 2009;**11**(4):361-370. DOI: 10.1111/j.1399-5618.2009.00683.x

[17] Ohayon MM. Epidemiology of insomnia: What we know and what we still need to learn. Sleep Medicine Reviews. 2002;**6**(2):97-111

[18] Stone KL, Ewing SK, Lui LY, Ensrud KE, Ancoli-Israel S, Bauer DC, et al. Self-reported sleep and nap habits and risk of falls and fractures in older women: The study of osteoporotic fractures. Journal of the American Geriatrics Society. 2006;**54**(8):1177-1183

[19] Yüksel A. Yaşlanma ve Uyku Fizyolojisi. In: Kılavuz SS, Akçiçek içinde F, editors. Yaşlı Fizyolojisi. US Akademi Publisher; 2018. pp. 223-237

[20] Delvecchio G, Mandolini GM, Arighi A, Prunas C, Mauri CM, Pietroboni AM, et al. Structural and metabolic cerebral alterations between elderly bipolar disorder and behavioural variant frontotemporal dementia: A combined MRI-PET study. The Australian and New Zealand Journal of Psychiatry. 2019;**53**(5):413-423. DOI: 10.1177/0004867418815976

[21] Haller S, Xekardaki A, Delaloye C, Canuto A, Lövblad KO, Gold G, et al. Combined analysis of grey matter voxel-based morphometry and white matter tract-based spatial statistics in late-life bipolar disorder. Journal of Psychiatry & Neuroscience. 2011;**36**(6):391-401. DOI: 10.1503/jpn.100140

[22] Rej S, Butters MA, Aizenstein HJ, Begley A, Tsay J, Reynolds CF, et al. Neuroimaging and neurocognitive abnormalities associated with bipolar disorder in old age. International Journal of Geriatric Psychiatry. 2014;**29**(4): 421-427. DOI: 10.1002/gps.4021

[23] Baez S, Pinasco C, Roca M, Ferrari J, Couto B, García-Cordero I, et al. Brain structural correlates of executive and social cognition profiles in behavioral variant frontotemporal dementia and elderly bipolar disorder. Neuropsychologia. 2019;**126**:159-169. DOI: 10.1016/j.neuropsychologia.2017.02.012

[24] Gunde E, Blagdon R, Hajek T. White matter hyperintensities—From medical comorbidities to bipolar disorders and back. Annals of Medicine. 2011;**43**(8):571-580. DOI: 10.3109/07853890.2011.595733

[25] Almeida OP, Dols A, Blanken MAJT, Rej S, Blumberg HP, Villa L, et al. Physical health burden among older men and women with bipolar disorder: Results from the gage-Bd collaboration. The American Journal of Geriatric Psychiatry. 2022;**30**(6):727-732. DOI: 10.1016/J.JAGP.2021.12.006

[26] Nabulsi L et al. Large-scale replication of bipolar disorder dysconnectivity: A diffusion MRI analysis of 959 individuals from the ENIGMA bipolar disorder working group. Biological Psychiatry. 2021;**89**(9):S185-S186

[27] Duffy A, Alda M, Hajek T, Sherry SB, Grof P. Early stages in the development of bipolar disorder. Journal of Affective Disorders. 2010;**121**(1-2):127-135

[28] Rantala MJ, Luoto S, Borráz-León JI, Krams I. Bipolar disorder: An evolutionary psychoneuroimmunological approach. Neuroscience and Biobehavioral Reviews. 2021;**122**:28-37

[29] Wang X, Luo Q, Tian F, Cheng B, Qiu L, Wang S, et al. Brain grey-matter volume alteration in adult patients with bipolar disorder under different conditions: A voxel-based meta-analysis. Journal of Psychiatry & Neuroscience. 2019;**44**(2):89-101. DOI: 10.1503/jpn.180002

[30] Dhingra U, Rabins PV. Mania in the elderly: A 5-7 year follow-up. Journal of the American Geriatrics Society. 1991;**39**:581-583

[31] Abé C, Ching CRK, Liberg B, Lebedev AV, Agartz I, Akudjedu TN, et al. Longitudinal structural brain changes in bipolar disorder: A multicenter neuroimaging study of 1232 individuals by the ENIGMA bipolar disorder working group. Biological Psychiatry. 2022;**91**(6):582-592

[32] Coryell W, Fiedorowicz J, Solomon D, Endicott J. Age transitions in the course of bipolar I disorder. Psychological Medicine. 2009;**39**(8):1247-1252

[33] Chen WY, Huang MC, Lee YC, Chang CE, Lin SK, Chiu CC, et al. The heterogeneity of longitudinal cognitive decline in euthymic bipolar I disorder with clinical characteristics and functional outcomes. Frontiers in Psychiatry. 2021;**12**:684813

[34] Montejo L, Montenegro H, López-Jaramillo C, González-Pinto A, Vieta E, Martínez-Arán A, et al. Aging in bipolar disorder: Cognitive performance and clinical factors based on an adulthood-lifespan perspective. Journal of Affective Disorders. 2022;**312**:292-302

[35] Depp CA, Jeste DV. Bipolar disorder in older adults: A critical review. Bipolar Disorders. 2004;**6**:343-367

[36] Berk M, Kapczinski F, Andreazza AC, et al. Pathwaysunderlying neuroprogression in bipolar disorder: Focuson inflammation, oxidative stress and neurotrophic fac-tors. Neuroscience and Biobehavioral Reviews. 2011;**35**:804-817

[37] Yildiz-Yesiloglu A, Ankerst DP. Neurochemical alterations of the brain in bipolar disorder and their implications for pathophysiology: A systematic review of the in vivo proton magnetic resonance spectroscopy findings. Progress in Neuro-Psychopharmacology & Biological Psychiatry. 2006;**30**:969-995

[38] Doty TJ, Payne ME, Steffens DC, Beyer JL, Krishnan KR, LaBar KS. Age-dependent reduction of amygdala volume in bipolar disorder. Psychiatry Research. 2008;**163**:84-94

[39] Gildengers AG, Chung KH, Huang SH, Begley A, Aizenstein HJ, Tsai SY. Neuroprogressive effects of life-time illness duration in older adults with bipolar disorder. Bipolar Disorders. 2014;**16**:617-623

[40] Osby U, Brandt L, Correia N, Ekbom A, Sparén P. Excess mortality in bipolar and unipolar disorder in Sweden. Archives of General Psychiatry. 2001;**58**(9):844-850

[41] Høyer EH, Mortensen PB, Olesen AV. Mortality and causes of death in a total national sample of patients with affective disorders admitted for the

first time between 1973 and 1993. The British Journal of Psychiatry. 2000;**177**(7):676-682

[42] Ya-Mei B, Tung-Ping S, Mu-Hong C, Tzeng-Ji C, Wen-Han C. Risk of developing diabetes mellitus and hyperlipidemia among patients with bipolar disorder, major depressive disorder, and schizophrenia: A 10-year nationwide population-based prospective cohort study. Journal of Affective Disorders. 2013;**150**(1):57-62

[43] Smith DJ, Langan J, McLean G, Guthrie B, Mercer S. Schizophrenia is associated with excess multiple physical comorbidities but low levels of cardiovascular disease in primary care: Cross-sectional study. BMJ Open. 2013;**3**(7):1-7

[44] Laursen TM, Munk-Olsen T, Agerbo E, Gasse C, Mortensen PB. Somatic hospital contacts, invasive cardiac procedures, and mortality from heart disease in patients with severe mental disorder. Archives of General Psychiatry. 2009;**66**(7):713-720

[45] Barnett K, Mercer SW, Norbury M, Watt G, Wyke S, Guthrie B. Epidemiology of multimorbidity and implications for health care, research, and medical education: A cross-sectional study. The Lancet. 2012;**380**(9836):37-43

[46] Smith DJ, Martin D, McLean G, Langan J, Guthrie B, Mercer SW. Multimorbidity in bipolar disorder and undertreatment of cardiovascular disease: A cross sectional study. BMC Medicine. 2013;**11**:1-11

[47] Hajek T, McIntyre R, Alda M. Bipolar disorders, type 2 diabetes mellitus, and the brain. Current Opinion in Psychiatry. 2016;**29**(1):1-6

[48] Ljubic N, Ueberberg B, Grunze H, Assion HJ. Treatment of bipolar disorders in older adults: A review. Focus. 2023;**21**(4):434-443

[49] Arnold I et al. Old age bipolar disorder—Epidemiology, aetiology and treatment. Medicina. 2021;**57**(6):587

[50] Shobassy A. Elderly bipolar disorder. Current Psychiatry Reports. 2021;**23**:1-10

[51] Tyler E et al. Developing a recovery-focused therapy for older people with bipolar disorder: A qualitative focus group study. BMJ Open. 2021;**11**(8):e049829

[52] Smilowitz S, Aftab A, Aebi M, Levin J, Tatsuoka C, Sajatovic M. Age-related differences in medication adherence, symptoms, and stigma in poorly adherent adults with bipolar disorder. Journal of Geriatric Psychiatry and Neurology. 2020;**33**(5):250-255

[53] Tyler E et al. A systematic review of psychosocial functioning and quality of life in older people with bipolar disorder. Journal of Affective Disorders Reports. 2022;**9**:100371

[54] Girelli F et al. Neural correlates of cognitive behavioral therapy-based interventions for bipolar disorder: A scoping review. Journal of Psychiatric Research. 2024;**172**(1):351-359

[55] Yang J et al. A preliminary study of the effects of mindfulness-based cognitive therapy on structural brain networks in mood-dysregulated youth with a familial risk for bipolar disorder. Early Intervention in Psychiatry. 2022;**16**(9):1011-1019

[56] Chiang KJ, Tsai JC, Liu D, Lin CH, Chiu HL, Chou KR. Efficacy of cognitive-behavioral therapy in patients

with bipolar disorder: A meta-analysis of randomized controlled trials. PLoS ONE. 2017;**12**(5):e0176849

[57] Pardo PJ, Olman CA, Pardo JV. Neuroimaging in psychiatry. In: The Medical Basis of Psychiatry. Springer; 2016. pp. 881-917

[58] Tahghighi H, Mortazavi H, Manteghi AA, Armat MR. The effect of comprehensive individual motivational-educational program on medication adherence in elderly patients with bipolar disorders: An experimental study. Journal of Education Health Promotion. 2023;**12**(1):70

[59] Van Dijk M, Sonnenberg CM, Triebels MCM, van Luijn A, van der Stel J, Stek ML, et al. Perspectives on recovery by older persons with bipolar disorder, their caregivers, and mental healthcare professionals: An exploratory approach using focus groups and social dialogue. Psychogeriatrics. 2021;**21**(6):945

Chapter 6

Secondary Mania of Medical and Neurological Disorders

Gregory M. Nikogosyan, Emma R. Torncello and Samuel I. MacDonald

Abstract

Secondary mania, also known as secondary bipolar disorder, is a mood disorder characterized by episodes of mania or hypomania that are attributed to an identifiable physical or medical condition rather than primary psychiatric origins. This condition can arise due to various factors, including neurological disorders, systemic illnesses, medications, or substance abuse. Secondary mania often presents diagnostic and therapeutic challenges as a comprehensive evaluation is required to identify the underlying cause. Understanding the pathophysiology, clinical manifestations, and treatment strategies for secondary mania is crucial for effective management. This chapter explores the etiology, diagnostic criteria, differential diagnosis, and evidence-based treatment approaches for secondary mania, highlighting the importance of interdisciplinary collaboration in managing this complex disorder.

Keywords: secondary mania, organic mania, bipolar disorder due to another medical condition, medication induced mania, neuropsychiatry of mania

1. Introduction

Bipolar and Related Disorder due to Another Medical Condition, often referred to as "Secondary Mania," is a distinct clinical syndrome characterized as a period of abnormally and persistently elevated, expansive, or irritable mood and a persistent increase in energy lasting at least one week [1]. Per the Diagnostic and Statistical Manual of Mental Disorders Five, Text Revision, there must be "evidence from the history, physical examination, or laboratory findings that the disturbance is the direct pathophysiological consequence of another medical condition. Additionally, the symptoms should not chronologically precede the organic illness, and the causal relationship between the symptoms and the condition should be plausible" [2].

The historical context of mania has had many interpretations as well. In contrast to his contemporaries, mania as a clinical syndrome was first systematically described by Hippocrates, who proposed it was a disease of the brain. Hippocrates described mania as a state of agitation attributed to excess yellow bile [3]. Aretaeus of Cappadocia was the first to link melancholia and mania as related diseases in the first century AD. However, it was not until the 1850s that Jean-Pierre Falret first proposed the modern conceptualization of bipolar disorder as 'folie circulaire,' characterized by a continuous cycle of depression, mania, and free intervals of varying length [4]. Following after that, Emil Kraeplin laid the foundation for our modern psychiatric classification of mania within his overarching diagnosis of "manic-depressive insanity" in the late 1800s [4].

The original version of the DSM allowed for a diagnosis of a singular manic state; it was not until the DSM-III, in 1980, that an idiopathic manic episode became sufficient for a diagnosis of bipolar disorder, reflecting the contemporary perception that mania was always the hallmark of a cycling mood disorder [5]. This historical precedent is the reason that secondary mania remains categorized under "bipolar and related disorders." Despite this categorization, it is worth noting that multiple episodes and the presence of depressive episodes are not necessary for the diagnosis. It is partly due to the misperceptions created by the name "Bipolar and Related Disorder due to Another Medical Condition" that we use more directly descriptive "Secondary Mania" here.

Because the symptoms of secondary mania do not differ significantly from those of primary mania, accurate evaluation of underlying organic causes of mania is essential to avoid delays in the initiation of effective treatment [1].

2. Secondary mania comprehensive overview

2.1 Epidemiology

The incidence and prevalence of secondary mania varies based upon the underlying medical condition. Not only does the epidemiology of each underlying medical condition differ, but the likelihood of developing manic symptoms in patients with each underlying disorder can vary widely. For instance, in Cushing syndrome, the estimated incidence of mania or hypomania varies from 2 to 37%. Conversely, after a Traumatic Brain Injury (TBI), the incidence of mania has been estimated at 9% [6]. The nature of the literature surrounding secondary mania, which consists primarily of case reports, case series, and case-control studies, makes confident assertions about risk factors difficult. To date, no epidemiological studies have been performed studying the incidence or prevalence of the construct of Bipolar and Related Disorders due to Another Medical Condition. The DSM-5-TR notes, "Gender differences [in prevalence] pertain to those associated with the medical condition (e.g. systemic lupus erythematosus is more common in females; stroke is somewhat more common in middle-aged males compared with females)" [2].

2.2 Pathophysiology

Secondary mania can occur due to many broad etiological causes, but some common aspects are shared. Predisposing factors for developing mania due to secondary causes include individuals who have family histories of bipolar disorder. This may highlight an increased vulnerability of specific individuals to developing mania after brain insult or dysregulation due to a medical or neurological illness.

2.2.1 Neurocircuitry

Secondary mania is classically associated with lateralization with lesions primarily in the right hemisphere [7]. Multiple brain regions are associated with mania when disrupted or damaged, as in the cases of stroke or traumatic brain injury. These associations include bilateral orbitofrontal, right temporoparietal, right basal and medial temporal, basal ganglia, thalamic, and right frontotemporal brain lesions [8]. Secondary mania due to a neurologic cause typically involves either hypoactivity of right-hemisphere limbic structures or hyperactivity of reward-processing areas of the left hemisphere [9, 10]. Some studies have alternatively shown secondary mania associated with left hemisphere pathology. However, this may be explained by pathology relating to the nondominant hemisphere [11]. Further contemporary challenges to the laterality of lesions may be evidence found in individuals with bipolar disorder. Recent studies from the working group ENIGMA Consortium examined structural brain MRI and clinical data from many individuals with bipolar disorder, who found thinner cortical gray matter in bilateral hemispheres, particularly orbitofrontal, temporal, and parietal regions [12]. In stroke patients, lesion locations contributing to the onset of secondary mania are spatially heterogeneous. Some highlighted areas for stroke patients include the right orbitofrontal and basotemporal cortex areas, the caudate, and the thalamus [13].

These diverse regions of possible brain lesions or insults appear to share disruption of common functional networks involving the orbitofrontal cortex, dorsolateral prefrontal cortex, and temporal lobes. Furthermore, thalamic lesions leading to mania seem to be due to the disruption of the salience network, which can lead to increased difficulty in focusing on what is most important or relevant. Dysconnectivity of structures such as the amygdala, hippocampi, and ventrolateral prefrontal cortex in secondary mania may also be responsible for emotion dysregulation and disinhibition [14]. In summary, the thalamus acts as a relay station of the brain, connecting different regions that involve emotional regulation and mood. Dysfunction can occur at this relay station, top-down from the frontal and temporal cortex, where damage to neurocircuitry can lead to poor impulse control and disinhibition, or it can be bottom-up from the limbic system, which is responsible for emotional regulation.

2.2.2 Neurotransmitter systems

Due to the diverse etiologies in secondary mania, it is vital to consider the neurotransmitter system. The monoamine view of bipolar disorder focuses primarily on the dopaminergic system, but the serotonin, glutamatergic, and GABAergic systems contribute as well. Increased striatal dopamine receptor availability leads to increased dopamine neurotransmission in many previously discussed brain regions of interest [15]. This is another bottom-up process from the basal ganglia that can lead to secondary mania presentation. This striatal system is responsible for reward processing and motivation, an essential aspect of mania symptoms. The neurotransmitter view of secondary mania can be associated more with etiological causes such as substance use, medication, and metabolic or endocrine dysregulations. It is believed there is increased dopamine reactivity for individuals susceptible to bipolar states, and it is well known that manic-like episodes occur from the administration of dopamine agonists such as L-dopa, amphetamines, or other medications altering the neuro-molecular dynamics of dopamine [16]. When interacting with dopamine, the serotonergic system may contribute to mood elevation, impulsivity, and even aggression. Data for serotonin is primarily available for unipolar depression, where high concentrations of 5-hydroxyindoleacetic acid (5-HIAA) were connected to suicide occurrence and aggressiveness [16]. The serotonin system can also modulate dopamine, which is best highlighted by the non-dopamine block antipsychotic pimavanserin. Furthermore, it has been shown that excitatory glutamatergic activity was increased at the left dorsolateral prefrontal cortex and cingulate gyrus for individuals with bipolar disorder. Additionally, bipolar treatment groups with the anti-glutamatergic mood stabilizer lamotrigine showed a significant reduction in glutamate levels compared to control and non-remission groups for stabilization [17]. Inhibitory GABAergic neurotransmission has been implicated in other mood disorders as excess glutamate activity and reduced GABAergic inhibition contributes to the hyperarousal state and emotional lability, also commonly seen in secondary mania. Increased levels of GABA were connected to mania treatment response with valproate in patients with bipolar disorder [16].

2.2.3 Neuroendocrine

The neuroendocrine system also can play a significant role in mania. The hypothalamic-pituitary-adrenal (HPA) axis has been shown to have increased cortisol and ACTH levels in mania [18]. The gonadal and thyroid endocrine system also have effects that can lead to mania. Hyperthyroidism was associated with a higher incidence of bipolar disorders than control patients, and hyperthyroidism itself may be another risk factor for the development of bipolar disorder [19]. Sex hormones such as testosterone have also been implicated in increased motor activity, energy, emotional instability, and aggressive behaviors. Speech rate and amount were also found to be positively correlated with testosterone levels in individuals with bipolar disorder [20]. Interestingly, there has been some evidence of estrogen and progesterone helping stabilize depressive mood, and anti-estrogen medications such as tamoxifen have some anti-manic effects [21].

2.3 Clinical features

2.3.1 Symptoms and presentation

The clinical presentation of secondary mania may seem very similar to primary mania and is often confused with delirium. Delirium can be differentiated due to its fluctuating course with a disturbance of consciousness. The symptoms of secondary mania typically occur within hours or days of the physiologic or toxic etiology and usually have a less fluctuating course [22]. Primary mania typically occurs before age 30, but secondary mania can occur at any age. Further complicating matters is the concept of *Bell's mania or Delirious mania*, a rare mania presentation not clearly placed under Bipolar Disorder Type I/II or physiological disorders leading to mania. This is typically a very late-onset mania with symptoms of confusion in the patient. Diagnostic workup typically excludes secondary causes. Typically, there is an absence of a personal or family history of bipolar disorder, and antipsychotic treatment may return the afflicted individual to their normal baseline. The Bond clinical criteria have been used to help classify this disorder but remain imperfect given the controversy regarding the importance of having a presence of a family history of bipolar disorder. The Bond criterion highlights key aspects, which include acute onset, presence of hypomania at some point in the episode, features of delirium, personal history of mania or depression, family history of a major affective disorder, and responsiveness to standard treatment of mania [23].

2.3.2 Difference between primary and secondary mania

Differentiating between primary and secondary mania has important clinical implications for prognosis, treatment selection, and duration of treatment. However, the two conditions are not reliably distinguishable based on symptomatic criteria alone. A thorough history and physical examination may support clinical suspicion of an underlying medical condition contributing to psychiatric symptoms. A recent history of medical illness, injury, or changes to medical treatment may raise suspicion for organic causes of mania. Laboratory or imaging abnormalities may also point to an underlying medical cause. Given the broad differential diagnosis for conditions resulting in secondary mania, a thorough review of systems can also help to guide medical workup by identifying any associated features such as headaches, unintentional weight loss, neurologic deficits, etc.

The age of initial symptom onset is an essential consideration. The average age of onset for bipolar disorder is typically between 15 to 25 years of age, accounting for fifty-three percent of cases, and less than five percent of cases were above the age of 45 [24]. The initial onset of psychiatric symptoms over the age of 50 raises concern for secondary mania. Although manic episodes in elderly patients are not uncommon (with an overall prevalence of approximately 6% in the inpatient psychiatry setting) [25] in a review of case reports of patients who experienced their first episode of mania or hypomania over the age of 50, 82% of cases were suspected of having an underlying organic cause [26]. In addition to the later age of onset, the absence of a family history of bipolar disorder may also support a diagnosis of secondary mania [27]. Some clues to whether presentation is secondary or primary mania are that typically, treatments for secondary mania may be less effective and a family history of bipolar is absent [22].

Finally, it is essential to consider that a medical condition alone does not necessarily indicate a causal relationship with mania. Biological factors may precipitate the onset of a manic episode, including a first episode of primary bipolar disorder in susceptible individuals.

2.4 Diagnostic criteria and assessment

2.4.1 DSM-5-TR and ICD-11 definitions of mania

The DSM-5-TR full criteria for Bipolar and Related Disorder Due to Another Medical Condition is as follows:

a. *A prominent and persistent disturbance in mood that predominates in the clinical picture and is characterized by abnormally elevated, expansive, or irritable mood and abnormally increased activity or energy.*

b. *There is evidence from the history, physical examination, or laboratory findings that the disturbance is the direct pathophysiological consequence of another medical condition.*

c. *The disturbance is not better explained by another mental disorder.*

d. *The disturbance does not occur exclusively during the course of a delirium.*

e. *The disturbance causes clinically significant distress or impairment in social, occupational, or other important areas of functioning, or necessitates hospitalization to prevent harm to self or others, or there are psychotic features* [2].

Additionally, the DSM-5-TR provides the specifiers with manic features if full criteria for mania are not met, with manic- or hypomanic-like episodes if full criteria for those respective episodes are met except Criterion D (for manic) or Criterion F (for hypomanic), and with mixed features if symptoms of depression are present but do not predominate in the clinical picture [2].

The closest ICD-11 corollary for Bipolar and Related Disorder Due to Another Medical Condition is *Secondary mood syndrome, with manic symptoms*, which is described as "A syndrome characterized by the presence of prominent manic symptoms such as elevated, euphoric, irritable, or expansive mood states, rapid changes among different mood states (i.e., mood lability), or increased energy or activity that is judged to be a direct pathophysiological consequence of a health condition not classified under mental and behavioral disorders based on evidence from the history, physical examination, or laboratory findings" [28].

Although full criteria for mania are not necessary for a diagnosis of Bipolar and Related Disorder Due to Another Medical Condition, a significant portion of the literature on secondary mania uses criterion A-C of the full DSM-5-TR criteria for a manic episode as outlined below:

a. *A distinct period of abnormally and persistently elevated, expansive, or irritable mood and abnormally and persistently increased activity or energy, lasting at least 1 week and present most of the day, nearly every day (or any duration if hospitalization is necessary).*

b. *During the period of mood disturbance and increased energy or activity, three (or more) of the following symptoms (four if the mood is only irritable) are present to a significant degree and represent a noticeable change from usual behavior:*

  1. *Inflated self-esteem or grandiosity.*

  2. *Decreased need for sleep (e.g., feels rested after only 3 hours of sleep).*

  3. *More talkative than usual or pressure to keep talking.*

  4. *Flight of ideas or subjective experience that thoughts are racing.*

  5. *Distractibility (i.e., attention too easily drawn to unimportant or irrelevant external stimuli), as reported or observed.*

  6. *Increase in goal-directed activity (either socially, at work or school, or sexually) or psychomotor agitation (i.e., purposeless non-goal-directed activity).*

  7. *Excessive involvement in activities that have a high potential for painful consequences (e.g., engaging in unrestrained buying sprees, sexual indiscretions, or foolish business investments).*

c. *The mood disturbance is sufficiently severe to cause marked impairment in social or occupational functioning or to necessitate hospitalization to prevent harm to self or others, or there are psychotic features* [2].

In this use, Criterion D of the DSM-5–TR manic episode, "The episode is not attributable to the physiological effects of a substance (e.g., a drug of abuse, a medication, other treatment) or another medical condition," is omitted [2]. This may highlight that mania due to physiological causes and mania due to Bipolar I Disorder may be different constructs.

The ICD-11 criteria for a manic episode are almost identical, although they do not require a specific number of associated symptoms (Criterion B in the above DSM criteria). Per the ICD-11, "A manic episode is an extreme mood state lasting at least one week unless shortened by a treatment intervention characterized by euphoria, irritability, or expansiveness, and by increased activity or a subjective experience of increased energy, accompanied by other characteristic symptoms such as rapid or pressured speech, flight of ideas, increased self-esteem or grandiosity, decreased need for sleep, distractibility, impulsive or reckless behavior, and rapid changes among different mood states (i.e., mood lability)" [28].

2.4.2 Differential diagnosis: Distinguishing from bipolar I disorder

The differential diagnosis for secondary mania is broad, encompassing "virtually any disorder or process that disrupts brain architecture or physiologic functioning" [22]. Given the wide array of possible causes, a medical workup should be guided by a careful history, physical examination, review of systems, and any available initial laboratory or imaging results. Section 2.5 provides some examples of previously identified causes of secondary mania but is not an exhaustive list of all possible causes.

2.4.3 Diagnostic workup

A comprehensive medical history is the cornerstone of evaluating secondary mania. Key aspects should focus on, as discussed, the onset and course of manic symptoms. Consider the later age of onset and an identifiable medical event, such as a stroke, head trauma, seizures, or infection for example. Explore medication and substances recently started that may have precipitated mania. In addition to these factors, identify family history and the patient's past psychiatric history as secondary mania typically will not have prior bipolar episodes.

A detailed examination is crucial to help identify possible secondary causes of mania. Neurological examination should explore for any focal deficits that may indicate an underlying brain lesion, stroke, or demyelinating lesion. A general physical examination should investigate for possible signs of systemic illness, such as infection or autoimmune disorders that may be contributing to symptom presentation. Pertinent findings on the exam should lead to further diagnostic inquiry, which may include laboratory testing and imaging.

Laboratory testing is often indicated to help identify mania's neurologic, metabolic, infectious, or endocrine causes. General lab testing can include complete blood count, comprehensive metabolic panel, thyroid function tests, vitamin levels particular thiamine, B12 and folate. Further tests include drug and toxin screening and inflammatory markers such as C-reactive protein (CRP) and erythrocyte sedimentation rate (ESR). Specific tests for HIV and RPR, and VDRL should be considered for possible neurosyphilis. If suspicion is high for autoimmune encephalitis, a lumbar puncture for cerebrospinal fluid (CSF) analysis may be indicated, particularly in paraneoplastic syndromes such as anti-NMDA receptor encephalitis. CSF studies can also aid in identifying viral encephalitis, neurosyphilis, and oligoclonal bands for multiple sclerosis, which is found in 95 percent of patients [29].

Electrophysiological studies can also be of great support in the workup of secondary mania. Given mania symptoms can occur with various forms of epilepsy, it may be helpful to obtain an electroencephalogram (EEG) study. Furthermore, EEG can effectively detect delirium or encephalopathy from other psychiatric causes of mental status changes with a sensitivity of 100% and a specificity of 99% [30]. Typically, EEG findings of delirium will show marked diffuse and slow wave ratio increases, occipital slowing, decrease in alpha, and increase in beta, delta, and theta power.

Neuroimaging should be utilized if indicated based on a neurological exam to identify structural brain abnormalities for mania. Common modalities used include magnetic resonance imaging (MRI) and computed tomography (CT) scans of the brain. MRI is the preferred imaging technique for identifying tumors, strokes, white matter lesions, or signs of traumatic brain injury. MRI also provides high-resolution images of the brain anatomy and can help identify focal brain damage, particularly in the frontal lobes, basal ganglia, or thalamus, common regions implicated in secondary mania. CT scans are typically used as an initial screening tool in emergency settings before MRI and help detect acute hemorrhage or large tumors. Remember that the posterior fossa is better visualized by MRI than by CT scan, particularly in posterior strokes, and may be reason enough to use MRI as the first line [31].

For individuals who have had a negative workup in the acute setting, considerations for neurocognitive disorders should be on the differential for suspected frontal temporal and other dementias. Neuropsychological testing for such individuals may prove helpful in determining if an underlying dementing illness is leading to secondary mania findings particularly in cases with normal EEG findings. With the advent of multiple markers, particularly for the CSF for various neurocognitive disorders, a specialist in neurocognitive disorders should be part of the evaluation and assessment to ensure appropriate diagnostic workup.

2.5 Common conditions associated with secondary mania

2.5.1 Traumatic brain injury

Diagnosis of mania in TBI is complicated due to irritability, impulsivity, and agitation commonly occurring in the absence of a mood disorder. Furthermore, mania in TBI is noted in one study to range up to 9% in individuals meeting criteria for mania at some point within twelve months after initial injury [6]. Although most cases appear right-sided, specific regions within the hemispheres seem to be implicated in TBI mania, including the temporal poles, orbitofrontal cortices, and limbic areas [32]. Separately, there is some evidence that cerebellar abnormalities, including cerebellar damage, may be associated with mood disorders [33]. In this same cohort of patients, it was noted that the duration of mania appeared to be short-lived, lasting up to two months, perhaps suggesting a higher occurrence rate of mania. There is also evidence that there can be a substantial delay in the onset of manic symptoms following TBI, with one study noting an onset of 4 to 5 years after the injury [11]. Mania in TBI is also reported to have more irritability than euphoria in a case series of 20 patients [34]. In our experience, following the diagnostic criteria from DSM 5-TR would be most appropriate to determine if the presentation is consistent with mania and allow appropriate treatment strategy. TBI irritability alone may benefit from antidepressants but may worsen symptoms if, instead, the patient has TBI-related mania.

DOI: http://dx.doi.org/10.5772/intechopen.1007693

2.5.2 Stroke and other vascular disorders

Post-stroke mania appears rare, ranging from 0.4 to 1.6% in retrospective case reviews highlighting right hemispheric lesions causing dysfunction to ventral limbic circuits, which involve the orbitofrontal and basotemporal cortices, dorsomedial thalamic nucleus and head of the caudate nucleus [35, 36]. Symptoms appeared in the initial days after the stroke and were most noted to be elevated mood, pressured speech, decreased need for sleep, and agitation in secondary mania due to stroke [36]. Further areas also implicated in mania due to stroke have also been the superior frontal gyrus, medial orbitofrontal cortex, hippocampus and parahippocampal gyrus, superior and middle temporal poles, middle and inferior temporal gyrus, fusiform gyrus, anterior cingulate gyrus, and thalamus [37].

2.5.3 Autoimmune disorders

Multiple sclerosis (MS) resulting in mania has been described in several case reports [38–41]. The high frequency of secondary mania in MS may likely be related to white matter changes which are also commonly seen in primary bipolar disorders [9, 37]. Features such as sensory or autonomic findings, cognitive changes, motor symptoms, and lack of response to standard treatment may warrant consideration of multiple sclerosis in the differential diagnosis [42]. In other disorders, such as systemic lupus erythematosus (SLE), mania is found at a rate of 3 to 6%, possibly due to severe inflammatory response or corticosteroid treatment [1, 9]. Certain antibody markers have also been associated with a higher risk of neuropsychiatric symptoms in SLE, such as anti-ribosomal P-proteins [43]. Following inflammatory markers of autoimmune disorders may help delineate if worsening mania is due to the progression of the disease or reaction to medication.

2.5.4 Epilepsy

Epilepsy can present with many psychiatric symptoms, including mania. Psychiatric symptoms can occur in the preictal, ictal, postictal, or interictal state [44] but are more commonly seen in postictal and post-temporal lobectomy patients [45]. Temporal lobe epilepsy itself has also been linked with manic or hypomanic symptoms [46]. However, frontal lobe epilepsy has been associated with the development of postictal mania in at least one case report, and presentations of frontal lobe epilepsy can very much mimic mania [47]. Satzer and Bond et al. have suggested that mania in epilepsy can present in three various ways mechanistically. The first is ictal mania due to left-sided hyperactivity; the second is ictal mania due to right-sided surgical resection for epilepsy, and the third is postictal rebound hypoactivity in right-hemisphere limbic structures [9]. Interestingly, both mania in bipolar disorder and partial seizures are described to have kindling and notable similar precipitating factors such as stress and sleep deprivation, which may highlight a shared pathophysiological mechanism [48].

2.5.5 Brain tumors

Brain neoplasms have been described as precipitants of manic episodes [49–51]. According to a systematic review and pooled lesion analysis, mania secondary to brain lesions tends to be more commonly involved in right-sided lesions [52] and primarily seen in the frontal lobe, temporal lobe, or subcortical limbic structures [37]. Psychiatric symptoms should be considered in the broader context of the diagnosis, treatment, and sequelae of brain neoplasms, including consideration for the contributing role of medications utilized in management (such as steroids and immunomodulating medications), as well as the influence of sequelae of primary lesions and treatment (e.g. resulting inflammation or hematoma).

2.5.6 Infectious causes

HIV-related secondary mania is a well-described phenomenon with low incidence in early infection but rising to up to 8% of individuals with AIDS [1]. There appears to be a higher prevalence of mania in HIV-positive individuals compared to non-HIV-positive individuals, with a greater risk of secondary mania associated with more advanced disease [53, 54]. Differences in psychiatric symptoms may also be present. When compared to patients with primary mania without HIV infection, those with HIV-associated secondary mania were more likely to be female, cognitively impaired, older in age, and with a lower level of education [55, 56]. They tended to have more irritability, aggressive behaviors, and talkativeness, and they experienced paranoid delusions and auditory and visual hallucinations at increased rates compared to HIV-negative individuals with primary mania [55]. Psychiatric symptoms of HIV may be a result of the direct impact of HIV infection on the central nervous system, the effect of medications used in the treatment of HIV, or HIV-related infections of the brain [57]. Some evidence suggests that treatment of HIV with antiretroviral therapy may protect against the development of mania [58]. Another infectious process to consider with neuropsychiatric symptoms in later stages is Syphilis. Syphilis, particularly neurosyphilis, has also been implicated in not only delirium but mania [59]. Other infectious causes include herpes simplex encephalitis, which has been present as both mania and hypomania [60, 61]. Behavioral changes in herpes simplex encephalitis, which can occur alongside hemiparesis, dysphasia, aphasia, ataxia, or focal seizures, can be similar to behavioral changes in primary mania, making early diagnosis difficult [62]. Fever is present in over 90% of cases [62]. A thorough clinical history, including immunosuppression, recent illnesses, and travel history, can be vital in exploring the causes of encephalitis such as herpes simplex. Further laboratory workup should be pursued if suspected, although HSV serologies are generally not clinically helpful in the acute setting. Lumbar puncture is critical for appropriate diagnosis with high sensitivity and specificity for HSV-1 and HSV-2 antibodies in the CSF, although antibodies may be negative early in the illness. MRI with and without contrast is abnormal in most cases of herpes simplex encephalitis. Early empiric initiation of acyclovir is key and should be continued for 14 to 21 days if the diagnosis is confirmed [63]. Mania secondary to cryptococcal meningitis has been described in a number of case reports, both in patients with comorbid HIV and without [64–69]. When seen in the absence of HIV infection, the most common manifestations of cryptococcal meningitis are headache, fever, vomiting, and altered mentation. These authors did not find relevant articles of toxoplasmosis gondi infection leading to secondary mania and most studies were associations with underlying mental illnesses [70].

2.5.7 Endocrine causes

Endocrine disorders, including hyperthyroidism and thyrotoxicosis, may cause symptoms of mania. The mechanism for behavioral changes in hyperthyroid states is unclear but may include the disrupted activity of the adrenergic pathway between the frontal lobe and locus ceruleus [71]. In addition to behavioral symptoms such as irritability, anxiety, and sleep disturbance, patients with hyperthyroidism-induced manic symptoms may experience other classic symptoms of hyperthyroidism, including fatigue, weight loss, tachycardia, tremor, perspiration, exophthalmos, and gastrointestinal symptoms. Psychosis can also occur. There are few case reports of hypothyroidism causing mania, though this appears to be much rarer [72, 73]. Cushing's syndrome has also been implicated in mania, with presentations ranging from milder mood lability or irritability to severe mania with psychotic features [1]. Exceedingly rare, B12 deficiency can also be a possible cause for secondary mania and has been identified in at least two case reports. In both cases, symptoms were effectively managed with B12 replacement [74, 75].

2.5.8 Substance-induced and medication-induced mania

Substance-induced mania typically occurs in the setting of intoxication or withdrawal. Drugs that can induce mania, whether intoxicated or in a withdrawal state, include alcohol, phencyclidine, hallucinogens, sedatives, hypnotics, anxiolytics, amphetamine, cocaine products, and newer synthetic products (i.e., bath salts) [1].

Certain medications have been demonstrated to cause manic symptoms. For example, the incidence of steroid-induced hypomania or mania is 3.25%, with increased risk at doses greater than 40 milligrams daily of prednisone or prednisolone. However, lower doses have been associated with manic symptoms as well [76]. Antibiotics have also been implicated, particularly antitubercular agents, macrolides, and quinolones [77]. Newer evidence suggests TNF-alpha inhibitors may also be associated with the onset of manic symptoms [78]. Medications commonly utilized in MS that can exacerbate or cause mania include steroids, baclofen, dantrolene, tizanidine, modafinil, and other stimulants [37]. When evaluating whether a medication may be contributing to manic symptoms in a patient, it is essential to consider the potential contribution of the underlying disease process being treated as well.

2.6 Treatment and management strategies

2.6.1 Managing underlying medical condition

If possible, the management of secondary mania should begin with treatment of the underlying illness. Examples can include antibiotics for acute central nervous system infection, controlling a thyroid storm, stabilizing frontal and temporal lobe seizures, aggressive treatment with autoimmune or paraneoplastic syndromes, and adjusting functional neurosurgical device-related side effects.

2.6.2 Pharmacological management

Although the literature is sparse, a general guide appears to utilize mood stabilizers and antipsychotics for the symptomatic management of mania. Little data is available for the treatment of mania among persons with TBI, but some insights include exacerbation of cognitive impairments with valproate but less so than carbamazepine and lithium [32]. Furthermore, intolerance of lithium, which is commonly used as the first-line in bipolar disorders, appears to be an issue with individuals with secondary mania due to TBI, as therapeutic doses are not readily reached [9]. Another reason to possibly avoid lithium is its propensity to lower the seizure threshold, particularly in the TBI population who are at risk of posttraumatic epilepsy [32]. Even less evidence but perhaps more tolerable for the management of mania include anticonvulsants such as lamotrigine and oxcarbazepine and atypical antipsychotics such as risperidone, olanzapine, ziprasidone, and aripiprazole. Jorge et al. colleagues recommend first-line treatment for secondary mania due to TBI as valproate or quetiapine as first-line treatments, given their effectiveness [32]. In secondary mania due to stroke, considerations of mood stabilizers and antipsychotics similarly remain. Still, caution is recommended to utilize agents that further minimize cardio-metabolic risk, as many stroke patients' cerebrovascular accidents are attributed to such factors. In individuals with epilepsy, treatment is focused on stabilization with the seizure, commonly using mood stabilizers that are also used for bipolar disorders. In mania following temporal lobectomy, where mood episodes can last for months, mood stabilizers and antipsychotics can be utilized successfully as well [9].

For individuals with secondary mania due to tumors, similar strategies above can be utilized, such as mood stabilizers and antipsychotics [9]. Still, cases have shown resolution of mania with chemotherapy, radiation therapy, and resection [1]. Furthermore, in patients with MS, it appears there is some more experience utilizing Lithium in addition to the treatments already mentioned. Still, there is a concern for diuresis, which is concerning in MS patients with a neurogenic bladder [9]. In the case of SLE, it may be pertinent to treat acute mania with increased corticosteroids if inflammatory markers are increasing, but if suspecting an iatrogenic corticosteroid cause, consider lowering corticosteroid dose and/or utilizing antipsychotics or mood stabilizers. In hyperthyroidism, caution is advised, particularly with lithium use, due to its effects on the thyroid gland. Lithium should also be avoided, if possible, in individuals with significant fluid and electrolyte shifts [1].

2.6.3 Non-pharmacological interventions

There appears to be no firm evidence for psychotherapeutic treatments for individuals with secondary mania. Supportive therapies aimed at facilitating effective medical and psychiatric management may be the most appropriate approach. As above, treatment of the underlying medical condition should be prioritized, and pharmacologic management of psychiatric symptoms may be considered if required. Providing targeted psychoeducation can help patients and their family members better understand the symptoms, prognosis, and rationale behind the recommended treatment plan. Involving the patient's primary support group in psychoeducation, when feasible, can also provide an opportunity to address family or caregiver concerns about behavior changes and set expectations for the treatment course. Collaborating with the patient and their support system can aid in developing strategies to promote treatment adherence and patient safety, including in the event of symptom recurrence.

2.6.4 Neuromodulation interventions

The utilization of electroconvulsive therapy (ECT) is well-documented for a broad range of neurological and psychiatric disorders. ECT may prove to be effective in many cases of secondary mania as well, but there is some evidence for bipolar depression switching to mania with ECT. Interestingly, in one particular case, ECT-induced mania was effectively stabilized by continuing ECT [79].

There appears to be no evidence of the treatment of mania with other non-invasive neuromodulation interventions. Transcranial magnetic stimulation (TMS) in the treatment of depression, whether unipolar or bipolar, is known to lead to switching to mania and hypomania with the treatment of the left dorsolateral prefrontal cortex seen by increased energy, insomnia, irritability, anxiety, and increased suicidality [80]. Furthermore, hypomania has been described for other non-invasive neuromodulation techniques, such as transcranial direct current stimulation [81].

Invasive functional neurosurgery or neurostimulation devices have no evidence currently for the treatment of mania. On the contrary, there has been evidence for the onset of mania with stimulating devices. Up to 4% of patients who undergo subthalamic nucleus (STN) deep brain stimulation (DBS) for Parkinson's disease have been found to develop mania [9]. Mania has also been implicated in DBS stimulation of the ventral capsule and ventral striatum (VC/VS) for obsessive-compulsive disorder treatment [82].

3. Conclusions

Secondary mania presents a unique and often complex clinical challenge, requiring clinicians to distinguish it from primary bipolar disorder through a detailed evaluation of underlying medical, neurological, or pharmacological causes. The need for an interdisciplinary approach in navigating the multifaceted nature of secondary mania, particularly as its pathophysiology and triggers span multiple domains of medicine, is crucial in successful diagnosis and management. Careful delineation of primary mania, mania, and delirium is essential. Accurate diagnosis and tailored treatment strategies are vital to mitigating the impact of the underlying conditions while managing mood symptoms, as not all treatments for primary mania would prove effective in secondary mania. As our understanding of secondary mania continues to evolve, a commitment to comprehensive patient care—through collaboration between psychiatry, neurology, and other specialties—remains the cornerstone of effective treatment. Early detection, appropriate intervention, and ongoing research are critical in improving outcomes for individuals affected by this complex disorder.

Future research on secondary mania is complicated since there are many diverse causes and mechanisms of pathology. Further research into brain neural networks and circuitry may, in the future, explain the symptoms of mania that are shared between all diverse causes that are not classically defined as non-organic bipolar disorders.

Conflict of interest

The authors declare no conflict of interest.

Author details

Gregory M. Nikogosyan[1*], Emma R. Torncello[2] and Samuel I. MacDonald[2]

1 Department of Psychiatry and Behavioral Sciences, Division of Behavioral Health Consultation and Integration, University of New Mexico School of Medicine, Albuquerque, NM, USA

2 Department of Psychiatry and Behavioral Sciences, University of New Mexico School of Medicine, Albuquerque, NM, USA

*Address all correspondence to: gnikogosyan@salud.unm.edu

References

[1] Torales J, González I, Barrios I, Ventriglio A, Bhugra D. Manic episodes due to medical illnesses. Journal of Nervous and Mental Disease. 2018;**206**(9):733-738

[2] American Psychiatric Association. Diagnostic and Statistical Manual of Mental Disorders. 5th-TR. Washington, DC: American Psychiatric Association; 2022

[3] Engelhardt E, Sudo FK, Alves GS, Laks J. Neuropsychiatric symptoms in brain diseases—Historical foundations. Dementia & neuropsychologia. 2020;**14**(3):324-328. DOI: 10.1590/1980-57642020dn14-030014

[4] Angst J, Marneros A. Bipolarity from ancient to modern times: Conception, birth and rebirth. Journal of Affective Disorders. 2001;**67**(1-3):3-19

[5] Mason BL, Brown ES, Croarkin PE, North C, Suris A. Historical underpinnings of bipolar disorder diagnostic criteria. Behavioral Sciences. 15 Jul 2016;**6**(3):14. DOI: 10.3390/bs6030014

[6] Jorge RE, Robinson RG, Starkstein SE, Arndt SV, Forrester AW, Geisler FH. Secondary mania following traumatic brain injury. The American Journal of Psychiatry. 1993;**150**(6):916-921

[7] Arciniegas DB, Yudofsky SC, Hales RE. The American Psychiatric Publishing Textbook of Neuropsychiatry and Behavioral Neuroscience. American Psychiatric Pub; 2018

[8] Brooks JO, Hoblyn JC. Secondary mania in older adults. American Journal of Psychiatry. 2005;**162**(11):2033-2038

[9] Satzer D, Bond DJ. Mania secondary to focal brain lesions: Implications for understanding the functional neuroanatomy of bipolar disorder. Bipolar Disorders. 2016;**18**(3):205-220

[10] Robinson RG. Primary mania versus secondary mania of HIV/AIDS in Uganda. Asian Journal of Pharmaceutics. 2006;**163**(8):1309-1311

[11] Kim E, Lauterbach EC, Reeve A, Arciniegas DB, Coburn KL, Mendez MF, et al. Neuropsychiatric complications of traumatic brain injury: A critical review of the literature (a report by the ANPA committee on research). The Journal of Neuropsychiatry and Clinical Neurosciences. 2007;**19**(2):106-127

[12] Hibar DP, Westlye LT, Doan NT, Jahanshad N, Cheung JW, Ching CRK, et al. Cortical abnormalities in bipolar disorder: An MRI analysis of 6503 individuals from the ENIGMA bipolar disorder working group. Molecular Psychiatry. 2017;**23**(4):932-942. Available from: https://www.nature.com/articles/mp201773

[13] Barahona-Corrêa JB, Cotovio G, Costa RM, Ribeiro R, Velosa A, Cruz V, et al. Right-Sided Brain Lesions Predominate among Patients with Lesional Mania: Evidence from a Systematic Review and Pooled Lesion Analysis. bioRxiv. London, UK: Cold Spring Harbor Laboratory; 2018

[14] Lee I, Nielsen K, Nawaz U, Hall MH, Öngür D, Keshavan M, et al. Diverse pathophysiological processes converge on network disruption in mania. Journal of Affective Disorders. 2019;**244**:115-123

[15] Ashok AH, Marques TR, Jauhar S, Nour MM, Goodwin GM, Young AH,

et al. The dopamine hypothesis of bipolar affective disorder: The state of the art and implications for treatment. Molecular Psychiatry. 2017;**22**(5):666-679. Available from: https://www.ncbi.nlm.nih.gov/pmc/articles/PMC5401767/

[16] Lee JG, Woo YS, Park SW, Seog DH, Seo MK, Bahk WM. Neuromolecular etiology of bipolar disorder: Possible therapeutic targets of mood stabilizers. Clinical Psychopharmacology and Neuroscience. 2022;**20**(2):228-239

[17] Jun C, Choi Y, Lim SM, Bae S, Hong YS, Kim JE, et al. Disturbance of the glutamatergic system in mood disorders. Experimental Neurobiology. 2014;**23**(1):28-35

[18] Belvederi Murri M, Prestia D, Mondelli V, Pariante C, Patti S, Olivieri B, et al. The HPA axis in bipolar disorder: Systematic review and meta-analysis. Psychoneuroendocrinology. 2016;**63**:327-342

[19] Hu LY, Shen CC, Hu YW, Chen MH, Tsai CF, Chiang HL, et al. Hyperthyroidism and risk for bipolar disorders: A nationwide population-based study. PLoS One. 2013;**8**(8):e73057

[20] Liu Y, Cai H, Han T, Wang YF, Li J, Xie X, et al. Network analysis of comorbid aggressive behavior and testosterone among bipolar disorder patients: A cross-sectional study. Translational Psychiatry. 2024;**14**(1):1-7. Available from: https://www.nature.com/articles/s41398-024-02957-1

[21] Nguyen TV, Low NCP. Hormonal treatments for bipolar disorder: A review of the literature. Journal of Behavioral and Brain Science. 2012;**02**(01):48-59

[22] Arora M, Daughton J. Mania in the medically ill. Current Psychiatry Reports. 2007;**9**(3):232-235

[23] Hansen M, Bering R, Spanggård A, Barata P. Late-onset delirious mania: Does it ring a bell? Bipolar Disorders. 2024;**26**(4):331-334

[24] Baldessarini RJ, Tondo L, Vázquez GH, Undurraga J, Bolzani L, Yildiz A, et al. Age at onset versus family history and clinical outcomes in 1,665 international bipolar-I disorder patients. World Psychiatry. 2012;**11**(1):40-46. Available from: https://www.ncbi.nlm.nih.gov/pmc/articles/PMC3266753/

[25] Dols A, Kupka RW, van Lammeren A, Beekman AT, Sajatovic M, Stek ML. The prevalence of late-life mania: A review. Bipolar Disorders. 2013;**16**(2):113-118

[26] Sami M, Khan H, Nilforooshan R. Late onset mania as an organic syndrome: A review of case reports in the literature. Journal of Affective Disorders. 2015;**188**:226-231

[27] Krauthammer C, Klerman GL. Secondary mania: Manic syndromes associated with antecedent physical illness or drugs. Archives of General Psychiatry. 1978;**35**(11):1333-1339

[28] World Health Organization. ICD-11 [Internet]. International Classification of Diseases 11th Revision. 2022. Available from: https://icd.who.int/en

[29] Graner M, Pointon T, Manton S, Green M, Dennison K, Davis M, et al. Oligoclonal IgG antibodies in multiple sclerosis target patient-specific peptides. PLoS One. 2020;**15**(2):e0228883

[30] Wilson JE, Mart MF, Cunningham C, Shehabi Y, Girard TD, MacLullich AMJ, et al. Delirium. Nature Reviews Disease Primers. 2020;**6**(1):1-26. Available from: https://www.nature.com/articles/s41572-020-00223-4

[31] Hwang DY, Silva GS, Furie KL, Greer DM. Comparative sensitivity of computed tomography vs. magnetic resonance imaging for detecting acute posterior fossa infarct. The Journal of Emergency Medicine. 2012;**42**(5):559-565. Available from: https://pubmed.ncbi.nlm.nih.gov/22305149/

[32] Jorge RE, Arciniegas DB. Mood Disorders After TBI. Psychiatric Clinics of North America. 2014;**37**(1):13-29. Available from: https://www.ncbi.nlm.nih.gov/pmc/articles/PMC3985339/

[33] Lupo M, Siciliano L, Leggio M. From cerebellar alterations to mood disorders: A systematic review. Neuroscience & Biobehavioral Reviews. 2019;**103**:21-28

[34] Shukla S, Bl C, Mukherjee S, Godwin C, Miller M. Mania following head trauma. American Journal of Psychiatry. 1987;**144**(1):93-96

[35] Starkstein SE, Boston JD, Robinson RG. Mechanisms of mania after brain injury. The Journal of Nervous and Mental Disease. 1988;**176**(2):87-100

[36] Santos CO, Caeiro L, Ferro JM, Figueira ML. Mania and stroke: A systematic review. Cerebrovascular Diseases. 2011;**32**(1):11-21

[37] Silbersweig D, Safar LT, Daffner KR. Neuropsychiatry and Behavioral Neurology: Principles and Practice. New York, NY: McGraw Hill Professional; 2020

[38] Heila H, Turpeinen P, Erkinjuntti T. Case study: Mania associated with multiple sclerosis. Journal of the American Academy of Child & Adolescent Psychiatry. 1995;**34**(12):1591-1595

[39] Garfield DH. Multiple sclerosis and affective disorder: 2 case reports of mania with psychosis. Psychotherapy and Psychosomatics. 1985;**44**(1):25-33

[40] Xin GN, Yee KOK, Kiat AJ. A case of bipolar disorder due to multiple sclerosis with episodes of mania. Malaysian Journal of Psychiatry. 2022;**31**(2):92

[41] Kwentus JA, Hart RP, Calabrese V, Hekmati A. Mania as a symptom of multiple sclerosis. Psychosomatics. 1986;**27**(10):729-731

[42] Salem H, Keele CT, Teixeira AL. Multiple sclerosis induced-mania: A clinical challenge. Neuropsychiatry. 2017;**07**(03) [cited 2024 Sep 14]. Available from: http://www.jneuropsychiatry.org/peer-review/multiple-sclerosis-inducedmania-a-clinical-challenge.html

[43] Ebert T, Chapman J, Shoenfeld Y. Anti-ribosomal P-protein and its role in psychiatric manifestations of systemic lupus erythematosus: Myth or reality? Lupus. 2005;**14**(8):571-575

[44] Rizvi S, Farooq F, Shagufta S, Khan AM, Masood Y, Saeed H. Postictal mania versus postictal psychosis. Cureus. 2018;**10**(9):e3338

[45] Schmitz B. Depression and mania in patients with epilepsy. Epilepsia. 2005;**46**:45-49

[46] Byrne A. Hypomania following increased epileptic activity. The British Journal of Psychiatry. 1988;**153**(4):573-574

[47] Nishida T, Kudo T, Nakamura F, Yoshimura M, Matsuda K, Yagi K. Postictal mania associated with frontal lobe epilepsy. Epilepsy & Behavior. 2005;**6**(1):102-110

[48] Bostock ECS, Kirkby KC, Garry MI, Taylor BVM. Comparison of precipitating factors for mania and partial seizures: Indicative of shared pathophysiology? Journal of Affective

Disorders. 2015;**183**:57-67. [cited 2020 May 9]. Available from: https://www.sciencedirect.com/science/article/abs/pii/S0165032715002906

[49] Dhandapani VR. Organic mania secondary to left arteriovenous malformation. Asian Journal of Psychiatry. 2016;**22**:81-82

[50] Wang C, Fipps DC. Primary CNS lymphoma and secondary causes of mania: A case report and literature review. JNP. 2022;**34**(1):84-88

[51] Sokolski KN, Denson TF. Exacerbation of mania secondary to right temporal lobe astrocytoma in a bipolar patient previously stabilized on valproate. Cognitive and Behavioral Neurology. 2003;**16**(4):234

[52] Barahona-Corrêa JB, Cotovio G, Costa RM, Ribeiro R, Velosa A, Silva VC, et al. Right-sided brain lesions predominate among patients with lesional mania: Evidence from a systematic review and pooled lesion analysis. Translational Psychiatry. 2020;**10**:139

[53] Ellen SR, Judd FK, Mijch AM, Cockram A. Secondary mania in patients with HIV infection. The Australian and New Zealand Journal of Psychiatry (London, UK: Sage Journals). 1999

[54] Owe-Larsson MB, Säll L, Salamon E, Allgulander C. HIV infection and psychiatric illness. African Journal of Psychiatry. 2009;**12**(2). [cited 2024 Sep 14]. Available from: https://www.ajol.info/index.php/ajpsy/article/view/43729

[55] Nakimuli-Mpungu E, Musisi S, Mpungu SK, Katabira E. Primary mania versus HIV-related secondary mania in Uganda. AJP. 2006;**163**(8):1349-1354

[56] Nakimuli-Mpungu E, Musisi S, Kiwuwa Mpungu S, Katabira E. Clinical presentation of bipolar mania in HIV-positive patients in Uganda. Psychosomatics. 2009;**50**(4):325-330

[57] Owe-Larsson M, Säll L, Salamon E, Allgulander C. HIV infection and psychiatric illness. African Journal of Psychiatry. 2009;**12**(2):115-128

[58] Mijch AM, Judd FK, Lyketsos CG, Ellen S, Cockram A. Secondary mania in patients with HIV infection. JNP. 1999;**11**(4):475-480

[59] Mitsonis CH, Kararizou E, Dimopoulos N, Triantafyllou N, Kapaki E, Mitropoulos P, et al. Incidence and clinical presentation of neurosyphilis: A retrospective study of 81 cases. International Journal of Neuroscience. 2008;**118**(9):1251-1257

[60] Koehler K, Guth W. The mimicking of mania in "benign" herpes simplex encephalitis. Biological Psychiatry. 1979;**14**(2):405-411

[61] Fisher CM. Hypomanic symptoms caused by herpes simplex encephalitis. Neurology. 1996;**47**(6):1374-1378. DOI: 10.1212/WNL.47.6.1374

[62] Levitz RE. Herpes simplex encephalitis: A review. Heart & Lung. 1998;**27**(3):209-212. DOI: 10.1016/s0147-9563(98)90009-7

[63] Bradshaw MJ, Venkatesan A. Herpes simplex virus-1 encephalitis in adults: Pathophysiology, diagnosis, and management. Neurotherapeutics. 2016;**13**(3):493-508. DOI: 10.1007/s13311-016-0433-7

[64] Chou PH, Ouyang WC, Lan TH, Chan CH. Secondary mania due to AIDS and cryptococcal meningitis in a 78-year-old patient. Psychogeriatrics. 2016;**16**(2):135-138. DOI: 10.1111/psyg.12127

[65] Holikatti PC, Kar N. Psychiatric manifestations in a patient with HIV-associated neurocognitive symptoms and cryptococcal meningitis. Indian Journal of Psychological Medicine. 2012;**34**(4):381-382. DOI: 10.4103/0253-7176.108226

[66] Liang CS, Yang FW. Secondary mania associated with enterococcal meningitis in an elderly patient. General Hospital Psychiatry. 2011;**33**(3):301.e1-301.e3012. DOI: 10.1016/j.genhosppsych.2010.11.002

[67] Spiegel DR, Bayne CE, Wilcox L, Somova M. A case of mania due to cryptococcal meningitis, successfully treated with adjunctive olanzapine, in a patient with acquired immunodeficiency syndrome. General Hospital Psychiatry. 2011;**33**(3):301.e3-301.e301006. DOI: 10.1016/j.genhosppsych.2010.11.004

[68] Johannessen DJ, Wilson LG. Mania with cryptococcal meningitis in two AIDS patients. The Journal of Clinical Psychiatry. 1988;**49**(5):200-201

[69] Tang WK, Hui M, UngvariGS LCM. Cryptococcal meningitis mimicking primary mania in a young female. General Hospital Psychiatry. 2005;**27**(4):301-303. DOI: 10.1016/j.genhosppsych.2005.03.003

[70] Liu T, Gao P, Bu D, Liu D. Association between toxoplasma gondii infection and psychiatric disorders: A cross-sectional study in China. Scientific Reports. 2022;**12**(1):15092. DOI: 10.1038/s41598-022-16420-y

[71] Lekurwale V, Acharya S, Shukla S, Kumar S. Neuropsychiatric manifestations of thyroid diseases. Cureus. 2023;**15**(1):e33987

[72] Sathya A, Radhika R, Mahadevan S, Sriram U. Mania as a presentation of primary hypothyroidism. Singapore Medical Journal. 2009;**50**(2):e65-e67

[73] Stowell CP, Barnhill JW. Acute mania in the setting of severe hypothyroidism. Psychosomatics. 2005;**46**(3):259-261

[74] Goggans FC. A case of mania secondary to vitamin B12 deficiency. American Journal of Psychiatry. 1984;**141**(2):300-301

[75] Gomez-Bernal GJ, Bernal-Perez M. Vitamin B12 deficiency manifested as mania: A case report. Primary Care Companion to Journal Clinical Psychiatry. 2007;**9**(3):238

[76] De Bock M, Sienaert P. Corticosteroids and mania: A systematic review. The World Journal of Biological Psychiatry. 2024;**25**(3):161-174

[77] Lambrichts S, Van Oudenhove L, Sienaert P. Antibiotics and mania: A systematic review. Journal of Affective Disorders. 2017;**219**:149-156

[78] Miola A, Dal Porto V, Meda N, Perini G, Solmi M, Sambataro F. Secondary mania induced by TNF -α inhibitors: A systematic review. Psychiatry and Clinical Neurosciences. 2022;**76**(1):15-21

[79] Thomas RK, White PJ, Dursun S. Treating electroconvulsive therapy–induced mania with more electroconvulsive therapy: Evidence for electroconvulsive therapy as the ultra-mood stabilizer. SAGE Open Medical Case Reports. 2018;**6**:2050313X1879923

[80] Miuli A, Sepede G, Stigliano G, Mosca A, Di Carlo F, d'Andrea G, et al. Hypomanic/manic switch after transcranial magnetic stimulation in mood disorders: A systematic review and meta-analysis. World Journal of Psychiatry. 2021;**11**(8):477-490

[81] Gupta A, Adnan M. Hypomania risk in noninvasive brain stimulation. Cureus. 2018;**10**(2):e2204

[82] Greenberg BD, Malone DA, Friehs GM, Rezai AR, Kubu CS, Malloy PF, et al. Three-year outcomes in deep brain stimulation for highly resistant obsessive–compulsive disorder. Neuropsychopharmacology. 2006;**31**(11):2384-2393

Section 3

What's New in Neuroinflammation in Psychiatry?

Chapter 7

The Role and Importance of Neuroinflammation in Biopsychiatry

Hayriye Soytürk, Ümit Kiliç, Cansu Önal, Ayşegül Yildiz, Özge Kaya and Ayla Gencan

Abstract

Neuroinflammation is an inflammatory response that affects the central nervous system. This process involves the activation of immune cells like microglia and astrocytes, as well as the production of inflammatory chemicals like cytokines and chemokines. Neuroinflammation can be caused by a variety of circumstances, including trauma, infection, autoimmune illnesses, environmental factors, any stress scenario, and neurodegenerative diseases. Neuroinflammation is thought to be connected with a variety of psychiatric disorders. These illnesses include depression, anxiety disorders, schizophrenia, and bipolar disorder. Research in biological neuropsychiatry can assist in establishing future treatment options by demonstrating how neuroinflammation contributes to illness. This book chapter explains how neuroinflammation is a major contributor to mental illnesses, as well as how this topic is significant in study and therapy.

Keywords: psychiatric disorders, inflammation, neuroinflammation, biomarkers, cytokines

1. Introduction

Psychiatric disorders are complex conditions that affect millions of people worldwide, significantly reducing the quality of life. Psychiatric illnesses such as depression, schizophrenia, bipolar disorder, and anxiety disorders impact emotional, cognitive, and social functions, leading to serious consequences on both individual and societal levels. These disorders are associated with critical risk factors such as physical health issues, loss of productivity, and suicide. However, the challenges encountered in diagnosis and treatment further complicate the nature of psychiatric disorders [1]. Schizophrenia (SCZ), major depressive disorder (MDD), and alcohol use disorder are among the psychiatric illnesses that most frequently lead to hospital admissions [2, 3]. Currently, treatment strategies are generally determined based on the clinical course and symptoms of the patient. However, certain symptoms or specific patients may exhibit variations that do not fit established categories. The changing nature of symptoms over time can result in multiple diagnoses for the same individual. Neurological and psychiatric disorders can arise from exogenous stress factors and genetic predispositions. When mental disorders are left untreated, neurophysiological changes may occur, potentially leading to neurological and psychiatric diseases [4]. Although recent advancements in neurobiology, genetics, and neuroendocrinology have contributed to a better understanding of the pathophysiology of psychiatric disorders, there remain many unknowns awaiting further exploration in this field. Biological research on psychiatric disorders indicates that neurotransmitter imbalances in the brain play a crucial role in the development of these conditions. Specifically, imbalances in neurotransmitters such as dopamine, serotonin, and glutamate are significant in the pathophysiology of disorders like depression, schizophrenia, and bipolar disorder. Disruptions in the functioning of these neurotransmitters can lead to severe impairments in mood, motivation, and cognitive functions. Inflammation seems to rise with disease and is one of the body's primary defenses against damage or infection. The nonspecific reaction known as acute inflammation is typified by pain, swelling, and fever. Blood flow rises and blood vessels become more permeable when leukocytes migrate and become activated at the site of damage. This enables cells and molecules to leave the blood vessels and reach the wounded tissue [5].

The signs of chronic inflammation are often systemic and less evident than those of acute infection. Numerous chronic illnesses, such as diabetes, Alzheimer's disease, cardiovascular and cerebrovascular disease, and some types of cancer, are influenced by chronic inflammation. Chronic inflammation in the brain has relatively distinct features than inflammation in other tissues [6].

2. Pathophysiology of psychiatric disorders: Neuroinflammation, physiological mechanisms, biomarkers, treatment methods, and genetic-environmental dynamics

2.1 Brain and neuroinflammation

Neuroinflammation is defined as an inflammatory response of the central nervous system (CNS). This response involves immune system cells located in the CNS, infiltration of immune system cells from peripheral tissues into the brain tissue, and interaction of inflammation-related mediator molecules (cytokines, chemokines, free oxygen radicals, etc.) with brain tissue cells. The CNS has a special structure called the blood-brain barrier, which restricts the passage of ions, molecules, and cells from the circulation into the brain and spinal cord. This restrictive barrier helps to protect the CNS from toxins, pathogens, inflammation, injury, and various diseases, as well as tightly regulate CNS homeostasis, which is critical for proper neuronal function. For many years, the brain was considered a privileged region in terms of immunity due to the silent inflammatory response and the presence of protective brain barriers. Today, it is thought that immune cells are present in the meninges, that there is a bidirectional relationship between the immune system and the CNS, and that neuroinflammation may play an important role in psychiatric disorders. The best example of the bidirectional relationship between the immune system and the brain among psychiatric disorders is major depressive disorder. The hypothesis that proinflammatory cytokine increase plays a role in the etiopathogenesis of depression is called the "Neuroinflammatory Hypothesis of Depression." This cytokine increase may play a role in many mechanisms such as dysregulation in the hypothalamic-pituitary-adrenal axis underlying depression, changes in monoamine and glutamate systems, and impaired neuroplasticity. In light of the current evidence, it can be said that increased inflammation is a feature detected in almost all psychiatric disorders [7].

The complement system, a collection of proteins that, when triggered, combine to form a complex molecular structure that kills cells—typically bacteria and parasites—is also involved in inflammation. Cytokines are the most significant of these proteins. Cytokines are essential molecules that control inflammation and have a significant impact on the immune system. Numerous immune cells as well as cells outside the immune system manufacture them. In addition to their many other uses, cytokines can affect how inflammatory cells behave [7].

Microglial activation is a key factor in neuroinflammation. Inflammatory cells outside the brain are comparatively few in the brain. Peripheral inflammatory cells, which are linked to microglia, carry out some of the same defensive tasks as these cells do throughout the body. Other roles of microglia in the brain include transporting neurotransmitters, maintaining and pruning synapses, and phagocytosing—or engulfing—damaged and fragmented cells [8].

Activated microglia phagocytose the cells or proteins that initiate the inflammatory response and release inflammatory cytokines. The blood-brain barrier (BBB) can be disrupted by microglial activation and the release of proinflammatory cytokines [9].

Studies have also been conducted on the use of anti-inflammatory medications in the treatment of persistent mental illnesses, albeit not yet, to a degree that can direct clinical practice. It is generally known that a portion of individuals with schizophrenia have neuroinflammation, particularly in the dorsolateral prefrontal cortex, with considerable elevations in inflammatory markers, such as different cytokines. It is still unclear what causes cortical inflammation in schizophrenia, though. One can go upstream of effector immune molecules to transcription factors for clues to possible microenvironmental triggers and/or intracellular abnormalities in immunoregulation [10].

Regulates the expression of inflammatory genes. Here, we concentrate on nuclear factor kappa B (NF-κB), the "master immune regulator," and examine the data that suggests NF-κB dysregulation either causes or contributes to neuroinflammation in patients. In contrast to research that treat patients as a single, homogenous group, we highlight the usefulness of "immune biotyping" as a technique for analyzing immune-related transcripts and proteins in patient tissue as well as cerebral insights into NF-κB in schizophrenia. Targeting this important immune regulator is a relatively under-studied topic that might help lessen symptoms in schizophrenia by creating new or revised medications, despite the fact that NF-κB's ubiquitous nature presents significant challenges to drug development [11].

2.2 The complex pathophysiology of psychiatric disorders

Neurotransmitter systems, particularly dopamine and serotonin, play a central role in the pathophysiology of mental disorders [12]. However, the limited efficacy of current treatments suggests that additional biological pathways may be involved in these disorders [13]. The concept of homeostatic processes highlights how disruptions in both physiological and psychological systems can lead to psychopathology. Therefore, it is emphasized that a multi-layered analysis of these processes is required [14].

The complexity of mental disorders makes it challenging to unravel the intricate interactions between genetic, epigenetic, and environmental factors. This complexity not only increases the need for ongoing research but also raises concerns about the potential effects of genetic determinism and the stigma associated with mental illness [13]. For instance, in diseases such as schizophrenia and major depressive disorder, genetic predisposition, involving the role of hundreds of genes, is a significant factor [12]. Furthermore, epigenetic mechanisms that alter gene expression in response to environmental factors are increasingly recognized as critical to understanding mental disorders. Specifically, environmental influences such as early-life stress can lead to epigenetic changes that heighten the risk of developing conditions like post-traumatic stress disorder (PTSD) [15].

In addition to neurotransmitter imbalances, neurotrophic factors that regulate synaptic plasticity and neuronal survival also play a critical role in the pathophysiology of psychiatric disorders. Among these factors, brain-derived neurotrophic factor (BDNF) is a key mechanism that supports the strengthening of synaptic connections and the survival of neurons in the brain. BDNF binds to TrkB receptors, activating signaling pathways such as MAPK-ERK and PI3K-Akt, which promote synaptic plasticity [16]. This mechanism fosters neuronal survival, strengthens synaptic connections, and promotes synaptogenesis. BDNF's ability to enhance neurotransmitter release and modulate synaptic activity is particularly critical in regulating neuroplasticity in disorders such as depression, schizophrenia, and bipolar disorder [17]. Additionally, BDNF's role in regulating synaptic function is seen as an important target for improving the efficacy of psychiatric treatments. Similar to signaling pathways governed by neurotransmitters like glutamate and gamma-aminobutyric acid (GABA), BDNF induces various permissive and instructive effects in synaptic signaling, sometimes leading to seemingly contradictory forms of regulation [18]. While BDNF's full role in disease pathophysiology remains unclear, it is understood that BDNF serves as a crucial mechanism in the efficacy of psychiatric treatments, particularly antidepressants and mood stabilizers.

In addition to BDNF's effects on neuroplasticity, the endocannabinoid system (ECS) is also known to play a critical role in the development of psychiatric disorders. This system is composed of cannabinoids, endocannabinoids (eCBs), and cannabinoid receptors (CBRs), which are activated by metabolic enzymes. ECS demonstrates biological and therapeutic effects in psychiatric disorders, particularly through modulating signaling pathways at ion channels and in glial cells *via* G protein-coupled receptors (GPCRs) [19]. Specifically, it regulates neurotransmitter release at synapses in the central nervous system (CNS) through retrograde signaling, revealing that both GABAergic and glutamatergic systems are influenced by the ECS. Endocannabinoids such as anandamide (AEA) and 2-arachidonoylglycerol (2-AG) have been shown to inhibit neurotransmitter release *via* retrograde signaling at presynaptic CB1R receptors, which plays a crucial role in identifying molecular targets for psychiatric disorders like depression and anxiety [20]. Mechanisms such as depolarization-induced suppression of inhibition (DSI) and long-term depression (LTD) further support the role of retrograde eCB signaling in the brain in the development of psychiatric disorders [21].

The ECS also plays a key role in synaptic communication between neurons and microglia, and alterations in this system are associated with various psychiatric disorders. Notably, the conditional deletion of CB2 receptors in microglia and dopaminergic neurons highlights neuro-immune cross-talk, emphasizing the significance of ECS in neurological functions and dysfunctions [22, 23]. Consequently, therapies targeting endocannabinoid signaling offer potential in the treatment of psychiatric illnesses.

The components of the endocannabinoid system (ECS) participate in numerous physiological processes, including immune and metabolic regulatory functions that help maintain the organism's homeostasis. Microglial cells, the primary contributors to innate immune responses within the brain, play a critical role in neuroinflammation, which is pivotal in the progression of neuropsychiatric disorders [24]. The increased stress-induced levels of neuro-immune signaling molecules in the brain are among the key factors contributing to the development of these disorders. In this context, CB2 receptors play an essential role in regulating immune responses during these processes [25].

Schizophrenia (SCZ) is a severe psychiatric syndrome affecting 1% of the global population, and its treatment is challenging, with antipsychotic medications not being effective for every patient. Although the etiology and pathogenesis of schizophrenia are not fully understood, the role of the endocannabinoid system (ECS) in this disorder is receiving increasing attention [26]. According to the DSM-V, the diagnosis of schizophrenia requires the presence of at least two characteristic criteria (delusions, hallucinations, disorganized speech, severely disorganized or catatonic behavior, and negative symptoms) for more than 6 months. This diagnosis is purely clinical. Currently, there are no reliable physical examination findings or biomarkers to aid in diagnosis; however, magnetic resonance spectroscopy has shown that alterations in glutamatergic transmission in various brain regions are associated with SCZ [27, 28]. Since the 1960s, the pathogenetic theory of SCZ has been based on neurotransmitters, particularly dopamine. Some experimental and clinical data support this theory. Genetic studies have highlighted the link between SCZ and mutations in the DRD2 gene, which encodes the dopamine D2 receptor [29]. An increased density of dopamine receptors in the striatum has been observed in patients with SCZ [30]. Schizophrenia is characterized by dysregulation of glutamate and dopamine systems, leading to cognitive impairments and psychotic symptoms. Excessive glutamate release affects prefrontal-striatal-cerebellar and thalamocortical pathways, contributing to cognitive dysfunction [31].

Another disorder, depression, is associated with monoaminergic axon degeneration affecting serotonin and norepinephrine pathways. This degeneration results in hypomonoaminergic states that manifest as negative symptoms [32]. Changes in ECS components, particularly CB1 receptors (CB1R), have been reported in the brains of patients with schizophrenia [33]. However, these changes show inconsistencies depending on factors such as age, sex, and schizophrenia subtypes. While postmortem studies suggest alterations in CB1R and gene expression in schizophrenic brains, these findings have not yet led to definitive conclusions. Additionally, the role of CB2 receptors (CB2R) in schizophrenia has been less studied compared to CB1Rs, partly due to limited evidence of neural CB2Rs in healthy brains [26, 34]. In schizophrenia, changes in gamma band oscillations associated with GABAergic interneuron dysfunction are common and suggest a neuroinflammatory component [35]. In contrast to the hypermonoaminergic states observed in schizophrenia, the pathophysiology of depression involves neurodegenerative processes without loss of monoaminergic neurons [32].

The endocannabinoid system (ECS) plays a significant role in various psychiatric disorders, including autism spectrum disorder (ASD), attention deficit hyperactivity disorder (ADHD), anxiety, major depression, bipolar disorder, and schizophrenia [36, 37]. In autism, the ECS is known to regulate metabolic and cellular pathways such as nutrient intake, energy metabolism, and immune system control. ASD is also characterized by immune system irregularities, and dysregulation of CB2 receptors and ECS enzymes supports the role of ECS in immunological disturbances associated with these disorders. Changes in endocannabinoid (eCB) signaling in neurodevelopmental disorders may be related to exposure to cannabis and cannabinoids during the prenatal period or adolescence. Specifically, cannabis use during pregnancy may increase adverse outcomes for women and neonates [37–39].

Many neurological disorders, such as epilepsy, migraine, Alzheimer's disease, Parkinson's disease, and multiple sclerosis, are commonly comorbid with psychiatric disorders [40]. Traumatic brain injury (TBI), a common injury that leads to changes in brain function, is highly comorbid with psychiatric disorders. TBI is associated with issues such as substance abuse, antisocial behaviors, and impulsivity. In relation to neuro-immune-microbiome cross-talk, the role of the ECS in these comorbidities is gaining importance. However, these comorbidities both increase disease burden and complicate treatment. Early research on the comorbidity of psychiatric and neurological disorders also faces challenges, including the inability to determine the temporal sequence of relationships [41, 42].

Understanding the biological processes associated with psychiatric disorders highlights the importance of neuro-immune interactions. Specifically, neuroinflammation mediated by microglial cells plays a significant role in the pathophysiology of psychiatric diseases such as depression, schizophrenia, and bipolar disorder. The regulatory function of the endocannabinoid system in immune responses and its interactions with microglial cells are considered critical mechanisms in the development and progression of psychiatric disorders.

In addition to the regulatory effects of the endocannabinoid system on neurotransmitter functions, tryptophan metabolism is also an important factor in the development of psychiatric disorders. The tryptophan metabolic pathway is increasingly recognized as a critical link between various systems, including the immune-inflammatory response in the nervous system, and plays a significant role in stress, inflammation, and neurotransmission involving the kynurenine pathway, serotonin (5-HT), and glutamate [43]. Enzymes and metabolites within this pathway are highly associated with both neurological disorders, such as Alzheimer's, Parkinson's, Huntington's diseases, multiple sclerosis, autism, and epilepsy, as well as psychiatric disorders, including depression, schizophrenia, and bipolar disorder, all of which exhibit high rates of comorbidity [44]. Understanding the upstream and downstream effects of tryptophan metabolism is essential for gaining a comprehensive understanding of its mechanism of action. This knowledge supports the shift from mechanism-oriented to disease-oriented drug development, particularly in neuropsychiatric disorders [45].

Tryptophan (TRP), chemically known as 2-amino-3-(1H-indol-3-yl) propanoic acid, is an essential alpha-amino acid required for protein synthesis, yet it is one of the least abundant amino acids in cells and proteins [46]. TRP can only be obtained through diet and serves as a crucial substrate in the synthesis of various bioactive compounds, including serotonin, melatonin, kynurenine (KYN), indole, tryptamine, vitamin B3, and proteins [47]. The metabolism of TRP regulates various physiological processes and homeostasis through the production of these bioactive compounds. However, only free TRP can participate in metabolism and cross the blood-brain barrier (BBB) [48].

TRP is metabolized through three pathways: the kynurenine pathway (KP), the serotonin pathway (SP), and the indole pathway (IP):

Kynurenine pathway (KP): A significant portion of TRP metabolism is directed toward the kynurenine pathway, which plays important roles in the nervous system, immune response, and inflammation. TRP is metabolized by the enzymes indoleamine 2,3-dioxygenase (IDO) and tryptophan 2,3-dioxygenase (TDO) to produce bioactive compounds like kynurenine (KYN) [49]. These metabolites are associated with neurological and psychiatric disorders. Notably, the conversion of TRP to neurotoxic metabolites such as quinolinic acid (QUIN) in microglia and macrophages contributes to neuronal cell death and chronic brain dysfunction. This process plays a significant role in the pathophysiology of depression, schizophrenia, and other psychiatric disorders. Levels of QUIN and other kynurenine metabolites are closely related to the severity and progression of these disorders [50].

Serotonin pathway (SP): A small portion of TRP is metabolized by tryptophan hydroxylase (TPH) to 5-hydroxytryptophan (5-HTP) and subsequently by aromatic amino acid decarboxylase (AAAD) to serotonin. Serotonin regulates many neurological functions, including mood, cognition, and behavior. The serotonin transporter (SERT) plays a crucial role in maintaining serotonin levels in the brain. Serotonin is further metabolized by monoamine oxidase (MAO) to 5-hydroxyindoleacetic acid (5-HIAA) or to N-acetylserotonin (NAS), which is then converted to melatonin. Melatonin is involved in regulating circadian rhythms and gut health, contributing to the regulation of altered rhythms and gut permeability in psychiatric disorders. These processes play a significant role in the pathophysiology of depression, anxiety, and other psychiatric disorders [46, 51].

Indole pathway (IP): Microorganisms in the gastrointestinal system convert TRP into molecules like indole and its derivatives, regulating gut health and inflammatory responses. These metabolites can enhance serotonin release and may play a role in the development of psychiatric disorders such as depression and anxiety through gut-microbiome-brain interactions [52].

2.3 Gene therapy of psychiatric disorders

Gene therapy can provide significant therapeutic benefits in the treatment of neurodegenerative diseases through a variety of pathways, including correction of pathogenic mechanisms, neuroprotection, neurorestoration, and symptom control. Therapeutic efficacy depends on the correct timing and spatial specificity of disease pathogenesis and gene expression. Furthermore, ensuring the most complete gene delivery in the target structure while preventing leakage to neighboring regions is a significant challenge. Recently, interventional MRI-guided convection-enhanced delivery (iMRI-CED) technique has become the gold standard for real-time verification of accurate vector delivery, and this development may accelerate the translation of gene therapies for the treatment of diseases such as Parkinson's, Huntington's, and Alzheimer's [53].

In addition, Psychological diseases are a complex set of disorders, with high clinical variability in terms of onset, severity, and progression of the disease. It will require progressive research efforts such as identifying the genetic factors of the disease, developing specific biomarkers, and designing effective therapeutic methods. Gene therapy in the treatment of psychological diseases is a relatively new and experimental field, and research in this area is progressing rapidly. However, genetic intervention holds promise in the future for the treatment of some psychological diseases (Depression, Schizophrenia, Bipolar or Anxiety Disorders, OCD) known to develop under the influence of genetic factors based on their genetic and biological basis [54–57]. Gene therapy aims to target and change genetic variants that cause psychological disorders. Gene therapy can be designed to correct or prevent these mutations. Some genes associated with psychiatric disorders have been identified, but these types of genes are not genetic disorders with a complete Mendelian inheritance [57]. Therefore, it is difficult to develop a gene therapy that allows them to cure a disease gene by replacing it with a healthy gene. For this reason, in experimental neuroscience studies, there are limited studies showing that gene therapy approaches have an effect by changing behavioral parameters through molecular and cellular interventions in animal models of various psychiatric disorders such as drug addiction, affective disorders, psychoses, and dementia [58].

The challenge in gene therapy in the neurological and psychiatric fields is to find suitable vectors to transfer genes into the nervous system. First, neurons in the adult brain are postmitotic, and the most effective gene therapy vectors, modified retroviruses, work by integrating their transgenes into the host DNA during cell division [59]. Second, the brain is heterogeneous, and certain gene transfer vectors infect certain types of neurons more easily than others, making target cell selection difficult [60]. Psychological illnesses are often associated with imbalances in brain chemistry. Therefore, gene therapy in psychological illnesses can target biological and neurological mechanisms related to the brain and nervous system. For example, due to the clinical and etiological heterogeneity of major depressive disorder, it has been difficult to explain its pathophysiology. Current neurobiological theories are based on studies involving psychosocial stress and stress hormones, neurotransmitters such as serotonin, norepinephrine, dopamine, glutamate and gamma-aminobutyric acid (GABA), neurocircuitry, neurotrophic factors, and circadian rhythms [61]. (Hasler) Some conditions are resistant to oral pharmacotherapies. Levels of neurotransmitters such as serotonin, dopamine, or GABA can be regulated by gene therapy. Antidepressant treatments, including psychological and biological approaches, should be specifically tailored to the patient and their disease state [62]. Schizophrenia is a disease that can cause genetic defects in the dopamine and glutamate systems. To correct these defects, gene therapy techniques can correct neurotransmitter imbalances by targeting the relevant genes [63]. Additionally, efforts have been made to restore dopamine synthesis and neurotransmission through viral gene therapy for Parkinson's disease. Current treatments, such as dopamine agonists, monoamine oxidase inhibitors, and other symptomatic medications, have limited efficacy. Gene therapy using rAAV2 (recombinant adeno-associated virus) has shown promising results when targeted to the putamen or midbrain. Clinical trials have shown improvements in motor function, cognitive skills, and other symptoms, particularly with early intervention. Upstaza™, a gene therapy approved by the European Medicines Agency (EMA) and the Medicines and Healthcare Products Regulatory Agency (MHRA), has consistently improved motor development, autonomic symptoms, and Cerebrospinal fluid (CSF) markers, with a decreased frequency of oculogyric crises (OGCs), and improved motor scores [64]. More advanced approaches aim to directly target dopaminergic deficits in midbrain structures such as the substantia nigra and ventral tegmental area (VTA). Midbrain treatments with rAAV2-AADC gene therapy have resulted in significant improvements in motor function and resolution of OGC, with high success rates in children under 10 years of age. Additionally, antisense oligonucleotide (ASO) strategies have been shown to increase levels of Dopa Decarboxylase (DDC) protein, as well as its downstream product serotonin, in lymphoblastoid cells derived from patients with Aromatic l-amino acid decarboxylase deficiency (AADCD) to restore normal mRNA splicing [64, 65].

With the recent development of other gene therapies such as CRISPR (clustered regularly interspaced short 2 palindromic repeats) studies (GWAS), deletion of target genes and addition of others have been shown to reduce certain traits and tendencies associated with psychiatric disorders such as depression, bipolar disorder, and schizophrenia [66].

Genome editing technologies clustered regularly interspaced short palindromic repeats (CRISPR/Cas9) are a very promising tool for treating genetic diseases. CRISPR/Cas9 can reveal the biological mechanisms of psychiatric disorders at the basic research level and provide a convenient clinical approach for use in the diagnosis and treatment of psychiatric disorders [67]. CRISPR/Cas systems make it possible to detect and investigate the complex relationship between the genotype and phenotype of neuronal cells by creating new genetic tools that can both alter the DNA sequence and affect its function at higher levels of the genetic information flow [68].

iPSCs (induced pluripotent stem cells) are an important tool for studying neurodevelopmental disorders (NDD) because they mimic the differentiation process of the developing embryo into neurons. These cells can be used to study the genetic and molecular basis of neuropsychiatric diseases such as schizophrenia (SZ) and autism spectrum disorder (ASD). Neurons derived from iPSCs can be compared with patients and healthy controls to investigate abnormalities such as neurodevelopmental changes, cell proliferation rate, migration ability, neurite morphology, and electrophysiological properties. However, genetic and epigenetic differences in iPSCs can affect the differentiation ability of the cells [69]. Therefore, isogenic cell models are useful for studying the effects of specific mutations. For example, alternative neuronal cell models, such as SH-SY5Y cell lines, have been used to study the functional effects of mutations such as SHANK2. Increased glutamatergic markers were observed in cells cultured with B-27, and this was interpreted as B-27 may produce glutamatergic SH-SY5Y cells. These findings provide important information about the molecular basis of neuropsychiatric diseases [70].

While most current clinical trials using viral gene therapy have focused on neurodegenerative disorders, these trials have demonstrated its applicability to treat CNS diseases by altering specific networks in the brain [71]. Carlezon et al. (1998) demonstrated that drug-seeking behavior was significantly altered in a rat model of cocaine addiction using viral gene transfer techniques [72]. Even if suitable working models are available, detailed exploration of the brain circuits and various brain regions thought to be involved in the disease process is critical to generating a gene therapy. Human functional imaging has been particularly important for this process in psychiatric disorders because targets identified through this research can be studied at a more molecular level in animal systems [71].

Alexander and colleagues have suggested that the p11 protein expressed in the nucleus accumbens region is an important mediator of depression in humans and mice. They have shown that mice overexpressing p11, which plays a role in the activation of two receptors for serotonin, 5-HT1B and 5-HT4, have increased the activity of 5-HT1B serotonin receptors expressed by striatal neurons in the nucleus accumbens. In addition, in order to investigate whether these results have any relevance to depression in humans, they have reported that p11 expression in postmortem nucleus accumbens brain tissues from individuals with and without depression at the time of death was much lower in the nucleus accumbens of depressed individuals compared to healthy individuals. These new findings may indicate the nucleus accumbens p11 protein is an important mediator of depression and may be considered as one of the new therapeutic targets for drug development [73].

The primary tools currently used are modified viruses called viral vectors that exploit the ability of viruses such as herpes simplex virus type 1 (HSV-1) to transfer their genetic material into target cells and thereby efficiently integrate the therapeutic gene of interest. In this approach, replication-incompetent amplicons derived from HSV-1 are used to deliver genetic material to brain regions. These amplicons offer the advantages of low toxicity, broad DNA carrying capacity, widespread cellular tropism, and low insertional mutagenicity [74].

Another example is lentivirus, an RNA-based retrovirus from the human immunodeficiency virus family. Lentivirus (LV) is derived from HIV-1, which can transfer genes to both dividing and non-dividing cells and provides long-term transgene expression. However, integration of LV into the host genome can lead to undesirable consequences. To overcome this problem, non-integrating Integration-deficient LV vectors (IDLVs) have been developed. Although IDLVs are commonly used for vaccine delivery and immunotherapy, their use in neurological disorders is rare. The use of IDLV-modified stem cells in the treatment of diseases such as X-ALD and Metachromatic leukodystrophy (MLD) has reached the clinical stage of application [75].

The first study to use a lentiviral vector for gene delivery in the human brain, lentivirus, has been initiated in a clinical trial to increase dopamine synthesis in the striatum of patients with Parkinson's disease (PD) Also gene delivery vehicle for neurological gene transfer in PD gene therapy is adeno-associated virus (AAV) [76].

In the treatment of neuropsychological diseases, the efficient delivery of drugs to the brain is a major challenge because most drugs cannot cross the blood-brain barrier (BBB). This hurdle poses a significant challenge in the development of effective treatments for neuropsychological diseases such as Alzheimer's, Parkinson's, and depression. Among the most recent studies, nanocarrier-based drug delivery systems can enable drugs to cross the BBB and reach brain tissue directly. However, the short residence time of these carriers in the body limits the effectiveness of the treatment. Therefore, modification of carrier surfaces with polymers, cell-penetrating peptides and glycoproteins can help extend the residence time in brain regions and increase bioavailability. These modifications may promise important solutions for more targeted and effective drug delivery in the treatment of neuropsychological diseases [77].

Extracellular vesicles (EVs) are promising tools in gene therapy as biocompatible and non-immunogenic carriers. EVs can be engineered to carry therapeutic molecules and are capable of crossing the blood-brain barrier. However, effective EV therapy requires a better understanding of the basic biological processes such as cellular production, loading, distribution, and cellular delivery [78]. A study examining protein markers in small extracellular vesicles (PsEVs) derived from plasma from patients with Alzheimer's disease (AD) and mild cognitive impairment (MCI) showed that PsEV concentrations were higher in AD and MCI patients than in healthy controls, and that amyloid-β (1–42) and p-Tau expression was increased. Additionally, markers of synaptic dysfunction and neuroinflammation (synaptophysin, TNF-α, IL-1β, GFAP) were increased in MCI and AD. These biomarkers in PsEVs may improve the diagnostic accuracy of AD and highlight the role of synaptic dysfunction and neuroinflammation in disease progression [79]. Although the production of EVs at a clinical scale is challenging, packaging proteins, small hairpin RNAs (shRNAs), miRNAs, circular RNAs (circRNAs), and mRNAs into EVs to produce EVs offers significant potential in treating genetic diseases [78].

In a study investigating the potential of cell-penetrating peptides (CPPs) to cross the blood-brain barrier (BBB), CPPs such as Tat 47–57, penetratin, apidaesin, and oncocin were tested for their ability to cross the BBB. Tat 47–57 and apidaesin were able to penetrate human brain capillary endothelial cells, whereas penetratin was not. Furthermore, CPPs facilitate the passage of efflux markers such as mannitol and propranolol, providing a potential pathway for brain delivery. These results may enable the development of brain delivery strategies *via* CPPs [80].

Studies combining psychiatric disorders may increase sample size to identify small effect genes and examine rare genetic variants to predict treatment response. Identifying these genetic variants may pave the way for personalized medicine, improving clinical outcomes and reducing morbidity and mortality. Targeted gene therapy has made significant progress in the treatment of neurological disorders. Recent technological innovations include methods such as viral vectors, nanoparticles, polymer-mediated gene delivery, engineered microRNA, and CRISPR-based therapeutics. These techniques have profound applications in the treatment of common diseases such as Parkinson's, Alzheimer's, autism spectrum disorder, as well as Amyotrofik lateral skleroz (ALS), spinal muscular atrophy, and rare genetic diseases [81].

2.4 Epigenetics

Epigenetics refers to molecular modifications that regulate gene expression without altering the underlying DNA sequence. These changes, which include DNA methylation, histone modifications, and the activity of non-coding RNAs (ncRNAs), can influence cellular processes such as chromatin accessibility, transcriptional regulation, RNA stability, and protein translation [82, 83]. These epigenetic mechanisms collectively play a critical role in orchestrating normal development and physiological processes, as well as mediating interactions between the environment and genetic material [84, 85]. While some epigenetic changes are heritable across cell divisions or even generations, many are dynamic and occur in response to environmental factors such as dietary habits, stress, toxin exposure, and lifestyle [86].

Psychiatric disorders, such as depression, anxiety disorders, bipolar disorder (BD), and post-traumatic stress disorder (PTSD), are increasingly understood to result from a complex interplay between genetic predisposition and environmental influences [87]. While these conditions often have a genetic basis, external factors such as stressful life events, poverty, migration, alcohol consumption, and microbiota alterations significantly shape the expression of susceptibility genes [88]. In particular, specific epigenetic modifications, such as DNA methylation, have been linked to an increased risk of mental illnesses like schizophrenia and depression. These methylation changes affect genes involved in critical processes, including neuronal signaling, neuroendocrine regulation, and immune function, further emphasizing the role of epigenetic regulation in psychiatric conditions [89]. One critical pathway involves the activation of the hypothalamic-pituitary-adrenal (HPA) axis in response to chronic stress, which induces molecular changes affecting stress regulation and emotional functioning [90].

In this context, epigenetics, as a rapidly advancing field in biological research, has emerged as a crucial area of study in psychiatry [91]. Epigenetic mechanisms influence diverse physiological and pathological processes by altering chromatin accessibility, thereby regulating gene expression at both localized and genome-wide scales [84, 92, 93]. Its importance lies in its ability to elucidate how environmental factors regulate gene expression through mechanisms such as DNA methylation, histone modifications, and non-coding RNAs. These epigenetic processes provide a robust framework for understanding the dual contributions of genetic and environmental factors to the onset and progression of psychiatric disorders [94]. Neuroepigenetic research continues to uncover specific patterns of gene regulation linked to mental health conditions, emphasizing the transformative potential of this field [95]. By bridging genetic predispositions and environmental exposures, epigenetics offers a powerful lens to study psychiatric vulnerability [96]. In the next section, we will explore specific examples of how epigenetic research has illuminated the mechanisms underlying various psychiatric disorders, providing insights into both their pathophysiology and potential therapeutic approaches.

The glucocorticoid system plays a pivotal role in the regulation of emotional responses and stress adaptation, making it a critical area of interest in the study of fear-related psychiatric disorders such as post-traumatic stress disorder (PTSD) and specific phobias. Extensive evidence from both animal and human studies highlights the system's influence on memory processes, particularly in the consolidation, retrieval, and extinction of emotional memories [96, 97]. Dysregulation of the hypothalamic-pituitary-adrenal (HPA) axis, often mediated through altered glucocorticoid signaling, has been implicated in the persistence of maladaptive emotional states and aversive memories, which are hallmark features of these disorders [98].

In their 2004 study, Weaver et al. investigated how maternal behavior affects the stress responses of offspring through epigenetic changes in rats. High levels of maternal care (frequent licking, grooming, and arched-back nursing) were shown to reduce DNA methylation at the glucocorticoid receptor (GR) gene promoter in the hippocampus, increasing GR expression. This reduced methylation emerged within the first week of life, persisted into adulthood, and was associated with improved stress regulation *via* the hypothalamic-pituitary-adrenal (HPA) axis. Cross-fostering experiments confirmed that maternal behavior was responsible for these epigenetic changes. Additionally, histone acetylation and transcription factor (NGFI-A) binding were identified as critical mechanisms. Importantly, the study demonstrated that these epigenetic changes were reversible, as treatment with a histone deacetylase inhibitor normalized GR expression and stress responses. The authors concluded that maternal care programs the offspring's epigenome, highlighting how early-life experiences can shape long-term health and behavior [99].

Building on this work, explored whether similar epigenetic mechanisms operate in humans, focusing on the effects of childhood abuse on the glucocorticoid receptor gene (NR3C1-encoding the GR, is integral to regulating the HPA axis response to stress *via* cortisol binding). Researchers focus on the methylation status of the NR3C1 promoter and its expression patterns, as these epigenetic modifications influence GR expression and contribute to stress reactivity and anxiety-related phenotypes in the hippocampus [100]. In suicide victims with a history of childhood abuse, they observed increased DNA methylation at the NR3C1 promoter, reduced glucocorticoid receptor mRNA levels, and disrupted NGFI-A transcription factor binding, leading to decreased GR activity. These changes were absent in suicide victims without childhood abuse or individuals with no history of abuse or suicide. The findings suggest that childhood adversity induces long-lasting epigenetic modifications that impair HPA axis regulation, increasing vulnerability to stress-related disorders and suicide. McGowan et al. concluded that early-life experiences leave "epigenetic marks" on the brain, influencing mental health outcomes later in life.

Together, these studies demonstrate a shared mechanism in animals and humans, where early-life experiences program the epigenome of stress-related genes. Both studies underscore the critical role of the epigenetic regulation of the glucocorticoid receptor in shaping stress responses and highlight the long-term impact of early environmental influences on mental health [101].

The study of the Bakusic et al. [102] builds upon the foundational work of Weaver et al. [99] and McGowan et al. [101] by extending the exploration of epigenetic regulation of stress responses to a clinical population with major depressive disorder (MDD). Unlike the earlier studies, which focused on maternal care in rats and childhood abuse in humans, this study examined the role of DNA methylation in both the glucocorticoid receptor gene (NR3C1) and the serotonin transporter gene (SLC6A4), highlighting a broader scope of epigenetic targets involved in HPA axis dysregulation. It also added a prospective clinical dimension by linking NR3C1 methylation at specific CpG sites to symptom improvement, emphasizing the potential of epigenetic markers for predicting treatment outcomes in MDD [102]. The incorporation of the Trier Social Stress Test (TSST) provided a direct measurement of HPA axis reactivity, allowing the study to quantify the functional impact of epigenetic dysregulation. Importantly, the finding that NR3C1 and SLC6A4 methylation collectively explained a portion of the variability in cortisol responses bridges the gap between molecular changes and physiological stress regulation [102].

Together, these studies reinforce the role of epigenetic mechanisms in stress-related disorders. This evolution of research from animal models to human post-mortem analyses and, ultimately, to living clinical populations underscores the translational value of epigenetic studies in psychiatry.

PTSD is a mental health condition triggered by experiencing or witnessing a traumatic event, with epigenetic modifications playing a critical role in its development and persistence. Yehuda et al. [103] demonstrated that trauma exposure can lead to changes in DNA methylation patterns in stress-regulating genes, such as the glucocorticoid receptor gene (NR3C1), influencing neuroendocrine responses. Their study, conducted on adult offspring of Holocaust survivors, revealed differential methylation patterns associated with parental PTSD, highlighting both individual and intergenerational effects of trauma. These findings not only link trauma-induced epigenetic changes to the persistence of PTSD symptoms but also suggest potential mechanisms for intergenerational transmission of trauma-related vulnerabilities [103].

In addition to DNA methylation, there are studies showing PTSD patients have also exhibited alterations in histone modifications and non-coding RNAs, further highlighting the complex epigenetic landscape underlying trauma-related disorders [104].

In their review, Föcking et al. [105] emphasize that although schizophrenia has a significant genetic component, with heritability estimates around 64%, strong evidence directly linking specific genetic loci to the disease remains limited. The authors propose that epigenetic mechanisms may play a central role in mediating disease risk. They highlight the importance of investigating how epigenetic regulation bridges the gap between weakly acting genetic variants and the complex neurodevelopmental processes underlying schizophrenia. Notably, many identified risk loci are closely associated with epigenetic markers, such as DNA methylation quantitative trait loci (QTLs), suggesting that epigenetic regulation mediates the relationship between genetic variants and disease phenotypes. Furthermore, findings of transcriptional changes and chromatin features linked to schizophrenia risk loci reinforce the critical role of epigenetic mechanisms in gene regulation [105].

3. Conclusion

In conclusion, the pathophysiology of psychiatric disorders is based on the complex interactions of various biological mechanisms, including neurotransmitter imbalances, neurotrophic factors, the endocannabinoid system, and tryptophan metabolism. Better understanding these mechanisms will facilitate the development of more effective treatment approaches for these disorders. However, given the complexity of psychiatric disorders, further research is needed to fully understand these mechanisms and to develop targeted therapeutic strategies.

As epigenetics continues to advance at the forefront of molecular biology, its ability to bridge genetic predispositions and environmental influences highlights its critical importance in understanding psychiatric disorders, where both factors play a pivotal role. This growing field not only provides profound insights into the mechanisms underlying these complex conditions but also opens promising avenues for the development of targeted therapeutic interventions.

In the treatment of neuropsychological diseases, most drugs cannot cross the blood-brain barrier (BBB) and therefore have difficulty in affecting the brain. This difficulty creates some problems in the development of effective treatments for neuropsychological diseases such as Alzheimer's, Parkinson's and depression. Nanocarrier-based drug delivery systems can facilitate drugs to cross the BBB and reach brain tissue directly. However, the short residence time of these carriers in the body limits the effectiveness of the treatment. Therefore, modification of carrier surfaces with polymers, cell-penetrating peptides, and glycoproteins can help extend the residence time in brain regions and increase bioavailability. These modifications may promise important solutions for more targeted and effective drug delivery in the treatment of neuropsychological diseases.

Conflict of interest

No conflict of interest was declared by the authors.

Author details

Hayriye Soytürk[1*], Ümit Kiliç[2], Cansu Önal[3], Ayşegül Yildiz[4], Özge Kaya[5] and Ayla Gencan[5]

1 Institute of Graduate Studies Interdisciplinary Neuroscience, Bolu Abant Izzet Baysal University, Bolu, Turkey

2 Duzce University Vocational School of Health Services, Duzce, Turkey

3 Department of Molecular Biology and Genetics, Faculty of Scıence, Zonguldak Bulent Ecevit Unıversity, Zonguldak, Turkey

4 Department of Physiology, Bolu Abant İzzet Baysal University, Bolu, Turkey

5 Bolu Abant İzzet Baysal University, Bolu, Turkey

*Address all correspondence to: hayriyesoyturk1@gmail.com

References

[1] Kim Y, Vadodaria KC, Lenkei Z, Kato T, Gage FH, Marchetto MC, et al. Mitochondria, metabolism, and redox mechanisms in psychiatric disorders. Antioxidants & Redox Signaling. 2019;**31**(4):275-317. DOI: 10.1089/ars.2018.7606

[2] Smothers BA, Yahr HT, Ruhl CE. Detection of alcohol use disorders in general hospital admissions in the United States. Archives of Internal Medicine. 2004;**164**(7):749-756. DOI: 10.1001/archinte.164.7.749

[3] Weller BE, Faulkner M, Doyle O, Daniel SS, Goldston DB. Impact of patients' psychiatric hospitalization on caregivers: A systematic review. Psychiatric Services. 2015;**66**(5):527-535

[4] Lu Z. Nano-Aromatic Drugs for the Treatments of Neuropsychiatric Disorders. University of Chinese Academy of Sciences; 2021

[5] Aricioğlu F. Development in neurobiology of depression: Neuroplasticity, neurotrophic factors and cytokines. Turkiye Klinikleri Journal of Psychiatry Special Topics. 2010;**3**(1):20-27

[6] Kirkpatrick B, Miller BJ. Inflammation and schizophrenia. Schizophrenia Bulletin. 2013;**39**(6):1174-1179. DOI: 10.1093/schbul/sbt141

[7] O'Brien SM, Scully P, Fitzgerald P, Scott LV, Dinan TG. Plasma cytokine profiles in depressed patients who fail to respond to selective serotonin reuptake inhibitor therapy. Journal of Psychiatric Research. 2007;**41**(3-4):326-331. DOI: 10.1016/j.jpsychires.2006.05.013. Epub 2006 Jul 25

[8] Meyer U, Schwarz MJ, Müller N. Inflammatory processes in schizophrenia: A promising neuroimmunological target for the treatment of negative/cognitive symptoms and beyond. Pharmacology & Therapeutics. 2011;**132**(1):96-110. DOI: 10.1016/j.pharmthera.2011.06.003. Epub 2011 Jun 15

[9] Saijo K, Glass CK. Microglial cell origin and phenotypes in health and disease. Nature Reviews. Immunology. 2011;**11**(11):775-787. DOI: 10.1038/nri3086

[10] Miller BJ, Buckley P, Seabolt W, Mellor A, Kirkpatrick B. Meta-analysis of cytokine alterations in schizophrenia: Clinical status and antipsychotic effects. Biological Psychiatry. 2011;**70**(7):663-671. DOI: 10.1016/j.biopsych.2011.04.013. Epub 2011 Jun 8

[11] Murphy CE, Walker AK, Weickert CS. Neuroinflammation in schizophrenia: The role of nuclear factor kappa B. Translational Psychiatry. 2021;**11**:528. DOI: 10.1038/s41398-021-01607-0

[12] Blokhin IO, Khorkova O, Saveanu RV, Wahlestedt C. Molecular mechanisms of psychiatric diseases. Neurobiology of Disease. 2020;**146**(April):105136. DOI: 10.1016/j.nbd.2020.105136

[13] Hyman SE. The biology of mental disorders: Progress at last. Daedalus. 2023;**152**(4):186-211. DOI: 10.1162/daed_a_02038

[14] Nigg JT. Considerations toward an epigenetic and common pathways theory of mental disorder. Journal of Psychopathology and Clinical Science. 2023;**132**(3):297-313. DOI: 10.1037/abn0000748

[15] Hernandez J. From environment to gene expression: Epigenetics and the development of mental health disorders. International Neuropsychiatric Disease Journal. 2023;**20**(2):22-26. DOI: 10.9734/indj/2023/v20i2391

[16] Minichiello L. TrkB signalling pathways in LTP and learning. Nature Reviews. Neuroscience. 2009;**10**(12):850-860. DOI: 10.1038/nrn2738

[17] Shimojo M, Courchet J, Pieraut S, Torabi-Rander N, Sando R 3rd, Polleux F, et al. SNAREs controlling vesicular release of BDNF and development of callosal axons. Cell Reports. 2015;**11**(7):1054-1066. DOI: 10.1016/j.celrep.2015.04.032

[18] Wang CS, Kavalali ET, Monteggia LM. BDNF signaling in context: From synaptic regulation to psychiatric disorders. Cell. 2022;**185**(1):62-76. DOI: 10.1016/j.cell.2021.12.003

[19] Zou S, Kumar U. Cannabinoid receptors and endocannabinoid system: Signaling and function in the central nervous system. International Journal of Molecular Sciences. 2019;**19**:833. DOI: 10.3390/ijms19030833

[20] Joshi N, Onaivi ES. Psychiatric disorders and cannabinoid receptors. Advances in Experimental Medicine and Biology. 2021;**1264**:131-153. DOI: 10.1007/978-3-030-57369-0_9

[21] Ohno-Shosaku T, Kano M. Endocannabinoid-mediated retrograde modulation of synaptic transmission. Current Opinion in Neurobiology. 2014;**29**:1-8

[22] Onaivi ES, Canseco-Alba BD, Sanabria BD, Zhang HY, Eita M, Rohani T, et al. Identification of cannabinoid CB2 receptor neuro-immune crosstalk following conditional deletion of type 2 cannabinoid receptors in microglia and dopamine neurons. Society for Neuroscience Abstracts San Diego. 2018

[23] Canseco-Alba A, Schanz N, Sanabria B, Zhao J, Lin Z, Liu QR, et al. Behavioral effects of psychostimulants in mutant mice with cell-type specific deletion of CB2 cannabinoid receptors in dopamine neurons. Behavioural Brain Research. 2019;**360**:286-297. DOI: 10.1016/j.bbr.2018.11.043

[24] Crews FT, Lawrimore CJ, Walter TJ, Coleman LG Jr. The role of neuroimmune signaling in alcoholism. Neuropharmacology. 2017;**122**:56-73

[25] Onaivi ES, Ishiguro H, Gu S, Liu QR. CNS effects of CB2 cannabinoid receptors: Beyond neuro-immunocannabinoid activity. Journal of Psychopharmacology. 2012;**26**:92-103

[26] Ibarra-Lecue I, Pilar-Cuellar F, Muguruza C, Florensa-Zanuy E, Diaz A, Uriguen L, et al. The endocannabinoid system in mental disorders: Evidence from human brain studies. Biochemical Pharmacology. 2018;**151**:97-107

[27] Egerton A, Fusar-Poli P, Stone JM. Glutamate and psychosis risk. Current Pharmaceutical Design. 2012;**18**(4):466-478

[28] Poels EMP et al. Glutamatergic abnormalities in schizophrenia: A review of proton MRS findings. Schizophrenia Research. 2014;**152**(2-3):325-332

[29] Pantelis C et al. Biological insights from 108 schizophrenia-associated genetic loci. Nature. 2014;**511**(7510):421-427

[30] Kaalund SS et al. Contrasting changes in DRD1 and DRD2 splice

variant expression in schizophrenia and affective disorders, and associations with SNPs in postmortem brain. Molecular Psychiatry. 2014;**19**(12):1258-1266

[31] Cai R, Huang C, Ni L, Liu Z, Zhang S, Qiu Y, et al. The motivation and pleasure deficits but not expressivity affects social functioning through cognitive function in male patients with schizophrenia: A structural equation model. Asian Journal of Psychiatry. 2023;**85**:103616. DOI: 10.1016/j.ajp.2023.103616

[32] Nakamura S. Integrated pathophysiology of schizophrenia, major depression, and bipolar disorder as monoamine axon disorder. Frontiers in Bioscience (Scholar Edition). 2022;**14**(1):4. DOI: 10.31083/j.fbs1401004

[33] Castillo PE, Younts TJ, Chavez AE, Hashimotodani Y. Endocannabinoid signaling and synaptic function. Neuron. 2012;**76**:70-81

[34] Koethe D, Llenos IC, Dulay JR, Hoyer C, Torrey EF, Leweke FM, et al. Expression of CB 1 cannabinoid receptor in the anterior cingulate cortex in schizophrenia, bipolar disorder, and major depression. Journal of Neural Transmission. 2007;**114**(8):1055

[35] Palmisano A, Pandit S, Smeralda CL, Demchenko I, Rossi S, Battelli L, et al. The pathophysiological underpinnings of gamma-band alterations in psychiatric disorders. Life (Basel). 2024;**14**(5):578. DOI: 10.3390/life14050578

[36] Zou M, Li D, Wu L, Sun C. Role of the endocannabinoid system in neurological disorders. International Journal of Developmental Neuroscience. 2019;**76**:95-102

[37] Krebs MO, Kebir O, Jay TM. Exposure to cannabinoids can lead to persistent cognitive and psychiatric disorders. European Journal of Pain. 2019;**23**:1225-1233

[38] Crume TL, Juhl AL, Brooks-Russel A, Hall KE, Wymore E, Borgelt LM. Cannabis use during the perinatal period in a state with legalized recreational and medical marijuana: The association between maternal characteristics, breastfeeding patterns, and neonatal outcomes. The Journal of Pediatrics. 2018;**197**:90-96

[39] Gunn JK, Rosales CB, Center KE, Nunez A, Gibson SJ, Christ C, et al. Prenatal exposure to cannabis and maternal and child health outcomes: A systematic review and meta-analysis. BMJ Open. 2016;**6**(4):e009986. DOI: 10.1136/bmjopen-2015-009986

[40] Hesdorffer DC. Comorbidity between neurological illness and psychiatric disorders. CNS Spectrums. 2016;**21**(3):230-238. DOI: 10.1017/S1092852915000929

[41] Vaughn MG, Sala-Wright CP, John R, Holzer KJ, Qian Z, Veeh C. Traumatic brain injury and psychiatric co-morbidity in the United States. The Psychiatric Quarterly. 2019;**90**(1):151-158. DOI: 10.1007/s11126-018-9617-0

[42] Turner NE, McDonald AJ, Lalomiteanu AR, Mann RE, McCready J, Millstone D, et al. Moderate to severe gambling problems and traumatic brain injury: A population-based study. Psychiatry Research. 2019;**272**:692-697. DOI: 10.1016/j.psychres.2018.12.170

[43] Florensa-Zanuy E, Garro-Martínez E, Adell A, Castro E, Díaz Á, Pazos Á, et al. Cannabidiol antidepressant-like effect in the lipopolysaccharide model in mice: Modulation of inflammatory pathways. Biochemical Pharmacology.

2021;**185**:114433. DOI: 10.1016/j.bcp.2021.114433

[44] Chen B, Li J, Xie Y, Ming X, Li G, Wang J, et al. Cang-ai volatile oil improves depressive-like behaviors and regulates DA and 5-HT metabolism in the brains of CUMS-induced rats. Journal of Ethnopharmacology. 2019;**244**:112088. DOI: 10.1016/j.jep.2019.112088

[45] Li D, Yu S, Long Y, Shi A, Deng J, Ma Y, et al. Tryptophan metabolism: Mechanism-oriented therapy for neurological and psychiatric disorders. Frontiers in Immunology. 2022;**13**:985378. DOI: 10.3389/fimmu.2022.985378

[46] Zhang X, Li R, Wang J, Huang S, Li G, Wang S, et al. Advances in the regulation of tryptophan on animal physiological function. Special Wild Economic Animal and Plant Research. 2019;**41**(01):104-108. DOI: 10.16720/j.cnki.tcyj.2019.01.023

[47] Ramprasath T, Han Y-M, Zhang D, Yu C-J, Zou M-H. Tryptophan catabolism and inflammation: A novel therapeutic target for aortic diseases. Frontiers in Immunology. 2021;**12**:731701. DOI: 10.3389/fimmu.2021.731701

[48] Kong H, Zhu D. Tryptophan/kynurenine metabolic pathway and cardiovascular disease. Chinese Journal of Hypertension. 2012;**20**(05):433-435. DOI: 10.16439/j.cnki.1673-7245.2012.05.010

[49] Tanaka M, Tóth F, Polyák H, Szabó Á, Mándi Y, Vécsei L. Immune influencers in action: Metabolites and enzymes of the tryptophan-kynurenine metabolic pathway. Biomedicine. 2021;**9**(7):734. DOI: 10.3390/biomedicines9070734

[50] Fujigaki H, Yamamoto Y, Saito K. L-tryptophan-kynurenine pathway enzymes are therapeutic target for neuropsychiatric diseases: Focus on cell type differences. Neuropharmacology. 2017;**112**(Pt B):264-274. DOI: 10.1016/j.neuropharm.2016.01.011

[51] Anderson G, Maes M. Bipolar disorder: Role of immune-inflammatory cytokines, oxidative and nitrosative stress and tryptophan catabolites. Current Psychiatry Reports. 2015;**17**(2):8. DOI: 10.1007/s11920-014-0541-1

[52] Agus A, Planchais J, Sokol H. Gut microbiota regulation of tryptophan metabolism in health and disease. Cell Host & Microbe. 2018;**23**(6):716-724. DOI: 10.1016/j.chom.2018.05.003

[53] Sudhakar V, Mark Richardson R. Gene therapy for neurodegenerative diseases. Neurotherapeutics. 2019;**16**:166-175. DOI: 10.1007/s13311-018-00694-0

[54] Singh MK, Gorelik AJ, Stave C, Gotlib IH. Genetics, epigenetics, and neurobiology of childhood-onset depression: An umbrella review. Molecular Psychiatry. 2024;**29**(3):553-565. DOI: 10.1038/s41380-023-02347-x. Epub 2023 Dec 15

[55] Forrest MP, Hill MJ, Kavanagh DH, Tansey KE, Waite AJ, Blake DJ. The psychiatric risk gene transcription factor 4 (TCF4) regulates neurodevelopmental pathways associated with schizophrenia, autism, and intellectual disability. Schizophrenia Bulletin. 2018;**44**(5):1100-1110. DOI: 10.1093/schbul/sbx164

[56] Farsi Z, Sheng M. Molecular mechanisms of schizophrenia: Insights from human genetics. Current Opinion in Neurobiology. 2023;**81**:102731

[57] Mahjani B, Bey K, Boberg J, Burton C. Genetics of obsessivecompulsive disorder.

Psychological Medicine. 2021;**51**:2247-2259. DOI: 10.1017/S0033291721001744

[58] Thome J, Hässler F, Zachariou V. The World Journal of Biological Psychiatry. 2011;**12**(Suppl. 1):16-18. DOI: 10.3109/15622975.2011.601927

[59] Sapolsky RM. Gene therapy for psychiatric disorders. American Journal of Psychiatry. **160**(2):208-220. DOI: 10.1176/appi.ajp.160.2.208

[60] Zlokovic B, Apuzzo M. Cellular and molecular neurosurgery, pathways from concept to reality, part II: Vector systems and delivery methodologies for gene therapy of the central nervous system. Neurosurgery. 1997;**40**:805-815

[61] Hasler G. Pathophysıology of depression: Do we have any solid evidence of interest to clinicians? World Psychiatry. 2010;**9**(3):155-161. DOI: 10.1002/J.2051-5545.2010.Tb00298.X

[62] Tingyan W, Cai W, Chen X. Epigenetic regulation of neurotransmitter signaling in neurological disorders. Neurobiology of Disease. 2023;**184**:106232. DOI: 10.1016/j.nbd.2023.106232

[63] McCutcheon RA, Krystal JH, Howes OD. Dopamine and glutamate in schizophrenia: Biology, symptoms and treatment. World Psychiatry. 2020;**19**:15-33

[64] Chu WS, Ng J, Waddington SN, Kurian MA. Gene therapy for neurotransmitter-related disorders. Journal of Inherited Metabolic Disease. 2024;**47**:176-191. DOI: 10.1002/jimd.12697

[65] Tsai C-R, Lee H-F, Chi C-S, Yang M-T, Hsu C-C. Antisense oligonucleotides modulate dopa decarboxylase function in aromatic l-amino acid decarboxylase deficiency. Human Mutation. 2018;**39**:2072-2082. DOI: 10.1002/humu.23659

[66] Henry R. The Role of Gene Therapy in Psychiatry. In: Peterson JS, editor. BIOB 275: General Genetics. Helena College University of Montana; 2022

[67] Gutiérrez-Rodríguez A, Cruz-Fuentes CS, Genis-Mendoza AD, Nicolini H. CRISPR/Cas9 genome editing approaches for psychiatric research, Braz. Journal of Psychiatry. 2023;**45**(2):137-145. DOI: 10.47626/1516-4446-2022-2913

[68] Kurishev AO, Karpov DS, Nadolinskaia NI, Goncharenko AV, Golimbet VE. CRISPR/Cas-based approaches to study schizophrenia and other neurodevelopmental disorders. International Journal of Molecular Sciences. 2022;**24**(1):241. DOI: 10.3390/ijms24010241

[69] Schrode N, Ho SM, Yamamuro K, Dobbyn A, Huckins L, Matos MR, et al. Synergistic effects of common schizophrenia risk variants. Nature Genetics. 2019;**51**:1475-1485

[70] Martin ER, Gandawijaya J, Oguro-Ando A. A novel method for generating glutamatergic SH-SY5Y neuron-like cells utilizing B-27 supplement. Frontiers in Pharmacology. 2022;**13**:943627

[71] Gelfand Y, Kaplitt MG. Gene therapy for psychiatric disorders. World Neurosurgery. 2013;**80**(3-4):S32.e11-S32.e18

[72] Carlezon WA Jr, Thome J, Olson VG, Lane-Ladd SB, Brodkin ES, Hiroi N, et al. Regulation of cocaine reward by CREB. Science. 1998;**282**:2272-2275

[73] Alexander B, Warner-Schmidt J, Eriksson TM, Tamminga C,

Arango-Lievano M, Ghose S, et al. Reversal of depressed behaviors in mice by p11 gene therapy in the nucleus accumbens. Science Translational Medicine. 2010;**2**(54):54ra76. DOI: 10.1126/scitranslmed.3001079

[74] Jerusalinsky D, Baez MV, Epstein AL. Herpes simplex virus type 1-based amplicon vectors for fundamental research in neurosciences and gene therapy of neurological diseases. Journal of Physiology - Paris. 2012;**106**:2-11. DOI: 10.1016/j.jphysparis.2011.11.003

[75] Peng J, Zou W-W, Wang X-L, Zhang Z-G, Huo R, Yang L. Viral-mediated gene therapy in pediatric neurological disorders. World Journal of Pediatrics. 2024;**20**:533-555

[76] Du B, Wu P, Boldt-Houle DM, Terwilliger EF. Efficient transduction of human neurons with an adeno-associated virus vector. Gene Therapy. 1996;**3**:254-261

[77] Sharma S, Dang S. Nanocarrier-based drug delivery to brain: Interventions of surface modification. Current Neuropharmacology. 2023;**21**(3):517-535. DOI: 10.2174/1570159X20666220706121412

[78] Cecchin R, Troyer Z, Witwer K, Morris KV. Extracellular vesicles: The next generation in gene therapy delivery. Molecular Therapy. 2023;**31**(5):1225-1230. DOI: 10.1016/j.ymthe.2023.01.021. Epub 2023 Jan 25

[79] Singh R, Rai S, Bharti PS, et al. Circulating small extracellular vesicles in Alzheimer's disease: A case–control study of neuro-inflammation and synaptic dysfunction. BMC Medicine. 2024;**22**:254. DOI: 10.1186/s12916-024-03475-z

[80] Frøslev P, Franzyk H, Ozgür B, Brodin B, Kristensen M. Highly cationic cell-penetrating peptides affect the barrier integrity and facilitates mannitol permeation in a human stem cell-based blood-brain barrier model. European Journal of Pharmaceutical Sciences. 2022;**168**:106054. DOI: 10.1016/j.ejps.2021.106054

[81] Pena SA, Iyengar R, Eshraghi RS. Gene therapy for neurological disorders: Challenges and recent advancements. Journal of Drug Targeting. 2020;**28**(2):111-128. DOI: 10.1080/1061186X.2019.1630415

[82] Holliday R. Epigenetics: A historical overview. Epigenetics. 2006;**1**(2):76-80

[83] Schiele MA, Domschke K. Epigenetics at the crossroads between genes, environment and resilience in anxiety disorders. Genes, Brain and Behavior. Mar 2018;**17**(3):e12423. DOI: 10.1111/gbb.12423. Epub 2017 Sep 26

[84] Kouzarides T. Chromatin modifications and their function. Cell. 2007;**128**(4):693-705. DOI: 10.1016/j.cell.2007.02.005

[85] Li Y. Modern epigenetics methods in biological research. Methods. 2021;**187**:104-113. DOI: 10.1016/j.ymeth.2020.06.022

[86] Yegnasubramanian S, De Marzo AM, Nelson WG. Prostate cancer epigenetics: From basic mechanisms to clinical implications. Cold Spring Harbor Perspectives in Medicine. 2019;**9**(4):a030445

[87] Caspi A, Moffitt TE. Gene-environment interactions in psychiatry: Joining forces with neuroscience. Nature Reviews Neuroscience. 2006;7(7):583-590

[88] Nestler EJ, Aghajanian GK. Molecular and cellular basis of addiction. Science. 1997;**278**(5335):58-63

[89] Abdolmaleky HM, Smith CL, Faraone SV, et al. Methylomics in psychiatry: Modulation of gene–environment interactions may be through DNA methylation. American Journal of Medical Genetics Part B: Neuropsychiatric Genetics. 2004;**127B**(1):51-59

[90] Pariante CM, Lightman SL. The HPA axis in major depression: Classical theories and new developments. Trends in Neurosciences. 2008;**31**(9):464-468

[91] Colită CI, Udristoiu I, Ancuta DL, Hermann DM, Colita D, Colita E, et al. Epigenetics of ageing and psychiatric disorders. Journal of Integrative Neuroscience. 2024;**23**(1):13

[92] Baylin SB, Ohm JE. Epigenetic gene silencing in cancer—A mechanism for early oncogenic pathway addiction? Nature Reviews. Cancer. 2006;**6**(2):107-116

[93] Egger G, Liang G, Aparicio A, Jones PA. Epigenetics in human disease and prospects for epigenetic therapy. Nature. 2004;**429**(6990):457-463

[94] Kuehner JN, Bruggeman EC, Wen Z, Yao B. Epigenetic regulations in neuropsychiatric disorders. Frontiers in Genetics. 2019;**10**:268

[95] Conley BT. Neuroepigenetic mechanisms of psychiatric disorders: Implications for the Adlerian therapist [doctoral dissertation]. Adler Graduate School; 2018

[96] de Quervain D, Schwabe L, Roozendaal B. Stress, glucocorticoids and memory: Implications for treating fear-related disorders. Nature Reviews. Neuroscience. 2017;**18**:7-19

[97] de Quervain D, Wolf OT, Roozendaal B. Glucocorticoid-induced enhancement of extinction-from animal models to clinical trials. Psychopharmacology. 2019;**236**:183-199

[98] Wingenfeld K, Wolf OT. HPA axis alterations in mental disorders: Impact on memory and its relevance for therapeutic interventions. CNS Neuroscience & Therapeutics. 2011;**17**(6):714-722

[99] Weaver IC, Cervoni N, Champagne FA, D'Alessio AC, Sharma S, Seckl JR, et al. Epigenetic programming by maternal behavior. Nature Neuroscience. 2004;**7**(8):847-854

[100] Persaud NS, Cates HM. The epigenetics of anxiety pathophysiology: A DNA methylation and histone modification focused review. eNeuro. 2023;**10**(4):ENEURO.0109-21.2021. DOI: 10.1523/ENEURO.0109-21.2021

[101] McGowan PO, Sasaki A, D'Alessio AC, Dymov S, Labonté B, Szyf M, et al. Epigenetic regulation of the glucocorticoid receptor in human brain associates with childhood abuse. Nature Neuroscience. 2009;**12**(3):342-348

[102] Bakusic J, Vrieze E, Ghosh M, Bekaert B, Claes S, Godderis L. Increased methylation of NR3C1 and SLC6A4 is associated with blunted cortisol reactivity to stress in major depression. Neurobiology of Stress. 2020;**13**:100272

[103] Yehuda R, Daskalakis NP, Bierer LM, Bader HN, Klengel T, Holsboer F, et al. Influences of maternal and paternal PTSD on epigenetic regulation of the glucocorticoid receptor gene in Holocaust survivor offspring. American Journal of Psychiatry. 2014;**171**(8):872-880

[104] Zovkic IB, Guintivano J, Mouzon E. Epigenetic mechanisms in post-traumatic stress disorder. Neuropsychopharmacology. 2013;**38**(10):1776-1792

[105] Föcking M, Doyle B, Munawar N, Dillon ET, Cotter D, Cagney G. Epigenetic factors in schizophrenia: Mechanisms and experimental approaches. Molecular Neuropsychiatry. 2019;**5**:6-12